MW00695509

The REAL
WITCHES'
YEAR

The REAL
WITCHES'
YEAR

Spells, rituals and
meditations for every day
of the year

KATE WEST

Element
An Imprint of HarperCollins*Publishers*
77–85 Fulham Palace Road
Hammersmith, London W6 8JB

The website address is:
www.thorsonselement.com

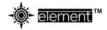

and *Element* are trademarks of
HarperCollins*Publishers* Limited

First published 2004

1 3 5 7 9 10 8 6 4 2

© Kate West 2004

Kate West asserts the moral right to
be identified as the author of this work

A catalogue record for this book
is available from the British Library

ISBN 0 00 718951 6

Printed and bound in the U.S.A.

CONTENTS

For Steve, who is with me
every day of the year.

ACKNOWLEDGEMENTS

My heartfelt thanks to everyone who has supported me through the months of writing this volume, including all those who wished me well. To Keith, Angela, Debbie, Fiona and Mike for ideas, inspiration, information and proof-reading. To Katy for her infinite patience. And above all to Steve and Tali who, as ever, lose a wife and mother to the keyboard.

BEGINNING

Few people enjoy a long drawn out introduction, so I'll try to keep my comments to the point. However, there are a few points which will benefit from a little explanation.

This book has an entry for every day of the year, all of which are aspects of, or related to, the Craft. There are things to do, make, think or learn about. And there are Spells, Rites and meditations and magical ideas. The entries are not intended to be a full discussion on the topic at hand; there would be nowhere like enough room to do this in a single book. They will however provide an insight and perhaps encourage you to find out more. Whilst each entry is assigned to a date, only those relating to the Sabbats, Astrology, Tree Months and a handful of others are date-specific, so there is no reason why you shouldn't use them whenever you feel is best. Or you can use the book on a daily basis as it is. There is also a daily thought which you can take with you and which I trust will help you cope with the complexities of daily life. Where these are not my own I have tried to attribute them, but a few have been in common circulation for so long that it is impossible to be certain who originated them; to these people I apologize. The four major Sabbats of Imbolg, Beltane, Lughnasadh and Samhain are here on both their modern and ancient dates, although they would originally have been timed by seasonal indicators, rather than a calendar. To explain: in 1582 the Pope introduced the Gregorian Calendar which spread gradually over the next couple of centuries, with Britain holding out until 1751. The actual implementation resulted in the 'loss' of eleven days: 2 September being followed by 14 September. For some time people celebrated festivals and feasts on both dates, but eventually the new calendar became the only one.

Readers with an interest in Astrology will quickly notice that I have placed information on the Sun signs on the 23rd of each month. I've chosen this date, as the actual date when the Sun enters any sign varies from year to year, but is usually completed by the 23rd.

There are also entries referring to the Celtic Tree Calendar. There are in fact several schools of thought as to the species and sequence of trees, the dates of transition from one to another, and indeed the number of trees in a year. I have chosen to work here with the version which I first encountered, but you may wish to look at others.

Some of the entries here are seasonal so I apologize to my readers living in the Southern hemisphere whose seasons are reversed. However, most of the entries in this book are not seasonal and I trust that you will be able to make the necessary adjustment for the few which are.

Other than that I trust you enjoy your journey through the year.

Blessed Be

Kate

NEW YEAR'S RESOLUTIONS

New Year's resolutions are a modern tradition but despite being neither a Wiccan tradition nor linked to the Witches' year, which begins and ends at Samhain, many Witches still practise this.

Rather than setting yourself one or two difficult-to-attain targets, make a list of 6 to 12 things you would like to achieve during the coming year. Some could be linked to self-improvement like eating in a more healthy way or learning a new skill, whilst others are perhaps more in the way of personal treats; for example saving for a balloon flight or a weekend at a health spa. Try to include one or more things associated with your Craft, like remembering to observe the cycles of the Moon or writing up your Book of Shadows, for example. It can also be helpful to apply a 'rule of three' approach to this: for each item for self-improvement, have one for the benefit of others, the land or the Craft, and one which is for pleasure. Ensure that your list includes things which are relatively simple to achieve as well as more difficult goals.

Write a list of all your targets and, whilst burning a gold candle, recite them to yourself, repeating after each: *"As is my will so mote it be."* Pin the list in a place where you will see it every day. If you don't want to announce your intentions to the world, you could place it on the inside of your wardrobe door. Now select one goal from your list and start work towards achieving it as soon as you can.

"The best way to succeed is to start."

A PROSPERITY CHARM

To ensure that money will enter the house
all year round, take one silver or golden coin
for each external door to the house.

The coins will almost certainly be gold or silver coloured rather than actually made of the metals concerned. Then take the same number of circular pieces of paper. Wash the coin(s) carefully under running water for 10 minutes and then dry them in a new cloth or tissue. On the paper(s) draw a picture of your family and around it draw pictures to represent all the things you need (not want) money for. Remember to include rent, taxes, light, heat, food, transport, pets, etc. Wrap each coin in one of the papers and, if you are able, bury one just outside the threshold of each door. Whilst you are burying the coin(s) say, *"I call upon the Old Gods to help us make the most of opportunities to bring money into this house. May those who live here ever have enough for their needs and commitments. Give each of us the true rewards of our work and may our family be happy and secure in this home. Blessed Be."* Whilst you are doing this, visualize members of the family with coins in their pockets entering the home. If it is not possible to actually bury them, then slip them down a crack at the base of the door, or just under the carpet on the inside. It is important that everyone who enters the house, and all post, must pass over the coins.

*"Never give an empty purse, lest both giver
and taker be likewise coinless."*

TO FIND YOUR TOTEM ANIMAL

*Everyone has an animal, bird or fish which holds
a special meaning for them. This is not necessarily
a pet or even a domestic animal; it could be wild,
foreign or even mythical.*

Mine is the Raven. I was born and raised in the area of Ravensbourne and wherever I have lived or worked Ravens have always been around. I've even hand-reared one. Whenever I see one, whether in life, in art, or in a dream, it always indicates something important is about to happen in my life.

To find your own Totem Animal, take a walk in the woods just before dusk. Take time to look at the trees and plants, to inhale the scent of the woods and to listen to the sounds around you. Find an old tree and sit down beneath it. Close your eyes and lay your hands flat on the soil to each side of you and take several slow deep breaths. Ask the Goddess to send your Totem Animal to you. Open your eyes and pick up the first thing you see lying on the ground near you. Take this home and place it under your pillow for three nights and your Totem Animal will come to you in your dreams. When you know what your Totem Animal is, remember to look out for it in the world around you, and to acknowledge this gift of the Goddess each time you see it.

*"Remember; manners maketh man,
woman and Witch."*

HOME-MADE COUGH SYRUP

**Whilst most pharmacies provide a wide range of
cold remedies, there is no harm in supplementing
them with a home-produced one.**

Take the juice of 1 orange and 2 lemons, 2 tablespoons of glycerin (from your chemist), 2 tablespoons of honey (locally made is best), ½ crushed cinnamon stick, 6 cloves, a large pinch of grated nutmeg, and ½ teaspoon of grated ginger. Heat gently for 10 to 20 minutes, stirring all the time. Do not allow to boil. Strain and place in a clean jar to cool.

The syrup will keep in a refrigerator for several days, but I find it rarely lasts that long as it is quite pleasant to taste. Adults may take a teaspoonful or two whenever needed. This can be given to children as young as 5 yrs but it should be diluted in 3 times as much water.

Note that whilst the addition of of brandy or whisky to this recipe might make you feel better, alcohol actually reduces the body's ability to heal itself!

If your home is centrally heated try to make sure that you get enough moisture into the air by placing a bowl of water near to your heaters or a damp flannel over radiators. Try to get out at least once a day for a reasonably brisk walk. If you believe in prevention rather than cure, try to reduce the amount you heat your home just a little and wear thicker clothes instead. This also has positive effects on your heating bills as well as the environment.

*"Into every life a little rain will fall,
so buy some boots and go splash in the puddles."*

USING A PENDULUM

The pendulum is one of a great variety of methods
of divination, and can be asked questions to which
the answer is yes or no.

Whilst many beautiful pendulums can be purchased, almost any weight suspended on a string or thread will act as a pendulum so long as it hangs freely. As with many tools of the Craft it can be better if you can find or make your own. Look for a stone with a hole in it and then suspend it on a piece of violet thread.

Before using your pendulum you should 'set' it, that is find the way in which it will respond. Ideally you should do this before every use. First, hold the string in your strong hand (the right if you are right hand-ed) and suspend it over your other hand. Hold it as steady as you can and then think of the strongest 'yes' you can. Observe the way the pendulum moves, whether it is back and forth, left and right, or round in a circle. Once you are sure you have established 'yes', stop the pendulum and clear your mind. Now repeat the process with the strongest 'no' you can visualize, again observing the pendulum's direction of movement. Now you are ready to ask your question(s). Remember to phrase it in such a way that the answer can only be yes or no. If you should get a different kind of movement then try again, but if it persists it could be that the answer is 'maybe' or that you are not meant to know.

"If you are not certain you want the answer,
don't ask the question."

TWELFTH NIGHT

Twelfth Night is the date in the Christian calendar for taking down the decorations.

Before you do this, go through all the greetings cards you received and update your address book. Then, if you do not use the cards yourself, separate the written half from the illustrated half and take the pictures to a charity store so that others can use them to create gift tags for next year, or to a children's nursery group so the pictures may be cut up for collage or other artwork.

Just recently I and a couple of friends have rebelled a bit against the technological and computer age. Instead of using email and the phone we write (yes, with a pen and paper!) letters to one another. Around about this time of year it can be really friendly to put a little extra effort into communicating properly with some of those old friends who you send cards to, but otherwise rarely communicate with properly. Forget all those 'thank you' letters you were forced to write as a child, think more along the lines of a chatty note to give your 'lost touch with' friends the highlights of your life over the last year or so. We tend to illustrate our letters with a few very rough sketches: matchstick men and almost cartoon-like animals, etc. Whilst I'm the first to say I'm no artist, these things do make for a more individual and personal communication.

> *"When every post seems to bring bills,*
> *write more letters."*

OBSIDIAN

As one of very many 'Witchy' stones, Obsidian is
both centring and protective. It is a volcanic stone
and also a form of naturally occurring glass.

Obsidian is often used in grounding or when you have trouble getting your physical self into order. As with all stones and crystals it is better to have one or two small off-cuts than a piece which has been blasted out of the earth for commercial reasons. Obsidian can be carried in a pouch or used in Ritual.

If you feel 'unconnected' with the 'real world' sit on the earth and place a tiny piece of Obsidian under each foot. Also plant your hands on the soil. Close your eyes and visualize the energy of the Earth flowing in through your hands and exiting via your feet, whilst also visualizing the Obsidian absorbing any excess non-physical energies. When you feel purified, take the Obsidian stones, wrap them in a dark cloth, and bury them in the place where you sat.

Should you feel threatened in any way, carry cleansed Obsidian in a pouch, close to your waist. It will deflect and absorb any negative energies which may come your way.

Obsidian also has many uses in Scrying. An Obsidian egg or sphere is a far easier scrying tool to use than one of Crystal as it is easier to let go of your conscious mind in the depths of a black stone.

"The inner meaning of our lives is written in the spell."
LEGEND, SECOND SIGHT

FEEDING THE BIRDS

At this time of year natural foods for birds are in
short supply, so it is more important than ever to
ensure that we supplement their diet. Whilst there
is a huge variety of commercial feeders and feed
available it can be more interesting, and usually
far cheaper, to create your own.

Fat balls can be hung in the kinds of net bag that fruit, and some vegetables, often come in. The basis for these can be lard or you can collect and save the residues of grilled sausages and the like. Add breadcrumbs and oatmeal, and search your kitchen cabinets for raisins, sultanas, seeds and shelled nuts. Even dried pulses can be added if you soak and soften them a little first. Mix everything together, roll into balls and chill in the refrigerator. Hang in the string or plastic nets in a safe place away from the reach of cats. These nets can also be used to put shelled peanuts (groundnuts) in, as the birds will have to peck through the mesh to reach the nuts. It is not a good idea to give them access to whole nuts as, once the breeding season starts, young birds cannot digest them.

Apples which have passed their best can be impaled on twigs and branches. If you had mistletoe in the house for the Yule period, this can also be put out for the birds, as the berries need to pass through the digestive system of a bird to aid germination. You never know, you might get your own Mistletoe plants in years to come.

"The life of the land is in all things living."

CANDLE MAGIC

Candle spells are one of the most popular forms of
magic, probably because they are simple as well as
effective. Not only that but if a non-Witch comes
into your home they are unlikely to notice, let
alone comment on, a burning candle.

There are many ways of using candles in magic. The easiest is to take a few
drops of oil and massage it into a candle of the appropriate colour (colours
are mentioned throughout this book), rubbing from the centre of the candle
out to the ends whilst visualizing the effect that you intend. Light the
candle and let it burn all the way down to set your spell into action.
Another way is to take a white candle and a length of thread of the appropriate
colour. Tie the thread around the candle, knotting it three times to
secure your spell. In this method the candle is only burnt down until the
thread is burnt. A third technique involves placing a pin in a candle and
burning it down until the pin drops in order to activate your magic.

Whichever method you use, only use the candle for the intended
spell. Do not be tempted to use the same one later for a different spell, or
for a different person, as this may result in some very confused magic!

It is as well to remember that a burning candle should always be
placed in a secure holder and on a heatproof dish. Furthermore, a burning
candle should never be left unattended.

*"In magic, as in all things, it is focus
and intent which make it work."*

THE CAT

No other animal is more frequently linked with Witches and the Craft than the cat, and in particular the black cat.

This is not just part of the mythology of the Craft, as many Witches live with cats. Notice I say 'live with', not 'own': no-one who knows cats will ever consider that you can have possession of one! Having said that, there is no reason why you have to live with a cat to be a Witch.

There is an enormous body of folklore surrounding the cat. A cat washing behind its ears is said to forecast rain; stroking an affected eye with a cat's tail was thought to cure a stye, and so forth. Whatever you feel about such sayings there is no doubt that the cat is a very magical animal. One of mine, now sadly dead, could tell the difference between a true Witch and a pretender. Certainly both my current cats pay great attention whenever I am practising the Craft, and can distinguish between a candle lit for magic and one lit for ambience.

Another way in which cats and Witches are linked is that cats are probably the best domestic animal for borrowing. That is when you transfer a part of your mind into the body of the animal so that you can travel in its shape and experience the things it sees and does. Indeed it is thought that the saying that a cat has nine lives is an indication of the number of times a Witch can ride with a cat in this way.

"All cats are grey at night."

OLD FRENCH PROVERB

ANIMAL HEALING SPELL

Magical healing is not just for humans: our pets and
other animal friends can also benefit. As with all
healing you should still consider whether professional
help is needed and you should also be careful not to
prolong pain or suffering.

For this spell you will need to gather a couple of hairs from the animal in
question; a gentle brush should provide you with plenty. If the 'patient'
in question is a bird collect a feather from its cage, and for a fish take a
few drops of water from its aquarium and place them on a small piece of
tissue. Take a brown candle and write on it the name of the animal (use
an old pencil), then using a little melted wax attach the hairs, feather or
tissue about half way down. Place the candle in a secure holder and lights
it saying, *"As the candle burns may sickness depart, as the hairs light
let healing come in. Blessed Be."* Watch the candle burn whilst visualizing
and focusing on your animal friend getting better. If your pet is very
poorly you may like to repeat this spell at the next Full Moon.

*"No-one who deliberately harms
an animal will ever be a true Witch."*

THE CHALICE

Whilst the Craft can be practised without tools most Witches will want at least one or two. Of these the Chalice is probably the most important, for whilst you can improvise many things, some kind of vessel to hold wine, juice or water is fairly necessary!

In the Craft the Chalice is not just a tool to hold liquid for enacting the Rite of Wine and Cakes, it is also the symbol of the Goddess. In the Great Rite it is actually the symbol of her physical body, and the wine it holds becomes the promise of new life. The Chalice is also symbolic of the Goddess as Wise One, where it becomes the cauldron where the magic of inspiration and knowledge is created by the Goddess Ceridwen.

In today's Craft the Chalice can be made of many things: pottery, stone, wood, metal, or glass. It can be highly decorated or plain and simple. It may have been specially made for the Craft or it may be an ordinary glass selected for the purpose. It is usual for every Witch to have his or her own personal one. In addition, where there is a group of Witches who meet regularly there is usually a communal Chalice, often somewhat larger to avoid frequent refilling. Whatever kind of vessel is chosen, it should be kept aside from daily use and only used in magical workings.

"For mine is the cup of the wine of life and the Cauldron of Ceridwen, which is the Holy Grail of Immortality."

THE CHARGE OF THE GODDESS

SOME OF THE FOLKLORE OF 13

The number 13 is often associated with Witches,
the Craft and all things occult, and in most cases
it is thought to be unlucky.

For many years, hotels and flats would be numbered without a number 13, either by missing it out altogether, or by using 12a in its place. It has long been considered unlucky to seat 13 at table for a meal. Where 13 people all sat down together it was important that everyone rose to leave the table at the same time, as should one person be first to leave they would die before the year has ended. Whilst it is often said that the origins of the superstition of 13 as an unlucky number come from the Last Supper, where Jesus sat down with 12 disciples, there is also a Norse legend that 12 Gods gathered for a feast and all was well until Loki, making the 13th, arrived to join them. This legend substantially pre-dates the Christian story.

Another belief is that there should be 13 Witches in a Coven, and that this is the reason why 13 is considered unlucky. Some say that a Coven should be made of 6 couples plus the High Priestess, whilst others go further and say that each person should be of a different sign of the Zodiac. Of course, were this 'rule' to be followed there would be very few Covens indeed!

Friday too was considered to be unlucky and therefore Friday 13th couples two fears in one. Personally speaking I have always found it to be a positive day. Fear of the number 13 is called 'triskaidekaphobia'.

"Bad luck may happen, but good luck can be made."

SELF-CLEANSING

*After the excesses of the festive season many
people choose to start a new dietary regime.
However, these New Year diets often fail,
usually because we ask too much of ourselves.*

It is unreasonable to go from what is effectively a life of excess to one of virtual deprivation, overnight. Also, we often tend to think of them in terms of good and bad foods rather than in terms of treating ourselves kindly. If you have tried one of these for the New Year and are now struggling, why not avail yourself of a little Witchy help?

Take a piece of Amber, a teaspoonful of Fennel seed (from your supermarket herb shelf), a teaspoon of Rock Salt granules and a tablespoonful of powdered milk. Wrap these in a cloth and secure tightly with string or a plastic bag tie. At dawn or dusk, run a fairly warm deep bath with your sachet in the tub. When it is ready, add 3 drops each of oil of Rosemary, Rose and Rosewood. Immerse yourself as completely as you can, ducking your head under the water three times. As you duck, say, in your head (otherwise you may inhale water): "*Water, water take away, all my cares from me today. Give me health, give me strength, help me prolong my life at length.*" On the last immersion say "*Blessed Be.*" Relax and soak away your worries. After you have got out of the bath, remove the sachet and dry the Amber. Carry this in your pocket, or somewhere you can readily touch it, until you have achieved your desire.

*"Food you eat but don't want is as
wasted as that thrown away."*

GOLD

*Gold is the colour linked to the Sun and to the
Element of Fire. It is used in spells for success, power,
prosperity, protection and wisdom. Symbol of the Sun
and the Solar Gods, gold is strongly linked to the male.*

In magic which uses gold it is usually in the form of burning gold candles or writing with a gold pen. However, gold itself is sometimes added to spells, usually in one of the following ways:

'Gold water' can be made by taking a piece of gold (usually jewellery) and placing it in a quantity of rainwater. This is then left in the light of the Full Moon for 3 nights, the jewellery removed and the water kept for use.

Seawater is sometimes used in recipes requiring gold. This is because seawater actually contains minute amounts of gold. If you have enough patience, collect a quantity of seawater and allow it to evaporate naturally. The remaining crystals, although mostly salt, will contain gold, albeit in infinitesimal quantities.

Small sheets of gold leaf can be obtained from art supply shops and pieces brushed off for use in dry spells, or applied to candles. As gold leaf is very tricky to handle, it is a good idea to practise first!

When it is impossible to use gold in any of the above forms then golden oranges and yellows can be substituted.

Wearing gold increases your personal power and energy, and will improve your self-confidence and self-control.

"Friends and family are the real gold of life."

ROSEMARY

An essential herb in my garden and kitchen,
Rosemary has many uses, both physical and magical.

When I was young I was taught that the saying "Rosemary for remembrance" referred to the use of Rosemary in funeral foliage or that it should be planted in memory of someone who has died. However, I now know that this actually refers to Rosemary's capacity for stimulating the memory. Sprigs of Rosemary were worn by Greek students to help them in their examinations, and drinking Rosemary tea definitely helps to focus the mind. Rosemary oil can be added to lotions and rubs and used wherever the circulation is poor. Grown close to more susceptible plants, Rosemary helps to deter pests.

In magic Rosemary is used in spells for love, protection, healing, and to improve mental powers. Give a sachet containing Rosemary to encourage a loved one to think of you. Although a stimulating herb, placed under the pillow it will ensure restful sleep and prevent nightmares. Rosemary water is used for cleansing, especially prior to undertaking any healing work. Rosemary in the bath water is rejuvenating and said to ensure a youthful appearance. Added to incense Rosemary will stimulate psychic powers.

It used to be said that where Rosemary grows well the woman is the 'master' of the house. I cannot vouch for this, but have found that despite a reputation for keeping Witches at bay, Rosemary invariably grows well wherever there are Witches in the house!

"Give your lover Rosemary in a knot,
far better than forget-me-not."

MAKING A WAND

One of the first home-made tools of any Witch is the wand, as it is usually relatively simple.

Most Witches would agree that a wand should be made from wood, preferably fallen not cut. First, find the tree your wood will come from; remember you want it to give you something of itself for your magical work, so take it an offering of some kind by way of introducing yourself. Once you have done this, look all around the tree to see if there is already something suitable on the ground. If there is not, come back at a later date. You may need to repeat this several times.

The piece you are looking for should be straight, about as thick as your thumb, and the length of the area between your elbow and your palm. Once you have something which seems likely, thank the tree, and then take it home to dry. It usually takes around 6 weeks of gentle drying before the wood is ready for working. Whilst you are waiting look several times at your wood and decide if it lends itself to any particular shaping and if you want to remove any bark. When it is ready shape it and remove the bark if you wish. Using sandpaper smooth down both ends and the length too if you wish. Start with a coarse paper and move down to the finest you can get. Then decorate it in the way you prefer and polish it with beeswax. It is now ready to be consecrated.

Good woods for wand making include Oak, Ash, Rowan, Willow and Hazel.

"People are like trees,
it takes time to grow a good one."

GIFTS AND GIVING

It is said that you should never take a gift from
a Witch without giving something in return,
lest you give them power over you.

I have often been asked why this should be; do Witches put curses on their gifts, or on people who don't return them? The short answer is; no we don't. However, here are two valid reasons why this might be said.

First, it is a very old belief that if you owe anyone anything you are in their debt until you have repaid them. Should someone do you a favour and you do not return it they will always be able to 'call it in', and not necessarily in a convenient way or at a good time. If someone gives you a gift, which presumably will have involved some time, effort or money, then you owe them until you have paid them back.

The second reason lies in the fact that in the Craft we do not charge for magical aid and spells (although many Witches may, not unreasonably, charge for ingredients). However, this can lead to excessive requests for magic, with little or no recompense for the time and effort which goes into them. Hence it is not unreasonable to expect something 'in kind' in return. Such items traditionally would have been left at the back door of the Cunning Man or Wise Woman who helped the village. Interestingly enough, I have seen this practised in recent years when parishioners would leave something at the back of the vicarage to repay the Priest who said prayers for them!

"Never take without giving in return,
lest you be beholden to the giver."

THE TRIPLE GODDESS

*The Goddess is seen in 3 aspects: Maiden, Mother
and Crone; which relate to the phases of the Moon, to
aspects of womanhood and to what we do in daily life.*

The Maiden is the New Moon; fresh starts and new beginnings. She is youth, enthusiasm and the season of Spring. She is seen as a young woman, dressed in white with flowers around her head. A woman was a Maiden, no matter how pregnant, until she gave birth to her first child. Hence the Moon's Maiden phase lasts up to the Full Moon. In daily life the Maiden marks the start of all things.

The Mother is the Full Moon; maturity, growth and fertility. She is caring, nurturing and healing. She is seen as a mature woman, dressed in red carrying a basket of fruits, flowers of the season and the harvest. The Full Moon is the time of the Mother Goddess, who cares for us all and gives life to the land. It is a time for reaping rewards. Today we invoke the Mother when we seek healing, understanding and growth.

As the term Crone is deemed somewhat derogatory these days She is often called the Wise One. Her time is marked by the Waning Moon; she is knowledge, wisdom and understanding. She is seen as an older woman with grey hair, dressed in purple or black. The phase of the Crone lasts into the Dark of the Moon (the 3 days each month when no moon appears) and is a time for scrying, divination and for taking our rest after the labours of life.

"The Three in One, the One made Three."

LEGEND, TRIPLE ASPECT

ST AGNES, HUSBAND FINDING EVE

Whilst not a Wiccan date, this night has long been popular with those who seek to find a husband.

There are many traditions associated with this night, all intended to bring dreams of the future husband. Here are some of them. Walking thrice backwards around a churchyard in silence at midnight, scattering hemp seed over the left shoulder. Boiling an egg, removing the yolk and filling the centre with salt and then eating the whole, shell included! Sticking 9 pins into a red onion, taking it backwards to the bedroom and sleeping with it under the pillow. But the most often repeated is that of making a Dumb Cake:

Three, 5 or 7 maidens should gather together on St Agnes Eve and make a cake from flour, salt, eggs and water. While they are mixing and baking the cake all the girls should stand on something different and which they have never stood on before. Each girl should take a hand in adding each of the ingredients and each girl should turn the cake once. When the cake is baked they should eat it all between them. Then, walking backwards, they should all retire to bed where they will dream of their future husbands. The whole process from start to finish should take place in complete silence and should be completed just before midnight.

It is interesting that all these methods include the elements of silence, walking backward and retiring to bed at midnight.

"Be careful what you wish for,
you just might get it!"

ROWAN MONTH

In the Celtic tree calendar this is the first day of the Rowan month.

The Rowan, Mountain Ash or Witchwood is a tree of protection and vision and is sacred to the Crone aspect of the Goddess. Take with you a small offering, such as a little wine or a small biscuit, and seek out a Rowan. You may need to take a guide with you to help you to identify it. When you find the tree, first make your offering to its spirit, saying, *"Graceful Rowan, if it pleases you, let me find some of your wood, that I might protect my home and all who live within it. I give this offering freely as I give my love to the land. Blessed Be."* Search carefully around the tree for fallen wood and take one piece for each of the doors which lead into your home. If you find a piece straight and long enough for a wand, you may also take this. A wand's length is the distance from your elbow to the centre of the palm of your strong hand. Thank the tree and take your wood home with you.

If you have been lucky enough to find a wand, it usually needs at least 6 weeks of gentle drying before it is ready to be worked. (Wand making instructions can be found at 17 January.)

Take your other pieces of fallen wood and tie a small length of red thread around each. Hang them over the doors which enter your home to protect against people bringing negative thoughts and feelings into the house.

"Grow like a tree, your roots in the earth,
yet reaching for the sky."

OLD IMBOLG

**Prior to the Christian tradition of removing
seasonal decorations at Epiphany (6 Jan) it was
the custom to remove Yule greenery and
decorations before Imbolg (2 Feb).**

It was considered very unlucky, possibly even to presage a death in the house, should so much as a leaf be left indoors by this date. Of course if we refer to the pre-1751 calendar, Imbolg would have fallen on 22 January, so if you really want to be on the safe side give your home a thorough check and remove any last traces of the December festive season today. If you had a wooden Yule log with candles you should put this away carefully as you will need it to start next year's Yule celebration.

Now is also the time to start looking for the first signs of approaching Spring. Traditionally Imbolg would not have been set by the calendar but rather by the first lambs being born, the first leaf buds appearing on the trees and the first snowdrops pushing up through the frozen ground. If you have snowdrops growing in your garden do not pick them until you can bring 13 blooms into the house at the same time, as less is considered to attract misfortune. When you have enough, cut them and place them in a small vase by a white candle which you light in honour of arrival of the Maiden Goddess. If you have a lot of snowdrop blooms it is also the time to split the plants and spread them so that next year you will have even more.

*"Welcome the snows, the Spring to impart,
for they in turn do play their part."*

THE SUN IN AQUARIUS

*The Sun has by now entered the zodiacal sign of
Aquarius (see my note on the Zodiac in the Introduction).*

Aquarius is one of the Air signs indicating thought, intellect and communication. It is also one of the Fixed signs bringing strong reactions to stimulus but also stability, reliability and a certain amount of stubbornness.

Those born under this Sun sign are generally intense, self-expressive, progressive, spontaneous, communicative and energetic. The typical Aquarian has strong feelings and embraces humanitarian causes. They will put a lot of energy into a cause but may allow their opinions to blind them to the truth. They are generally intelligent, intuitive and full of ideas. They work well with technology and things science based. Whilst usually faithful their detached manner and independent nature can lead to misunderstandings. On the negative side they can also be eccentric, contrary, tactless and erratic.

For Aquarians this period is one where both their strengths and weaknesses will be heightened, so they need to be careful to focus on putting their positive aspects to the fore. For them this is not the best of times to be working too closely with new people. They also need to be aware of the need to nurture their relationships and not to appear too distant or self-sufficient. Non-Aquarians will find this a good period for matters of the mind; thought, study and learning new things, and also for communication. It is a good time for projects which involve helping others.

> *"Learn to make only promises you are able
> and willing to keep."*

WEATHER PREDICTION

Anyone who has listened to a weather forecast will know that modern science seems no more accurate than the techniques of our forebears, especially if you require something a bit more local than the regional forecast.

The saying, *"Red sky at night, shepherd's delight. Red sky in the morning, shepherd's warning,"* is self-explanatory. But there are many other traditions of weather prediction of which these are just a few: A Cock crowing at bedtime forecasts rain, whilst one crowing during the rain predicts good weather. A Robin sitting in a hedge means it will soon rain. Seaweed hung outside the door will be limp when the weather is to be cold and wet, but if it curls up the weather will be dry.

To whistle at sea would be to summon up the wind, and in my family we were never allowed to whistle in the morning as this would bring rain that day. Another I can vouch for personally: whenever a person's nose becomes cold then rain will follow within the hour. Cold feet (when sensibly wrapped) advise of a cold night, whereas unusually hot feet predict warmer days. If it rains on St Swithin's day (15 July) the weather will be wet for 40 days and nights. A mild January will precede poor Spring weather, whereas a cool July brings a hot August. Cats and children become more boisterous than usual before strong winds, and when a cat sleeps with her face under her forepaws then the temperature is sure to drop.

If you would prefer to influence the weather rather than simply predicting it.

"The slower the journey the more you discover on the way."

SOWING SEEDS

*The weather may be bleak and the land resting but
you can start to bring new life by sowing seeds indoors.
Even if you don't have much of a garden of your own it
can be very rewarding to grow a few things inside.*

If you have plenty of space you may find it worthwhile to invest in commercially-made seed trays and covers, but if space is at a bit of a premium then a few plant pots on saucers with plastic bags over them will provide a good germinating environment. It is worth investing in a good-quality seed compost as this reduces the chances of weeds and diseases. Ensure that the pot will drain well by adding a good amount of gravel to the pot, top up with soil and sow the seeds about ⅔ up the pot. Cover with a little moist soil and place the whole pot under a plastic bag to keep warmth and moisture in. Label carefully and place in a moderately warm, well-lit place, out of direct sunlight, and make sure it does not dry out.

Broadly speaking you should sow annuals at this time of year. Whilst the ultimate choice will be personal, some interesting seeds to sow are Calendula, Campanula, Clary Sage, Delphinium, Nasturtium, Poppy, Marigold, Sunflower, Sweet Pea. Of course the easiest way to choose the plants to sow is a browse round your garden centre. You can also sow fruit seeds (pips) such as apple and orange or even some of the more exotic fruits, although you may have to maintain these as indoor plants for a much longer time.

*"Plant seeds of friendship
if you want love to grow."*

PAN, THE GOAT-FOOT GOD

Pan is one of the Horned Gods and his worship originated in Greece.

Primarily a God of nature, woodland and the countryside, with the feet and legs of a goat and a human body, he is often linked to shepherds and goatherds and depicted playing reed-pipes. He is strongly linked to music, seduction, fertility and protection of the land. He is also one of the 'trickster' Gods, so should be treated with the proper respect.

It is best to approach Pan in his own environment. Take a walk in the woodland at the start of dusk, taking with you some offerings, like a little wine, honey and raisins. Find a secluded tree and sit down under it. Take a few deep breaths and say, *"Pan, Lord of the woodland and glade, I seek knowledge of you and I bring this wine in honour of you."* Pour the wine on the ground. Then say, *"Pan, Lord of the meadow and the field, I seek understanding of you, and I bring this honey to show my respect of you."* Pour the honey on the ground. Now say, *"Pan, Lord of the land and all that lives upon it, I seek your Blessing, and I bring this fruit in offering to you."* Close your eyes and meditate on the God and on the land around you, thinking of all the things you saw on your way there and all the things that surround you. When you feel the presence of Pan, say, *"Bless me Great Pan, that I might know you and care for your land even as you do. Blessed Be."* Wait for a sign, give your thanks, then leave quietly.

"Respect the Old Gods and they may feel more inclined to respect you."

INTERPRETING DREAMS

**There are many books on dream interpretation
but by far and away the best interpretations
will be those you make for yourself.**

To illustrate; many years ago a young girl came to me in tears as she had dreamed that her teeth fell out. Looking in a dream interpretation book she found that this meant the death of someone close. It did not take much Witchcraft for me to ask if she had recently missed a dental appointment, and she had! Quite often our most powerful dreams have the most prosaic of meanings.

To interpret your own dreams try the following: If you feel your dream was significant on waking, write down as much of the dream as you can remember. It need not be in a continuous flow, notes will do. Review your list and make a note beside any aspects which you can easily interpret, e.g. a dream of your dog getting fat might occur if you had decided it was too cold to give it a proper walk. Now using coloured paints or crayons illustrate as much of the rest as possible. This can be in abstract rather than picture form. That evening just before retiring, burn a purple candle, and drink a cup of Rosemary tea whilst reading through your dream notes. Add to your picture if you feel like it. Place the picture and a sprig of Rosemary under your pillow, and your dreams this night should clarify your previous ones.

*"There are some things we
were never meant to know."*

MAKING OFFERINGS

*It is well understood that we should make offerings
to the Gods and the land, however there are good
and not-so-good ways of doing this.*

Most of us feel unhappy, if not actually angry, when we see litter in our parks, roads and countryside. But I also feel a great deal of sadness when I visit an ancient monument, or even a woodland area, and find evidence of previous visitors. This is not just confined to empty cans, packets and discarded cigarette ends, it also includes empty tealight (nightlight) holders, wax, ribbons, and other non-biodegradeable items. Ours is a nature-based belief system and it is up to every one of us to ensure that not only our daily lives but also our magical ones are in harmony with the land.

So what can we offer? Small gifts of things which will benefit the animals, birds and other life such as seeds, grain and fruit are perfectly acceptable. Drinks poured onto the ground are also acceptable in small quantities. For example, a little alcohol can represent an offering of value. Other unobtrusive but natural gifts can include plaits of grasses or even a few hairs tied together. In such cases it is the amount of effort which is put in which counts, not the size of the offering. If it can be easily seen from a couple of paces away then it is almost certainly too much. Remember that if every visitor to a popular site did as you do, would there be a mountain of offerings left to spoil the place for other users.

*"Leave nothing but footprints,
take nothing but memories."*

THE COUNTRYSIDE CODE

A ROMANTIC EVENING SPELL

When planning an evening at home for two it can never hurt to add a little Witchy help to the proceedings.

The first step is, I regret to say, to make sure the environment is tidy and, at the least, relatively clean. This also includes tucking away evidence of children, work brought home, and the like. Subdued lighting can cover a multitude of problems but it is hard to really relax when there is obvious dust and mess about. Next arrange the furnishings, cushions, etc so as to make an inviting place, turn lights down and have as many candles as you have safe holders for, reserving two for your spell. If you are eating, plan a menu of light finger foods which will need little preparation or serving time, so that you are free to actually enjoy the evening and not dashing about all the time.

Next make your magical preparations: You will need two red candles, each anointed with oil of Cardamom. Also, in an oil burner, place 2 drops each of the following oils: Cardamom, Frankincense, Neroli, Rose and Ylang Ylang in plenty of water. Start your burner off and have a bath in which you have also placed a couple of drops of oil of Camomile, Lavender and Neroli, as well as a small piece of Amber. As you bathe visualize the water washing away all the distractions and concerns of everyday life, freeing you to concentrate on your partner. When you are ready to commence your evening, top up the oil burner and light the candles. Now relax and enjoy.

*"When life is busy, focus on the
task ahead, not the one passed."*

THE ROBIN

The Robin is traditionally associated with the winter
months, but is actually around all year and can often
be seen waiting for a gardener to unearth a worm or
two. Traditionally Robins have always been considered
birds of omen and protected from harm.

Robins are very territorial and it is unusual to see more than one in any
location. To see two indicates prosperity for the person who sees them.
To encourage this you might like to have two bird tables at opposite ends
of your garden! It has long been held that it is very unlucky for a Robin
to come into the house, even to the point where cards bearing pictures of
Robins are discarded rather than kept or sent. Having said that, my own
family tradition held that a Robin on the doorstep meant a gift was on its
way. A Robin tapping on the window of a sick room was said to presage
the death of the person within. If it tapped on another window, it would
mean the death of a person in the family.

To harm a Robin would also bring ill-fortune, and anyone caught
doing so would risk being paraded through the town with the dead bird
around their neck. In certain parts of the country, stealing a Robin's egg
would mean being ostracised by the rest of the community. A feather
which has fallen from a Robin is a very powerful ingredient in prosperity magic when it is burned in the flame of a green candle.

*"He sees most clearly
who stands and looks."*

WART CHARMING

Warts are somehow inextricably linked to Witches.
The caricature Witch invariably has a wart on her
nose, and it used to be said that if someone was truly
a Witch they would have the power to cure warts.

Warts can be counted away. The sufferer should count their warts and give their name and the number to the healer, who would tell them to 'uncount' their warts. The warts should then vanish within two weeks. I have 'bought' warts by giving a person a coin for them which they then rub on and retain until the warts go. However, it is said that if someone who is not a true Witch tries this then they will gain the warts! Alternatively, cross each wart nine times with a new pin and cast it away (outdoors please) over your left shoulder.

Many plants are said to aid the healing of warts: cut a notch for each wart into a piece of Elder, then rub the stick on the warts and burn it on an open fire. Another version says the stick should be placed in the road so that another finds it and takes the warts! An apple cut in half should be rubbed on the wart, sewn together and buried. As the apple rots so the wart will go. This rubbing and burying also applies to meat, pieces of bread pinched out from inside a freshly baked loaf, and straw. The juice of a freshly-picked Dandelion is said to speed their removal, as is that of the Spurge, Celandine and Elderberry.

> "Ask not what the Craft can do for you,
> but what have you done for the Craft."

IMBOLG EVE

In Celtic times the day was considered to begin at
dusk the preceding night, so all major celebrations
would commence the night before the day of the
festival, much as New Year festivities start on its eve.

Also called Imbolc, Oimelc and Candlemas, this is the festival of Bride or
Bridget. It celebrates the Goddess's transformation from Crone to
Maiden and heralds the coming Spring and the change from dark to light.
One of the ways to celebrate this is with a Circle of lights.

Everyone gathers in a Circle, lit only by a single black candle; the
wick should be trimmed to give the smallest of flames. Each person has an
unlit white candle. When everyone is ready someone says, *"This is the fes-*
tival of Imbolg and the first signs of returning life tell us that Spring is on
its way. Let us light the path for the new season and say farewell to the old.
Blessed Be." They light their white candle from the black one, state something they wish for in the coming season, and extinguish the black candle.
Going around the group Deosil, each person states their own hopes and
lights their candle from that of the person next to them. When all the candles are lit, everyone says together, *"We welcome the Goddess as Maiden.*
We welcome the signs of new life. We welcome the coming Spring. Blessed
Be." The candles can be placed somewhere safe to burn whilst everyone
enjoys a feast or, if this is not a family celebration, they may be extinguished and taken home to *bring* Spring into everyone's homes.

"When you know you can't win,
consider another game."

IMBOLG

As with all the Sabbats it is a time to celebrate the
changes in the land around us. It is important to be
outside to see, feel, smell and appreciate the way that
nature is changing, to pay our respects to the Gods
and to seek their guidance for the coming season.

You can either take a walk to a favourite place, where you will be able to
appreciate the changes around you or, as this is a time of new beginnings,
it can be interesting to take a new route. Whichever your choice, take
with you a small amount of spring water, or collected rain water. As you
go, take care to notice the signs of new life and growth and whenever you
see new shoots, buds or leaves sprinkle a few drops on the plant and give
thanks to the Goddess.

If you should come across a well or a spring, take the time to make
an offering to the waters within. If you have finished the water you
brought then your offering should be something which will not contam-
inate the water in any way. Where a tree grows close to this water you can
also tie a single hair to one of its branches and ask for a Blessing for yourself or for someone close to you.

If you should be lucky enough to pass grazing land look out for the
first lambs of the year. If you see your first lamb of the year on this day
you can make a wish.

"Take pleasure in the journey,
as arriving is its end."

THE GODDESS BRIDE

As with many Goddesses, Bride has many names:
Bride (pronounced Bre-id), Brigantia, Brigid,
Brigandu, Brigit; and was taken over by the
Christians and renamed Bridget.

In her various guises she is a Goddess of smith-craft, poetry, inspiration, healing and medicine. She is also credited with inventing keening (the mourning song) and whistling. In Ireland she is known as the fire Goddess Brigid 'bright one' and Brigid of the bright (or fiery) arrow.

One of the older Imbolg rituals involves making Bride's bed. The women of the household make a corn doll and dress it with white cloth and coloured ribbons. The men make a phallic wand of the same length as the Bride doll. These would be placed together in the hearth, surrounded by candles, last thing at night. In the morning the ashes would be inspected for signs of the God's visit; perhaps the shape of the wand, or a footprint in the ashes. If something was found it would indicate that the Goddess and God had been united and fertility would follow.

For those without a real fire, a modern alternative is to place both Bride and the wand in a bed together. Then each person writes on a slip of paper something they wish fertility for in the coming year. These slips are then carefully burnt and the ashes collected and placed at the foot of the bed. Small candles are burnt around the bed and once they have finished everyone retires and leaves the bed until the morning. The following day the ashes are inspected and any markings and patterns are interpreted.

"The Gods are present in everyone;
you just have to work out which Gods!"

MAKING A CIRCLET OF LIGHTS

Yet another tradition associated with Imbolg is the
making of a circlet of lights which can be worn by a
Priestess taking the role of Bride in the Sabbat Ritual.
This 'crown' is placed on her head and she wears it
whilst moving around the circle to bring in the
light and fire of the Goddess.

The most usual method is to make a crown topped with a number of tiny
candles (the type placed on birthday cakes). Even though her hair is protected by a foil lining to the crown, this is still a risky business and the
wearer has to have good poise to avoid getting wax (or worse) in her hair,
not to mention nerves of steel. I can speak from experience here! Of
course someone good with electricity could create a similar effect with
'fairy' lights but it would need to operate off a battery pack, rather than
the mains current. A far safer and easier method is to create symbolic candles from paper and coloured foil. For younger members of the family it
can be fun to make a ring of paper with a cross piece over the crown of
the head. Onto this is placed a suitably decorated loo roll holder.

Alternatively, you can incorporate the circlet of lights into the
Bride's bed ritual, or make it the centre point of your feast, by weaving
spring flowers and leaves into a preformed florist's circle and placing
candles into this.

*"Magic and machinery rarely mix,
and magic's older!"*

CREATE YOUR ASTRAL TEMPLE

**An Astral Temple is a form of Sacred Space
which is created on the Astral (or psychic) plane.**

It has a number of advantages over the conventional Sacred Space. It can be located in any environment you choose, and will be available to you wherever and whenever you wish. It does not require the use of special tools or equipment and, created properly, will always be away from prying eyes and touching fingers. Some Covens will create one which provides them with a meeting place for magical working when they are physically distant from one another. Some Solitaries use one so that they have a private and safe place for meditation, pathworking and the like.

An Astral Temple is created through meditation and visualization, so you will need to make sure that you will be completely undisturbed during your working. Before you begin, decide what sort of setting you would like; indoor, outdoor, etc. Now settle yourself down comfortably, close your eyes and do a few breathing exercises to relax. Visualize yourself travelling to your chosen environment, taking with you something valuable by way of an offering. Call upon each of the Elements, the Goddess and the God, in your usual way, and ask each for their Blessing on your Sacred Space. Visualize yourself casting the Circle and making all secure. Now kneeling in the centre of your Sacred Space, visualize the Goddess and the God at your Altar, rise, greet them and make your offering. If they place the offering on your Altar, then your Astral Temple is ready for use. Otherwise, repeat the exercise another time.

*"The more you worship your Gods,
the greater in power they grow."*

FOOT SOOTHING LOTION

They support us, they take us everywhere we wish to
go, they affect our mood, the way we look and the
way we respond to others, and yet most of the time
we simply forget about them. But once in a while
it's a really good idea to give our feet a treat.

Make a soothing lotion by taking about 2 tablespoons of unscented hand
lotion and add 3 drops of oils of Peppermint, Lavender and Chamomile.
Before using the lotion give your feet a good scrub by adding a tablespoon of coarse salt to one of dried semolina and mixing to a stiff paste
with some warm water. Massage it into your feet for about 5 minutes.
Wash off thoroughly with warm water and pat them dry with a warm
towel. Now massage them again with your soothing lotion and then lie
down with your feet raised above your head for 15 minutes; on the sofa
with them on the arm is good.

There are many traditions associated with feet. When the soles itch
you will be going to walk on strange ground. If a woman's first toe is
longer than her big toe, then she will always be 'master' in her own
house. If this is seen in a man he will be unkind to his wife! In some
places webbed toes are said to indicate a person who will not drown. But
I have heard it said that if the toes be even slightly webbed it is the sign
of a Witch.

*"Care for 'the land and all
things living' includes yourself."*

JASMINE

Jasmine is a plant which has many species providing
flowers from the winter to the summer. It is closely
linked to the Goddess as Maiden and incenses made
with Jasmine flowers should be burnt in her honour.

Oil of Jasmine should be worn by the Priestess whenever she wishes to
invoke the Goddess as Maiden and a few of the flowers can be added to
a little mead to make a libation to the Goddess.

The scent of Jasmine has long been associated with love and romance
and a sachet made with Jasmine, Rose and Gardenia flowers will, if carried close to the heart, draw a true love to you. Jasmine flowers can be
burnt in the bedroom to induce sleep and bring prophetic dreams.
Jasmine flowers collected at midnight on the Full Moon can be worn to
attract money.

Jasmine oil is psychologically healing, helping to reduce anxieties,
stress, sadness, extreme moods and encouraging emotional expression. It
can also help to ward off colds if used in the bath as soon as the first signs
are felt. A syrup made from Jasmine flowers and honey is also held to
soothe coughs, although you would need a substantial quantity of flowers to make even a small amount. An alternative is to make Jasmine-
scented sugar by layering the flowers with sugar in a jar, covering with a
damp cloth and standing in a cool place for a few hours, before removing the flowers. However it is worth noting that the fruit of the Jasmine
is poisonous!

"Remember you own the phone,
not the other way around."

MAKING AN ASPERGER

An Asperger is used to sprinkle oil, water or even
occasionally wine. Whilst it is in no way an essential
tool for the Witch, as you can always use your fingers,
it is a simple and effective tool to make.

The resting season is a good time of year to make an Asperger, as you will be able to see and select the types of wood you need. If you have your own garden you can make this selection part of reshaping the tree or plant in question. Some plants which lend themselves to this are Broom, Rosemary and Sage (if you have a very well-developed plant). You will need to gather a few twigs about 20 to 30 cm long. Each should branch into several pieces about half way down. If the wood is green (living) you will need to thoroughly dry it out. Tie the twigs together just above the point where they branch, binding the un-branched ends together with a fine ribbon so that the whole resembles a sort of mini besom (broom-stick). Some people like to choose the colour of their binding ribbon or ribbons to honour the Gods: white, red and purple for the Triple Goddess; golden orange for the Sun God, and so on. Alternatively, you might choose greens and browns to celebrate the fact that this has actually come from a living plant.

Before using your Asperger in your Rites, take it outside and practise with water until you can be sure that you can achieve a light and even sprinkling, rather than sousing everything and everyone in sight!

*"Trying and failing achieves far more
than not even giving it a go."*

HOUSE CLEANSING

Whenever you move into a new home it is as well to
cleanse it to remove any residual negative energies which
may have been left behind by the previous occupants.
You may also like to do this after any period of upset in
your home to thoroughly drive out the problem, or if you
have been visited by someone who seems to have left
some of their negativity behind them.

You will need a broom, some sea water, or rain water with some sea salt
dissolved in it, and an Asperger. Open all the windows and doors in your
house and starting from the centre sweep the whole house. Move Deosil
as much as possible. As you go, visualize all negativity as wispy grey
cloud which you are driving out through the windows and doors. Now
take your salt water and Asperger and sprinkle the salt water around the
boundaries of your whole home, making sure that you include the sills of
all the doors and windows. Be very careful not to make every thing too
wet or to sprinkle any electrical equipment, switches or sockets, etc. As
you do each door or window say, "*I mark this boundary that no negativity be allowed to enter here. Blessed Be.*" and then close it.

If the weather is really inclement you may need to work room by
room rather than doing the whole house in one go. In this case make sure
you cover the boundaries between rooms and any passageways, stairs, etc
without windows.

*"Don't give negative
thoughts your energy."*

CRYSTAL MAGIC

Stones and crystals are often employed in magic and spells, a use which goes back thousands of years.

There are hundreds of kinds of stones, from pebbles to diamonds, and some of the more commonly used are discussed in this book. Each kind of stone has its own energy, described as vibrationary energy, and hence lends itself to different magical workings. We use them to hold, activate and enhance our spells. They are often used when working magic for another, as they provide a tangible reminder of the spell concerned, and they can be carried, like a talisman of protection. Crystals are also used in healing and in divination.

Whilst there are many accepted uses of different crystals, even within several of the same kind there will be some which are better for your purpose than others. The best way to determine which stone will be best for a particular purpose is to place several in front of you and with your eyes closed pass your strong hand, palm downwards, over each until you locate the one which feels right. The feeling you are seeking is a particular vibration of energy on the psychic plane. Many of the crystals we use today are mined using explosives and some are even prepared using child slave labour, and their properties will be affected by this. They will not be as true in their energy as a pebble you have collected yourself from the beach or on a walk. So, when you buy crystals, do ask about their origins, or use your inner sight to see if they feel right.

"Rarity is not a reliable measure of worth."

THE JAY

This brightly coloured bird has pink and blue feathers
much sought after in magical working, and is the
source of a number of omens. As with most
feather magic, it is, however, important that
the feather(s) should be fallen.

When a Jay's feather is found then the finder can expect to receive something they have long wanted. A Jay's feather worn in the hat means you
will never have empty pockets, but otherwise brought into the house
indicates there will never be silence. I sometimes wonder if there's a hidden Jay's feather in my home! A single Jay's feather placed in a small bag
together with a piece of Serpentine and hung around the neck will stop
excessive nosebleeds. A similar pouch with a Jay's feather and a green
stone, such as Malachite or Jade, will attract riches. Although you might
like to note that many spells to attract riches do not necessarily bring
monetary riches! A singed pink feather carried in the pocket will dispel
negative feelings.

On seeing a Jay you should always raise your hat, or otherwise salute
it. Two Jays together indicate a romantic meeting, but three or more will
indicate a quarrel. Should a Jay cross your path from right to left, something unwanted will be leaving you. If it flies the other way, you should
turn around three times to avoid something bad coming. When a Jay hops
in front of you, count the number of hops before it flies off: this indicates
the number days before you can expect a visitor.

"Thinking first beats regretting second."

WHITE

**White is one of the colours of the Maiden.
It is from this that its links with purity originate as
it is only from the Victorian era that white became
a popular colour for a wedding dress.**

In magic white represents the Moon, particularly the New Moon. It is linked to sleep and psychic abilities. Placing a white stone under your pillow will drive away nightmares and is particularly useful for children, as long as they are old enough to be trusted not to swallow it. White is protective and carrying a white stone in your pocket will give you extra protection during the hours of darkness, although it is no substitute for caution! Carrying a white stone in your pocket is also said to relieve headaches. White reflects back all light and is therefore illuminating, and the wearing of white, especially to sleep in, is said to enhance the ability to see clearly on both the psychic and physical planes. Whenever you feel that you cannot clearly see the cause and solution of a problem, place a white stone under your pillow, wear white to bed and sleep in the light of the Full Moon. The answer will come to you the following day.

White is also said to contain all colours and therefore white candles and white stones can be magically charged to represent any colour. To do this you need to visualize the colour you are intending and, in your mind's eye, change the colour before use.

*"The problem with common sense
is that it's not all that common."*

LOVE DIVINATION

Love divination traditionally takes place at many
times of the year, including St Agnes' Eve,
Midsummer's Eve, Halloween, Christmas Eve
and, of course, St Valentine's Eve.

Whilst historically these are usually carried out by girls, there is no reason why they should not work just as well for a boy. Here are just a few.

A blue thread should be thrown over the left shoulder and out of the window. Its shape will indicate the initial of the loved one.

Two girls should sit in silence from midnight to 1am. Each should pull as many hairs from her head as she is years old and place them in a clean white cloth with some Moonwort fern. At the stroke of 1, each should burn these hairs, one at a time in the flame of a white candle. Then, still not speaking, they should retire to bed where they will dream of their true love.

To bring your true love to you, you should sit on the doorstep shelling peas until you find a pod with nine peas in it. This should be placed on the threshold of the kitchen door and the next man to cross over it will be your sweetheart.

The new bride should give a piece of wedding cake to each of her unmarried friends, which, if they put it under their pillow on the night after the wedding, will give them dreams of their future partner.

Go out at dawn on St Valentine's Day and seek the trail of a snail. The first you see will have the shape of your future lover's initial.

*"Relationships are easy: it's
having good ones which is hard."*

VALENTINE'S DAY

**Whilst in no way a Wiccan festival Valentine's Day
has become so much a part of our modern calendar
that it seems unreasonable to omit it here.**

Having said that, whilst this day is named after one of two Christian
Martyrs of the same name, there have been fertility festivals around this
time far longer.

15 February is the Roman festival of Faunus, also known to the
ancient Greeks as Lupercalia or the festival of Pan. Both woodland
deities, Faunus and Pan are closely linked at this time to Priapus who
originated in Asia, definitely a fertility God. Images of the God were decorated and displayed through the streets, and the Priests would whip
members of the crowd, especially women, to bring about fertility.

In addition to the Gods and festivals of fertility there are a great
number of Gods and Goddesses who are linked to love, like Eros, Venus
and Hathor, and these are perhaps more appropriate deities to honour if
you are seeking love and romance. Light a pink candle to your chosen
deities and ask them to bring you a true love. Resist the temptation to
work magic to make someone love you: not only is it unethical but it also
invariably results in problems and disappointment.

Whilst today it is customary for us to send a greetings card, whether
romantic or humorous, to those we love, this only originated in the
Victorian era. Before this it was a country custom, which still exists in
some parts, for unattached girls and boys to draw names from which to
choose their partner for the day.

"Popularity is for people who can't tell right from wrong."

EROS

*In the centre of London's Piccadilly is a statue
of a winged youth carrying a bow with which to
shoot arrows into the hearts of couples he wishes
to fall in love with each other.*

Called Eros, this statue is very much a watered down version of the son of the Greek Goddess Aphrodite. This dilution of his power is taken further by representations in art of his Roman counterpart Cupid, son of Venus. The original Eros, far from being the son of Aphrodite, was one of the 'first Gods'. These four, including Gaia, Nyx and Erebus, headed the Greek pantheon, in much the same way that Isis, Osiris, Nepthys and Set were the four major Egyptian Gods. Rather than a sort of mischievous cherub, Eros was the God who determined and ruled over relationships and who brought peace and order from chaos. His is the middle ground between totally selfless love where the personality is submerged within another, and control where one seeks power over another. He is a God of balance and of the kind of relationship where both parties are equal and true partners.

Eros is a God to approach when a relationship seems to be at risk of being one-sided, or when a person has a blinkered approach to love. When a couple works a Rite to honour Eros it will bring greater depth and balance to the relationship, and can be particularly helpful in solving deep-seated disagreements.

*"Lost for words?
Then leave a space!"*

DRAWING PARTNERS
CLOSER TOGETHER

**Although an obvious Rite to perform around
Valentine's Day, this can be performed at any time.**

Before your ritual you should each make a circlet for the other. The man should weave Roses into the one for the woman and she should weave Bay leaves into his. Ensure you have some Rose petals and Bay leaves over. You will also need two wine glasses; each with a red and a pink ribbon tied around the stem, and some pleasant wine or fruit juice. Prepare a warm, clean and romantic environment, where you can be sure of being undisturbed. Spread cushions or pillows on the floor and scatter around some Bay leaves and Rose petals, saving some for an offering.

Seat yourselves comfortably facing one another and call upon Eros and his partner Psyche to join with you. Place the circlets on each other's heads. Now take a glass of wine each and toast each other, praising some aspect of your partner, take a small sip and then exchange glasses. Now take your circlet and remove one Rose petal or Bay leaf and place it in your partner's circlet. Repeat the toasting and sharing of leaf and flower until both circlets contain equal amounts of Bay and Roses. Finally, refill both glasses and add 3 petals and 3 leaves to one, together raise this to Eros and Psyche, giving thanks to the God and Goddess of loving relationships, later pour it onto the ground. Share the other glass between you.

*"Comfortable silence shows a better relationship
than mindless chatter."*

BEES AND HONEY

Bees, one of the staples of country living,
have a long and interesting folklore.

You should always tell them of family changes: births, deaths, marriages and most especially moves, lest they abandon the hive or even die. Bees should never be bought or sold, but exchanged for something of like value. If they must be paid for the exchange should involve a piece of gold. It is known that bees communicate with one another through movement, but it is also said that their movements can tell us things. A bee flying into the house indicates the coming of a visitor. One flying around a sleeping baby should never be shooed away as it foretells a happy life. Swarming bees are likewise watched for their actions; if they settle on a dead branch it is said to foretell a death nearby, on the roof of a house means good fortune, but on the walls bad luck is coming.

Honey has long been prized for its healing, health-giving and cosmetic properties. In the past it was used to dress wounds as it provides an antiseptic 'seal' under dressings and promotes rapid healing. A honey poultice, warmed and placed on a dressing, will 'draw' bruises and swellings. Honey is well known for its ability to help sore throats, coughs and colds, and local honey will help to prevent hay-fever. Applied to the skin, honey whitens and smoothes.

Bees are traditionally one of the creatures into which a Witch might put her mind to travel whilst asleep. Honey is often used as a magical payment, to recompense both the Gods and the individual Witch.

"Is getting your own back
worth spoiling your own life?"

ASH TREE MONTH

The Ash is one of the most magical trees.

Yggdrassil, the World Tree, the one from which Odin hung to gain the Runes, is thought to have been an Ash. The Ash was called a check on peace for it was from this tree that spears were made. It is a tree of Initiation and intelligence. It is said that the Ash should never be burnt or cut down, but it is permissible to take wood from the living tree if you make the appropriate offerings first. The Ash is a tree of protection and they were planted to keep Witches at bay, although as with many things thought to ward off Witches it is quite possible that this was invented to cover the magical uses of the tree.

As well as being used to make spear shafts, it was also used to make the quarterstaff. Ash is a healing tree and a staff would be placed over the door to keep illness at bay. Ash leaves placed in water would be placed by the bed to prevent sickness from entering overnight, the water and leaves being renewed each evening; a good idea if someone in the house has an illness which you do not want others to catch. Ash leaves are also carried in the pocket to attract the admiration of the opposite gender. Placed beneath the pillow the leaves will bring on prophetic dreams. Scattered around the house the leaves act as a protection.

Note that you should never stand under an Ash during a thunderstorm as they are said to attract lightning.

> *"The grass may be greener on the other side,*
> *but it also needs more mowing."*

QUARTZ

Quartz and crystal are terms which are often used interchangeably to refer to a wide range of stones.

However, there are many types of Quartz and each has its own energy. Many of these, such as Amethyst and Carnelian, are given their own names, while others are known as Quartzes, like Rose Quartz.

Crystal Quartz is often employed in the Craft; it is symbolic of the Great Mother, the Moon, the Sun, and the 5th Element, Spirit. It has powers of healing, protection and psychic enhancement. It can be worn to enhance these energies during ritual, placed on the Altar to represent the Goddess and the God or to act as a magical 'amplifier', attached to a silver chain to make a pendulum, and much more. Genuine Crystal will rarely be completely clear, so look for flaws in the stone to prove it is the real thing. Thirteen natural Crystals, or points, can be used to create a magic circle for divination or ritual. A single Crystal placed in a glass of spring water in the light of the Full Moon makes a healing drink, but remove the stone first!

Quartz is available on the beach, although it will rarely be clear. These stones, which have been tumbled by the sea, are excellent for use in spells and magic. To make a magical tool collect a number of such stones and enough sand to cover a dinner plate. Spread the sand over the plate and place the stones in a spiral. When working your spell trace the stones inward to the centre and then out to the edge, three times, whilst repeating your need.

"It's our faults that make us real."

THE ATHAME

The Athame (pronounced Ath-a-mee),
or Witch's Knife, is probably the second
most important tool for the Witch.

It is used by the Witch as an extension of both their hand and their will.
With regular use it actually builds up a reservoir of energy which the
owner can access. As a result an Athame becomes intensely personal to
the Witch and it is not only the height of bad manners to touch someone
else's Athame, but in some Covens can result in being disciplined.

Strictly speaking an Athame is a black-handled knife with a double-
edged blade which is 9 inches (23 cm) in length. Many Traditional
Witches do not take iron into the Circle so the blade needs to be of some
other metal. Indeed some do not take any metal into the Circle and will
use an Athame made of wood or some other material. Athames are frequently decorated with symbols prior to consecration, but traditionally
these should not be permanent. It used to be a tradition of the Craft that
a newly-acquired Athame was firstly placed under the pillow for a full
lunar cycle and then 'blooded' by its owner prior to consecration. Some
Witches advocate the making of your own magical tools but I am very
wary of entering the Circle with a home-made Athame, as I'm well aware
of what might happen if blade and handle part company! Many Covens,
presumably with large Altars, encourage everyone to place their Athame
on the Altar; others prefer to carry it in a holder at the waist.

"Never give a blade without a coin in return,
lest you cut your friendship."

TRADITIONAL.

CROCUS

One of the plants pushing its way through the chill ground is the spring Crocus.

A hardy plant, it is weather resistant and very welcome to the birds who will feast on its flowers unless you protect them. It is also known as Saffron, although only one variety, *Crocus Sativus*, yields the pistils known as the spice saffron used in cooking. Although very expensive, only a few strands of Saffron are needed in most recipes, and the pistils of other Crocuses can be used in magical working.

The Crocus is associated with the fertility Goddesses Astarte (or Ashtoreth) and Eos. It is used in spells for happiness, love, healing, lust and strength, as well as spells for women seeking to become pregnant, although the latter should not consume it. Saffron sachets were worn on the stomach during labour to induce a speedy delivery.

A drink made from Saffron aids the digestion; reducing flatulence and wind, it induces perspiration thereby speeding recovery from colds and flu, and helps to strengthen menstruation. It is also drunk to strengthen the mind and brighten the spirits. Used in Divination it increases clairvoyance. A couple of strands of Saffron are added to white wines or mead in the Chalice to honour the Goddess, and Crocus petals, or Saffron water, may be sprinkled around the Altar or Circle in Her honour.

Saffron has long been much prized as a dye, giving deep golden yellows and oranges, so care should be taken when handling it as it may stain.

"Smiles open better doors than frowns."

CHAKRA BALANCING

**One technique for whole body healing is
balancing the Chakras, the seven major
junctions in the energy lines of the body.**

When these are balanced, energy flows uninterrupted through the body, but an imbalance can lead to discomfort, lethargy and even illness.

The Chakras each have a function and colour of the rainbow. The Base Chakra, at the bottom of your torso, is red. Reproductive, just above the pelvic bone, is orange. Stomach, at the navel, is yellow. Heart, in the centre of the chest, is green. Throat, just below your Adam's apple, is blue. Third eye, in the centre of your forehead, is indigo. Crown, at the top of your head, is violet.

One way of Chakra balancing is through meditation and visualization. Find a warm, comfortable, private environment, lie flat on your back and close your eyes. Take several deep breaths to relax. Now visualize a red disc spinning over your base Chakra. When you can see it clearly, visualize an orange disc spinning over the reproductive Chakra, whilst still seeing the red one. Continue up through the Chakras, keeping the preceding discs spinning until you reach the crown. Here you visualize the energy rising up through your body and then down, covering you. Keep this going for a minute or so then, in reverse order, visualize each of the discs slowing and ceasing to spin until you reach the base again. At the base slow the spinning without stopping it completely. Take a few more breaths, and then ground yourself with something to eat and drink.

*"Pay attention when the Goddess drops you a hint;
next time it won't be just a hint."*

THE SUN IN PISCES

The Sun has entered Pisces, one of the Water signs
indicating the intangible world of feelings and
emotions. It is also one of the Mutable signs
bringing flexibility and problem solving.

Those born when the Sun is in this sign are generally sensitive, compassionate and easy going. They are receptive, imaginative, and many have strong intuitive and psychic abilities. A typical Piscean is very unworldly, and will react strongly to suffering, either doing everything to help or by recoiling. They are very fluid, hard to pin down, and do not easily conform. They work best where rational thought and control are not required, being good at caring and things artistic. In relationships they can be very intense and lovable but are less effective on the practical side. On the negative side they can be over-emotional and inclined to think of themselves as being the victim, and their very flexibility can also lead them to changing direction and to extremes of thought. Pisceans can also be submissive, gullible and easily disillusioned.

At this time Pisceans need to avoid making commitments, taking strangers on trust, and over-reacting to people and events. They should also avoid practical tasks such as DIY. It is however a good time for looking inward and working on deep-seated problems. Others should be aware that emotional swings are probable in this period. It is a good time for lavishing care and attention on the self, and also for water-based activities.

*"A good friend will always make you smile,
however wryly."*

IN THE GARDEN

By now the garden should be showing signs of Spring.
Before the growing season gets under way it is
a good idea to spend some time removing the
last of the winter debris.

You should be able to see clearly what has died back and needs tidying up. If you wait for a truly warm day then nature will start to get away from you! Remember that any task you dedicate to the Gods will go more easily.

Many birds which spent Winter elsewhere are now returning home, seeking mates and building nests. There are several ways that you can help them. If you had feeders out over the Winter this is the time to take them down, give them a good clean with a stiff brush and warm water, no chemicals please, dry and return them. Remember to keep filling them as small birds particularly need to eat almost their own bodyweight every day to survive, let alone feed a growing family. Many people do not recommend feeding whole peanuts at this time of year in case young birds choke. However, if you put them in mesh feeders then the adults will have to break them up to get them out. Stone bird baths and water holders can be cleaned using sand and a wire brush or scourer. Where you have the space put up nest boxes. If you groom your dog or cat, then place some of the groomings in the hedge so the birds can line their nests, although do not do this within a week of any treatment such as shampoo or flea drops.

"On a clear day you can see ...
all of the weeds!"

KNOW YOURSELF

We live in a strange world, where bookshop
shelves groan under the weight of self-help books,
where counsellors and therapists abound, yet
despite this we rarely see ourselves truly.

If you want to grow, you have to have an honest understanding of yourself. The following exercise is one I set most of those who come to me in the Craft.

Take a large sheet of paper and divide it into two columns. Head the first 'Things I like about me'. Under this heading write at least 20 things you like about yourself. They could be physical, like nice eyes; mental, like logical thinker; emotional, like true to my friends, or general. Most people find this a challenge, so give yourself a few days to come up with your list. Head the second column 'Things I dislike about me', and list 20 things you consider negative. Now, put the list aside for at least 2 days, before the next phase. Alongside your 'likes' note whether this is something you were born with or something you have learned or worked on in some way. Now take your dislikes and examine each one. Is it something you dislike because of the way you feel you 'ought' to be or look because of outside fashions, trends or stereotypes? Is it something you could change about yourself? When you have finished you should have a number of things to congratulate yourself on, some to work on, and some which are more a question of the world accepting you rather than you conforming to the advertisers' ideals!

"'What if' will never change the past,
but it can change the future."

THE WITCHES CIRCLE

Creating a magic Circle is one of the keystones of the Craft.

The Circle is our Sacred Space, and can be created wherever and whenever we need it. It helps focus our concentration, contain our energies until we are ready to release them, and protect us from outside negative influences. The Circle is created by invoking the Elements from within and without and by inviting the Goddess and the God, and is completed by Casting a Circle of containment and protection, which is in actual fact a sphere. The Circle should be created every time we perform a spell, work magic, celebrate Ritual and even when we meditate.

The traditional Circle is 9 feet (2.7 m) across and is often measured by placing the 4'6" (1.35 m) cord from your robes onto a peg in the centre and using the free end to describe a circle. Some groups mark the circumference with chalk or with salt, but most of us are limited by room size and have to make do with the space we can create there. When working outside it is common to mark the quarters of the Circle; the East, South, West and North points, with candles or Quarter Lights. When working in a group it is better to create a physical Circle with an Altar, using tools and invocations, but when on your own it can be done on the psychic plane.

Once the Ritual or working is over the Circle is removed by thanking the Elements, the Goddess and the God and by taking down the Circle.

"The Craft doesn't solve all your problems,
but it may bring a new set of interesting ones!"

SELF-CONFIDENCE CHARM

*Self-confidence and self-esteem make everything
seem easier; indeed things always seem to work better
for people with these qualities. Some are born with
them, but the rest of us sometimes need a little help.*

Take 2 pink candles, a mirror, a piece of Rose Quartz, a sliver of fresh
Ginger, a few Bergamot flowers, Ylang Ylang oil and a small bag of gold-
en fabric tied with a pink ribbon or cord. Take a bath or shower with
your favourite scents or soaps. Dress in something comfortable which
makes you feel special. Find yourself a comfortable position where you
can see your face in the mirror and stand the candles safely on either side
of it. Place your other magical ingredients in front of the mirror. Light
both candles and spend a few minutes looking at your reflection, concen-
trating until you can visualize a golden halo of light around your head.
Next take the Rose Quartz, pass it briefly over each of the candle flames,
saying, *"Great Mother, bring me confidence in the qualities you have
given me,"* and place it in the bag. Pass the Ginger over the flames, saying, *"Mighty Father, bring me confidence in the strengths you have given
me,"* and place that in the bag. Now add the Bergamot flowers and say,
"To inspire me by day." Finally add 2 drops of oil and say, *"To soothe me
by night."* Tie the cord around the bag and say, *"As is my will, so mote it
be. Blessed Be."* If it is safe, let the candles burn all the way down. Carry
the bag with you at all times.

*"You must be important,
otherwise you wouldn't care."*

PARSLEY

Parsley is another useful herb which has a history of being associated with Witchcraft.

Like others with this association it is said that where Parsley grows a woman rules. Folklore also says that it is bad luck to give or receive it, that only the wicked can grow it, and that in order for it to flourish, it must be planted by a woman (you have to wonder sometimes!). Whatever is said, though, Parsley is almost invaluable in cooking, medicinal herbalism and in magical work.

Parsley adds flavour to all kinds of foods and is excellent for the stomach and digestion. It is rich in vitamins A, B and C and counters strong-tasting foods, removing traces of even raw onion and garlic from the breath. A strong tea cleanses the blood and can help to regulate the kidneys, as well as being beneficial in cases of rheumatism. The roots of Parsley can be eaten as a vegetable. Moistened leaves placed over the eyes soothe and ease itchiness, or can be rubbed into insect bites and stings. An infusion of parsley is said to lighten the skin and remove freckles. It is even said that floating parsley on the garden pond helps to keep the fish healthy.

Parsley is used in baths for purification and protection prior to Ritual. It can be eaten in rituals to promote fertility and lust and it is said that when a woman seeks to be pregnant she should sow Parsley seed and pick the resultant crop, although she should not eat it. Parsley should always be picked and not cut, lest you cut your love and your luck.

"When in doubt, breathe deeply."

LEAP DAY

In our modern calendar 29 February comes once
every 4 years to make up for the fact that the Earth's
orbit around the Sun is not an exact number of days.

In some ways this corresponds to the intercalary days, or days outside of the calendar which existed previously. Although Samhain and Beltane occurred every year they were very much perceived as days apart. People stopped work at these festivals to attend to their spiritual work. They were days when the veil between the worlds was thin and spirits might pass between this world and the other. Whilst also being festivals associated with the agricultural cycle they were additionally days where the land and people needed protection against spirits which might deceive, mislead or beguile.

Samhain was, and is, the Feast of the Dead, a time for remembering those who have gone before. Beltane was a feast of life, the marriage of the Goddess and the God. But both are times for scrying and divination, to seek to know more. Both festivals, but more so Beltane, were times of the trickster Gods; times to remember that the Gods do not play 'fair' by our rules, but by their own.

Our modern intercalary day is a time to review the overall picture of our lives, to celebrate our successes and to plan the way ahead to future ones. Whilst we may not be able to devote a whole day to this, it is a good idea to spend some time in contemplation and to celebrate Leap Day with our friends.

*"It's not what you don't have,
but what you do have, which matters."*

THE HARE

Witches have long been associated with Hares.
In fact the Hare, like the egg, is sacred to the
Goddess Eostre or Ostara, whose festival is
celebrated at the Spring Equinox later this month.

When the festival was taken over and renamed Easter, the Hare's association with the Craft caused the substitution of the more 'friendly' rabbit
as a symbol of the festival. However, if you look carefully at the chocolate animals you will see that many have ears far too long for a rabbit!

It was believed that a Witch could turn herself into a Hare in order
to travel secretly across the land, and that any injury done to the animal
would show itself on the Witch in the morning. Hares were feared for
this reason. Also, should a pregnant woman meet one she would tear her
petticoat to avoid her child being born with a harelip. Even the name was
dreaded and if mentioned at sea the boat must return lest disaster follow.
Conversely, to see a Hare, and especially if it crosses your path, is considered a good omen.

The saying 'mad as a March Hare' refers to the fact that this is the
month when they enter their mating season and the males chase one
another and, standing on their hind legs, 'box' with their forepaws for
supremacy. If you can find the time, go out around the Full Moon and
look for Hares as they really do seem to dance in the moonlight. If you
live in the country, try to drive especially carefully at this time, as Hares
frequently dash across the road.

"Sometimes the best magic
is just waiting to be seen."

THE ELEMENTS

For magic, or indeed life, to work well,
the Elements of Air, Fire, Water,
Earth and Spirit must be in balance.

Each Element corresponds to things in our lives, has representations in magic and correspondences to help us know and associate with it. Knowledge of the Elements is essential to the Craft.

Air, from the gentlest breeze to the strongest wind, represents our thoughts, and therefore the beginning and planning stages of all actions. Air is represented in the Circle by the direction East, and the colour yellow. It is the season of Spring and the morning.

Fire, whether the flame of a candle or the brilliance of the Sun, is our passions and enthusiasms, our strongest energies and the aspect which makes us decide to carry out our plans. Its direction is South, its colour red. It is Summer and the afternoon.

Water, from the tiniest drop to the oceans, is our emotions, feelings, tears and laughter, the part which imbues a project with feeling. Its direction is West and its colour blue. It is Autumn and the evening.

Earth, the soil, rocks and mountains, is our physical body and the physical realm; it is putting plans into action. Its direction is North, the place of power, its colour is green. It is Winter and the night.

Spirit is the Goddess and the God; it is the spark of life. It is the self within and our individuality. It is the centre of the Circle and is represented by the colours violet, white and many others. It is all seasons and all times of day.

"Unbalanced magic is like a chair
with a short leg: wobbly."

AIR MEDITATION

Together with spending time experiencing the
Elements in nature, meditation and visualization are
excellent ways of gaining a greater understanding of
them. This Air meditation is best performed outside
where you can feel the Air around you, but not at
the risk of getting badly chilled.

Sit comfortably, close your eyes and take several deep breaths to relax. Imagine yourself at the top of a high hill, with a gentle breeze brushing your skin and the Spring sun warming the land. Focus until you can actually smell the moist fertile earth, and the young green plants just bursting through the soil. Listen to the sounds of the birds seeking partners and making nests; hear the sounds of new life all around you. Now let the breeze enter you and carry you high above the earth. Soar like a bird, feel the currents of Air carrying you effortlessly as high as you wish to go. See the land spread out before you, like a huge patchwork quilt. Fly through the clouds, swoop and dip and let your Spirit guide you. Feel the Air begin to gather strength, and dive down to the refuge of the forest. Settle yourself safely beneath a sturdy tree and listen to the wind gathering power, rustling the leaves and branches. Hear the sounds of old wood dropping to the ground and making way for new growth, providing homes for the smaller creatures of the woodland. Hear the wind subsiding and feel yourself returning to the here and now. When you are ready, open your eyes and have a little to eat and drink to ground you.

*"Give your heart,
but hold on to your spirit."*

AN AQUAMARINE SPELL

The Aquamarine is a clear light blue, sometimes blue-green, stone. It is a stone of the Moon and is linked to peace, purification, love, water and psychic powers.

When you and your loved one are to be parted for a while take 2 Aquamarines and place them in sea water (or water with a little sea salt added) overnight in the light of the Moon, if possible when it is full. In the morning remove the stones and wrap each one in a pale blue cloth. Each of you should then dip a finger in the water and anoint the other on the forehead, eyelids, lips, and over the heart. Each should keep their stone about them during the day and place it beneath their pillow at night, until they are reunited.

An Aquamarine can be placed in the bath to cleanse and purify before magical working, or can be rubbed over the body for the same effect. If worn it will increase psychic powers and holding the stone during meditation will also help to unlock the subconscious. A tincture to enhance psychic power can be made by standing the stone in spring water for the three nights of the Full Moon; this can then be sipped during acts of divination.

The Aquamarine is also carried to heal emotional problems and to ensure safe travel over water. Aquamarines are often exchanged by couples as they marry to smooth the path of true love and to promote happiness and well being in the relationship.

"Love becomes true only
when it is returned."

LAVENDER

Lavender is the healing herb.

The oil can be smoothed onto minor injuries of all kinds, and is useful in dispelling headaches, fevers and feelings of malaise. It is also used to encourage old bruises to fade. The flowers and leaves are used in pillows, sachets and cushions to induce peaceful sleep and pleasant dreams. The flowers, when added to all kinds of food and drink, enhance flavour and bring feelings of well being. The stems make a good Asperger, and can be used like incense sticks or placed around the house for their perfume. The scent soothes the mind, emotions and spirit and is excellent around the home for promoting peace. It also helps to keep moths from clothing. Bunches of Bay and Lavender hung in doorways and windows help to keep insects out and were thought to keep sickness and negative energies away. Lavender water is said to lighten and brighten the skin and protect against biting insects.

Magically, Lavender is used in spells for love, protection, purity, happiness and peace. Lavender placed in the bath will dispel negative thoughts and energies and allow greater focus during magical working. Lavender flowers are carried to attract a partner, and a few secretly placed in another's pocket will cause them to think about your last meeting. They will also protect against cruel or unfair treatment.

To see whether a wish will come true, place 9 sprigs under your pillow and before retiring speak your wish aloud 3 times. If you dream of your wish it will come true, otherwise it is not to be.

"Burn the candle at both ends and
you'll end up burning your fingers."

BLUEBELL

There is nothing like taking a walk in the woods
and coming across a great swathe of Bluebells
in bloom: it always seems to me that one day there
is nothing and the next there is an abundance.

The Bluebell, Harebell or Jacinth is a member of the Hyacinth family and it is important to remember that, like many other wild flowers, it is protected and the plants should never be taken from the wild. You should never step on the leaves, for not only is this considered to bring bad luck, it can also kill the plant. Whilst most of its flowers are a blue or bluish-purple, you may come across white, or rarely, pink ones. If you are lucky enough to have these plants in your garden you should wait until the first blooms begin to die off and then split the bulbs to encourage more growth next year, although you should not do this too energetically.

The Bluebell has magical properties of truth and luck, and it is said that if you can slip a Bluebell into someone's pocket without their knowledge, they will be compelled to tell the truth in answer to the first three questions they are asked. If you have an abundance of Bluebells in your garden you can cut the flowers, as close to the ground as possible, and then make a tincture by soaking the blooms only for a week in a little vodka. This can then be used to empower candles to bring good luck. It is also said that if you place a single bloom in your shoe you will have good fortune all that day.

"The truth is a fearsome weapon."

THE ALTAR

**An Altar is both your working table, and a place
where you honour the Goddess and the God.**

With these two complimentary purposes in mind it becomes easier to understand why and where you place the things you do onto the Altar. The Altar is usually placed in the North (power), East (beginnings) or Centre of the Circle.

First, ensure you have a surface sufficient for your needs, a comfortable height, and neither too large nor too small. It is usual to cover this with a cloth which protects the surface from accidental spills and denotes the change of use. On this place symbols of the Elements; incense for Air, a candle for Fire, a dish of Water for itself and Salt for Earth. Usually these are placed approximately in their compass positions, although the candles should always be placed so you can avoid reaching over them. You will also need either a pair of candles, statues or other representations of the Goddess and the God. It is usual to have an Altar Pentagram (a largish, flat version of the 5-pointed star in a circle) in the centre front to act as your working surface. You should have a Chalice of wine and some biscuits to perform the Rite of Wine and Cakes, or for grounding. In addition you will need matches to light the candles, a snuffer if you don't use your fingers, extra supplies of incense, and the ingredients for whatever spell(s) or magic you are working. You do not need to include other things which are not necessary for your Rites.

*"Create space in your life for the Goddess
and She will create space for you."*

CLEANSING CARPETS MAGICALLY

**Spring is almost upon us and as the days grow
longer we start to notice that our homes are no
longer as clean and fresh as we would like.**

Not only that, but there will be trace energies from everyone who has
been in the house and everything which has happened there. This has traditionally been a time of turning out and cleaning and whilst we no
longer scrub the whole house from top to bottom it is good to freshen up
the home on both the spiritual and physical levels.

Take 4oz (100g) of bicarbonate of soda and place in a jar with a lid.
Stir in 2 teaspoons of dried or fresh Lavender, 1 teaspoon of Rosemary,
1 teaspoon of Chamomile and 6 Bay leaves. Put the lid on tightly and
draw an invoking pentagram over it. Store in a cool, dark and dry place
for 2 weeks. When next you are going to do your vacuuming, sprinkle
some of the mixture over the carpet first and leave it for 5 minutes before
vacuuming it up again. You may find that it's best to remove the Bay
leaves before use if your vacuum is likely to struggle with them. When
you have finished the whole house, empty the vacuum so that any residual energies are not still in the home.

This mixture is also very good at removing smells from pets or spills
from carpets, although if they are very strong or persistent you will need
to brush it in and leave it for an hour before vacuuming it up again.

*"Clean your life,
one room at a time."*

THE HORNED GOD

Horned Gods have been worshipped since man began, and the wearing of horns has long been seen as a symbol of power and virility.

Not only that but they represent strong links with nature and the fertility of the land. There are many images of horned figures from cave paintings onwards. It was only in the Middle Ages that Satan began to be depicted with horns, cloven hoofs, etc as a way of 'proving' that Witches worshipped a demon or devil.

To Witches the Horned God is the consort of the Great Mother. He is seen as a young man in the spring, as her husband at Beltane, and her partner thereafter. He leads the Wild Hunt which starts at Samhain. The Horned God has many names, the Celtic ones being Herne or Cernunnos; Herne being the sound that the female deer makes when calling for the Stag. Cernunnos is possibly the earliest known written form of his name. Other names include Pan and Faunus, but he is also referred to as the Hunter and Hunted, the Stag God, Lord of the Forest and the All Father.

It is worth remembering that he is just as divine as the Goddess, and that the way to redress the gender imbalances of recent times is not by relegating him to second place, but by seeking a true balance. Just as day needs night, light needs dark, male needs female, so in the Craft we worship the Goddess and the God, equally and in balance, and we should seek that balance in our lives and ourselves.

*"Hear the Hunter call from a distant horn,
heralding a storm that is rising."*

LEGEND, SECOND SIGHT

YELLOW

**Yellow is the colour of Air and is ruled by Mercury,
hence it represents thought, intelligence and creativity.**

It is one of the colours of the Goddess as Maiden and is associated with the East, Spring, fresh starts and new beginnings. Yellow is a brightening colour in more than one respect: not only does it cheer and lift the spirits but it also lifts the intellect. Also a solar colour, it is protective and strengthening.

Wear yellow clothing when you feel down or when in the company of those who are saddened or depressed. Yellow is used in healing problems of the digestive and nervous systems and of the skin. Wearing or carrying a yellow stone, particularly around the neck, will increase confidence and eloquence if you have to speak in public. Also wear one if you have an interview or feel the need for assistance in communication of any kind. Wearing a yellow stone will also enhance the ability to visualize, so use them when meditating as well as when working magic. When studying place a large sheet of yellow paper under your books to increase mental awareness. Writers will also find that it increases creativity. Bring yellow flowers into the house in the spring to dispel the gloom of winter. A single pressed Buttercup, that most yellow of flowers, can be sewn into the clothing of a loved one to ensure constancy.

If you would like inspiration before starting a new project, make a small circlet of yellow flowers and place it around a yellow candle. Light the candle and let it burn right down before commencing work.

*"Just because it's simple,
doesn't mean it won't work."*

THE GARTER

A garter is a band worn around the upper thigh, often to hold up a stocking.

In the past garters were worn by both men and women, both for practical and symbolic reasons. A cave painting shows a Shaman wearing Ritual garters on both legs. It has been suggested that the Order of the Garter, originally founded by Edward III, actually involved a Witchcraft Coven. This is an interpretation of the events surrounding his rescue of the Countess of Salisbury's reputation when she dropped her garter at a court event.

In the Craft today the Garter is worn by the High Priestess during Ritual and all Coven meetings. Some traditions suggest that it should be made of green leather, lined with blue silk and have a silver buckle. However, I have seen them made from a variety of materials. As the Coven hives off then the High Priestess will add an extra buckle to represent each daughter Coven.

The Garter has long been held to have magical properties. If a woman should lose her garter then it means that her love is thinking of her. If a girl wears a garter of wheat straw whilst making love she will conceive a boy, whilst one of oats will ensure the birth of a girl. If a man removes a Bride's garter after her wedding then it will bring him good luck; and more recently, if it is hung in a vehicle it will ensure safe travel. A Bride's garter placed under a girl's pillow will bring dreams of her future husband, whilst wearing a red garter is said to cure rheumatism.

"Look beyond the visible to find the meaning within."

HELPING NATURE

**Any gardening guide will tell you that this is the time
to start work outside if you haven't already done so.**

On the practical side you need to be pruning Roses, hedges and shrubs, removing weeds, turning over soil and digging in compost. It's also the time to sow seeds, plant summer flowering bulbs and give the grass a light trim. House plants too should be looked over at this time; trimmed, cleaned, given their first feed and, if necessary, potted on.

Having said that, this is also the time to do some magical work to help the garden. Collect about a pint of rain water, place 3 green stones into it and stand it for 3 nights in the light of the Moon. It doesn't matter at which phase, so long as it is not the 3 nights just before the New Moon, as your magic is for both growth and defence. Take it into the garden together with your Asperger and one new plant or seed. With your hands either side of the water vessel, hold it in front of you, close your eyes and visualize the Goddess as Maiden. When you can see her, say, *"Gracious Maiden, I call upon you to bless this water. May it bring fertility to all in this space. May it protect against disease and all that might harm the growth here. Blessed Be."* Take your Asperger and lightly sprinkle the whole of your garden. Now plant your seed or plant and say, *"Gracious Goddess I plant this in honour of you and in payment for the fertility of the land. Blessed Be."*

"A weed is just a plant in another place."

MAGPIE

The Magpie is another creature that Witches
were believed to turn into, and possibly for that
reason it has long been held that you should raise
your hat or bow should you see one.

Like most of the Crow family the Magpie had a reputation as a bird of
omen. Tradition has it that to see one on your roof means your house will
never fall down, whilst one chattering towards it portends a visitor or the
coming of news. Having said that, a Magpie flying close to the windows
indicates a death, and should one cross your path from left to right you
will have bad luck. It is also said to be very bad luck to harm a Magpie or
to steal from its nest.

Here are two versions of a popular rhyme about the relevance of the
number of Magpies you see at any one time:

'*One for sorrow, two for joy, three for a girl, four for a boy, five for
silver, six for gold, seven for a secret never to be told;*' '*One for sorrow,
two for mirth, three a wedding, four a birth, five for heaven, six for hell,
seven you'll see the devil himself.*'

Another historical attribute of this bird is its desire for all things
shiny, and it has a reputation for taking such items. If you are in the habit
of cleansing or empowering objects by placing them outside and you
have Magpies in the area, I recommend that you bear this in mind as I
have seen Magpies make off with small objects.

> "*Learn to accept good things,
> rather than to question them.*"

CRYSTAL DIVINATION

For this you will need 9 coloured crystals or stones of roughly the same shape and size and a soft cloth bag large enough to get your hand into. If you cannot find or afford crystals, use coloured pebbles, or paint pebbles in the appropriate colours.

When you have a question, shake the bag and draw out a stone, and see if this provides your answer. If things are still unclear you may draw up to 2 more stones to help you clarify things. If you still do not have an answer, consider rephrasing your question. Sometimes you still will not have an answer, in which case take the stones you have pulled from the bag and sleep with them under your pillow, together with a slip of paper with the question written on it. Here are some suggested stones and their interpretations:

Red. Red Jasper, Carnelian. Anger, conflict, aggression, passion, lust, energy.
Pink. Rose Quartz, pink Tourmaline. Love, romance, friendship, relationships, self-respect.
Orange. Amber, Citrine. Power, growth, success, joy, the God.
Yellow. Tiger's eye, yellow Calcite. Thought, intellect, communication, creativity, self-control.
Green. Aventurine, Malachite. Growth, fertility, work, money, messages, news.
Blue. Sodalite, Lapis lazuli. Truth, wisdom, excess emotion, travel, the sea.
Purple. Amethyst, Sugilite. Healing, peace, tranquillity, rest.
Black. Obsidian, black Onyx. Concealment, silence, lies, the unknown.
White. Moonstone, white Chalcedony. Spirituality, psychism, dreams, the Goddess.

*"Remember there is often more than
one solution to a problem."*

CORDS

Lengths of cord have several uses in the Craft.

The material used should be natural, and the ends should be secured by stitching, not by tape or knots. It is usual for all Witches to have their own set of at least 3 cords.

Where a Witch wears robes, they are normally cinched at the waist by a cord 4'6" (1.35m) in length. This cord can then be used, with the Athame, to draw the traditional circle 9 feet (2.7m) in diameter. Many Covens allocate different colours to different degrees of Initiation. It is not uncommon for Witches to have a holder on this cord to carry their Athame.

Three cords are used to bind a person for Initiation. One, 9 feet in length, is used to tie the hands behind the back, and the ends are then taken over the shoulder and knotted at the front in such a way as to restrain but not endanger. The other two are 4'6" and one is tied around the right ankle, the other above the left knee.

Cords are sometimes used to raise power by binding, as restricting the flow of blood can cause an altered state of consciousness. Personally, I do not recommend this as accidents can happen and the resulting headlines can be embarrassing! Cords are also used in Circle to raise power in dancing. Opposite pairs each take an end and then the whole Circle revolves, faster and faster, around the High Priestess who holds the centre point up, until she feels sufficient energy has been created.

Cords are sometimes used in knot magic, although string, thread or ribbons are also used.

"Only focused energy
will result in change."

KNOT MAGIC

Knot spells are one of the oldest forms of magic.
It has long been a tradition for sailors to buy
the wind from a Witch.

She would give them a cord with three knots in it, and they would undo one for a breeze, two for a wind and three for a strong wind, usually to bring them home. A girl would knot her right garter nine times around her stocking and attach it to the bed to dream of her future husband. A groom would go to his wedding with one shoelace undone so that he might 'untie' his wife's virginity on the wedding night. A pregnant woman's image would have a knotted cord around her neck in order that the pregnancy might go full term. This would be cut at the onset of labour to ensure an easy delivery.; Knotted silk was tied around an affected part to ease the pain of rheumatism. And it used to be common to place a red thread with nine knots in it around a teething baby's neck.

A popular modern knot spell involves tying 9 knots in a length of appropriately coloured thread or cord whilst saying, "*By the knot of one, the spell's begun. By the knot of two, it cometh true. By the knot of three, so mote it be. By the knot of four, the open door. By the knot of five, the spell's alive. By the knot of six, the spell is fixed. By the knot of seven, the stars of heaven. By the knot of eight, the stroke of fate. By the knot of nine, the thing is mine!*"

*"The loosest knot marks
the weakest spot."*

PROPHETIC DREAM PILLOW

To encourage dreams of the future make
yourself a dream pillow. This is a sachet which
can be placed under the pillow on nights
when you seek answers in your sleep.

Take a rectangle of purple fabric about 5 by 10 inches (12x25cm). If you can find one with silver threads in so much the better. Fold in half with the good side inside. Using silver-grey thread, stitch the edges by hand to make a small bag, leaving a small gap to insert your herbs. Turn the bag right side out through this gap and insert 2 tablespoons of Lavender flowers, 4 Bay leaves and a teaspoonful each of at least three of the following: Ash leaves, Broom tops, Cinquefoil, Holly, Huckleberry, Jasmine flowers, Marigolds, Mimosa, Mugwort, Peppermint, or Rose petals. Then sew up the opening carefully.

It is best to use this on a night when you can be reasonably sure of being able to wake naturally in the morning, without an alarm. Before retiring you should also place pen and paper nearby so that you can note your dreams immediately on waking. Do not use a dream pillow more than 3 times a month or you will become too accustomed to the herbs.

Your dream pillow will be more effective if you use fresh leaves and flowers, however it may not keep for long, so you might like to use dried material instead. In this case it can be 'activated' by sprinkling it with a little water and warming it in a plastic bag before use. When not in use your dream pillow should be wrapped in white cloth to protect it.

"Sleep cures what life procures."

ALDER TREE MONTH

The Alder is the shield tree, both
on the physical and spiritual levels.

Called 'the protection of the heart', it was highly prized. The wood is easy to work, yet very tough and when first cut the sap is red, giving the tree the appearance of bleeding. No doubt all these were reasons for its use in shield making. Nearly all parts of the tree can be used in dye making; the bark giving black, red or yellow, depending on the mordant used. Green comes from the catkins, the wood yields pink, early shoots yellow and later ones cinnamon. The bark is boiled and the resulting liquid is used to alleviate swellings, inflammation and rheumatism.

The Alder is also a tree of balance, bearing male and female catkins, the male being larger with purple scales and yellow flowers, the female being smaller, somewhat cone shaped, purple and later developing into cones. Also, because the Alder often grows in moist places it is one of the trees which unite all four of the Elements.

Because of its defensive properties Alder is often carried as protection, and a piece of Alder worn from the neck is said to be a good protection on spiritual journeys, such as meditation and astral travel. An Alder shield, made on the psychic plane through visualization, is a good addition to your Astral Temple. Male catkins and female cones can be placed on the Altar to represent the God and the Goddess, during workings for balance, or added to a charm bag to bring balance into daily life.

"From every seed you sow,
may something wholesome grow."

VALERIAN

One of the folk names of Valerian root is All-heal,
which gives an indication of its medicinal
properties and the way in which it was valued.

Two of the reasons why it dropped out of favour are its vaguely unpleasant odour and slightly bitter flavour. Regrettably today we seem far more concerned that a thing should be pleasing to the palate, rather than effective in its use. However, Valerian tincture can be made more palatable by adding fruit juice and holding your nose when you drink it! Alternatively, tablets are also available.

Valerian acts as a calmative and nerve sedative, and reduces pain and promotes sleep. It can be used at times of stress to soothe and relax, and is useful if you are trying to give up any kind of habit; from drinking or smoking to regret or negative thinking.

Valerian is also anti-spasmodic and is helpful in relieving any kind of cramp, or even 'night jumps'. Valerian in the house is said to reduce friction and arguments, and can be hung over windows to reflect the negative thoughts of others. Valerian is sometimes added to incense when dispelling negative energies from the home, although it is best to burn it with the windows open! It has also been traditionally used in love sachets and potions. Powdered Valerian root is sometimes used as 'graveyard dust'.

As Valerian is extremely attractive to some cats, prompting them to roll in it, chew it, and apparently become intoxicated by it, you may need to protect the plant if you wish to grow some.

*"The more consequences you foresee,
the less to regret later."*

SPRING EQUINOX RITE

The Spring Equinox, when day and night are equal in length, is a time of balance.

Also known as Oestara it is the festival of Eostre or Ostara, the Anglo-Saxon Goddess of Spring. This is an excellent time for some personal 'spring cleaning', a time to be rid of the bad and encourage the good into your life.

Prepare by making two lists of 9 items each. The first should be things which you would like to be rid of. The first 3 are personal, perhaps bad habits; the next 3 affect your interaction with others, eg old resentments or guilt; and the final three affect the land, eg the loss of young life to cars on the road. Make a second list of 9, again in 3 parts, of things you would like to bring, maybe a new job for yourself, more patience in your dealing with others and the plentiful growth of crops.

Light a black candle and read the first list aloud three times. Burn the paper and ask the Goddess and the God to take these things from you. Visualize these negatives burning in the flames and being carried away in the smoke. When the paper has completely burnt, put the candle out. Now light a white candle and read aloud, three times, the list of things you would like to bring to your life. Burn this paper and ask the Goddess and the God to bring these things to you. Visualize your wishes being carried to the Gods in the smoke. Let this candle burn all the way down.

"Give your energy to positive thoughts, let negatives fade and pass from you."

OESTARA

The hours of daylight have increased
and are, briefly, equal to those of night.
From now until the Autumn Equinox,
there is more day than night.

This is the Spring Equinox, whose true date will actually vary slightly each year. Oestara is sacred to the Anglo-Saxon Dawn Goddess Ostara, or Eostre, who derived from Ishtar, Astarte and Isis, and whose symbols are the egg of rebirth and the Hare. It is the forerunner of that other festival of rebirth, Easter. To the Greeks this was the time when Persephone returned from the underworld and Demeter cast off her cloak of mourning, allowing life to return to the land. Our language still holds traces of Eostre, in the words oestrus and oestrogen.

Spring is with us now; there will be signs of growing life all around: leaves on the trees, flowers in bloom, creatures rearing their young. Try to get into the countryside to appreciate these changes; you will see much to tell you of the return of life to the land, you may even see a Hare. This festival is coloured light green and yellow. Look for yellow flowers like primroses and daffodils. When you see your first, make a wish to the Goddess and ask her Blessing. If, on your walk, you come across sheep's wool on a fence, take a little home with you and leave it outside for the birds to line their nests.

"Gracious Goddess, let us work your Rites in good season,
and not perform magic without reason."

EGGS

Long a symbol of the universe and of rebirth there are many traditions surrounding eggs.

In the days before commercially produced chocolate eggs in fancy packaging it was traditional to hard boil and decorate hens' eggs by hand: these were then given away as symbols of good fortune. Indeed, this tradition goes back to ancient Egyptian times. More recently, hand-painted eggs were hidden in the garden for children to find, and add to the Spring feast.

It was thought that Witches could take to the sea in eggshells and for this reason an empty shell would always be crushed, or have a hole poked into it. A variation on this is that the fairies could take up residence in the eggshell. Indeed I can remember my mother telling me to always knock a hole in the shell of a boiled egg after it had been eaten. Double-yolked eggs used to be thought very lucky, although now that they are tested and sold as such I'm not certain the magic still holds! It was also believed that to find a red streak in the yolk of an egg foretold bad luck, although this probably relates to the fact that this egg may have been under the hen long enough to start developing and therefore might not be fit to eat.

A very old spell to prevent pregnancy, although I'm not sure I'd trust it myself, was to take a raw egg, still in its shell, and pass a needle with a red thread through it lengthways. The thread was then knotted and the whole egg placed under the couple's bed.

"Advice can only be offered, never given."

THE SUN IN ARIES

*Aries is the first sign of the zodiac and a Fire sign,
indicating passion, energy and creativity. It is also a
Cardinal sign, bringing eagerness, the urge to reach
out and to take action, but also impatience.*

Those born when the Sun is in Aries are usually energetic, assertive, expressive and spontaneous. Typically they give off an air of activity and urgency, and often sexuality. It is hard to miss an Arian when they are in the room! They are impulsive and restless, often seeking quick results. Enterprising and courageous with an adventurous spirit, they can appear aggressive and self-centred. Whilst being quick thinking they rarely pay attention to detail, so the projects they conceive often run aground. Working well where initiative and enterprise are needed, they are great at exploring new avenues, so long as they are partnered with someone with a practical side. They are passionate in love, but may seem tactless and insensitive, especially as they are not good at listening. On the negative side they can be selfish, impatient, tactless and rude.

For Arians this is a time to play to your strengths but be aware of your weaknesses; conceive new plans but put off execution until the Sun enters a new house. Be particularly aware of the need to let partners feel that they are listened to and that their ideas and feelings are appreciated. For others this is the time to use the ambient energy to seek new solutions to stagnant problems. If you know an Arian, ask them for advice, but give it serious thought before taking action!

*"Would you leap off a cliff as quickly
as you leap to conclusions?"*

AMULETS, CHARMS, TALISMANS, INCANTATIONS AND SPELLS

*If you consult an everyday dictionary these will
all appear to have very similar definitions; however,
in the Craft they are distinctly, if subtly, different.*

A Talisman is usually a paper-based spell. It may be carried on the person, in the pocket or wallet, or placed in a special place. It will include pictures or symbols to signify its purpose.

An Amulet is an object which is worn or carried. It may, or may not, have been empowered to promote its natural or inherent properties. Pieces of jewellery are frequently used as amulets.

A Charm is usually more than one object, put together to create a 'carry-able' spell. Usually these are contained in a cloth bag, pouch, or the like. Again it is worn or carried. People sometimes use the word Charm when they mean Incantation, which is a number of words, frequently rhyming, used as a spell to focus and concentrate the energy put in by the practitioner.

A Chant is a verse, or verses, which are repeated regularly and rhythmically to raise energy which is to be used in magical working.

A Spell is a specific piece of magical working to solve a particular problem. Whilst it may involve the creation of one of the above, it might only involve the lighting of a candle or even just the direction of the energy of thought.

*"Learn to read between the lines;
it's often where the information is."*

LAKES, PONDS, STREAMS AND RIVERS

Water is one of the five Elements, which are so
important to the Craft. Wells, ponds, lakes, springs,
streams and rivers were extremely important to our
forebears, being seen as gateways to the other-world;
places of energy and power; sources of help and
assistance and homes of the Goddess.

As in the story of Excalibur, they could be places where mortals met with
those of the other realm. There are several water motifs through the
mythology of the Craft. It was thought that a Witch could never cross
running water, although it's never stopped any Witch I know! Also, an
'evil spirit' could not follow over running water, and there are good reasons why anything that tracks using scent or prints will lose its prey if
they pass through a stream. In the Craft we often use running water to
cleanse objects prior to use, and we know that 'natural waters' are definitely more magical than the stuff we get through our taps.

On the domestic side, if you have a pond this is the time to generally make all clean and tidy for a new season of growth. If you haven't done
so already, it could be time to think about having the Element of Water
in your home or garden. Even if you live in the tiniest flat you can still
have a 'water' garden: Fill an opaque vessel with clean stones and rainwater. Add cuttings of easy-to-grow plants, and a few shells or gemstones.

*"Listen to the sounds of the Elements
for this is the music of the land."*

THE 'MAGICIAN'S RULES'

The four precepts to magical working, or 'Magician's Rules', are below.

To Know. This does not just mean knowing the methods, correspondences, ways of raising power and directing intent. It also means to know yourself, what you intend and what you might, subconsciously, intend. For not truly understanding your inner feelings and motivations, may affect your magic.

To Dare. You must not only be prepared to do this thing, but you must know that it will happen. You must also be prepared to take this step confidently. Everything you do has the possiblity of going wrong or misfiring. So do you dare? Any doubts, don't do it!

To Will. 'Will' is again not just hoping or wishing, it is using your willpower, your personal energy, to actually force it into being. Imagine the person you most love about to come to harm – the 'will' you put into your magic should be as strong as the "no" you would scream.

To Keep Silent. Probably the hardest of all, this means exactly what it says: keep silent. Consider this: when you are upset, you talk to your friends and your upset begins to subside. In magic the same is true – as your feelings fade the more you talk about it, so does the energy put in. Moreover, the more people you tell, the more likely you are to find someone who has doubts about your spell, which will dilute your energy flow.

"Witchcraft is not about gaining power,
it's about knowing when and how to use it."

CLEANSING OBJECTS

*All the things we use in our Craft and magic should be
cleansed before use, because unless we only gather them
from nature, they will have been in contact with others.*

Other people leave traces of their thoughts and feelings on the things they
touch and this unwanted psychic energy may interfere with the magic or
spells we intend to use them for. The only exception to this is when you
have been given something by a Witch in whom you have absolute confidence and trust. There are several ways of cleansing objects, and a little
thought will tell you which method is best for which item.

Probably the most useful way of cleansing something is to place it
overnight in the light of the Full Moon. Whilst the direct light of the
Moon is preferable, you do need to ensure that your object will not be
taken, moved by animals, or fall off an external windowsill. Using moonlight has the advantage of empowering the objects it touches too.

Waterproof objects can be cleansed by holding them under running
water for 5 to 10 minutes. If you have access, a stream is best, otherwise
under a tap is fine. In either case you need to be sure that small items cannot be washed away and lost.

Where running water is not suitable and you really cannot wait for
the Full Moon, then draw a Pentagram with salt in one fluid line (you
may need to practise). Place the item in the centre overnight. In the morning dispose of the salt which will have absorbed all extraneous energies.

*"Spend time wisely;
it's more valuable than money."*

A CHARM TO DEFLECT NEGATIVITY

Sometimes those around us carry negative energies which they seem to disperse as they go.

It could be that things are not all well in their world and, where possible, we can try to help them in this. Others simply throw off the negatives in their lives, seemingly scattering them, so that anyone with even a slight psychic talent unwittingly picks them up. Whatever the cause of these negativities it is beneficial to be able to protect ourselves.

One of the best gemstones for this is the Smoky Quartz as it absorbs negative energy. In its natural state this stone appears as a light grey form of Quartz Crystal. Very dark grey-black stones have almost always been treated to enhance their colour. Smoky Quartz is often put into silver jewellery, making a very simple and unobtrusive way of protecting yourself. Alternatively, you can put a Smoky Quartz Crystal into a small charm bag, which can then be worn on a cord around your neck or carried in your purse or pocket.

At the time of the waning Moon, take some white fabric and make yourself a small charm bag, in the same way as the Dream Pillow (see 17 March), and place within it a small Smoky Quartz Crystal point, a small mirror, some dried Caraway seeds and Rosemary leaves. Wear or carry this whenever you feel you might come into contact with anyone who generates a level of negativity.

*"You can only really 'know best'
for yourself."*

COBWEBS

Picture a traditional Witch's cottage and the chances
are that you will imagine cobwebs. Now, this could be
because the folklore image of the Witch is as a poor
old woman, possibly no longer able to clean her home.

But I like to think it may have something to do with the uses of cobwebs,
for not only are they brilliant works of art and nature's highly efficient
fly traps, they have been used in healing and in healing magic.

Even when I was a child it was common to be told to place a clean
(i.e. not dusty) cobweb over a cut or bleeding wound to help stop the
bleeding, and if the wound is not too deep it will work. It used to be said
that, for every cobweb you see on waking, you will receive a kiss that day.
But if you find one across your door it indicates that your love is with
another. Cobwebs in the kitchen are said to indicate a house without kisses. If you can collect a cobweb with dew on it, without breaking it, place
it on a dish of water to attract love into your life. Cobwebs are frequently used in spells to promote communication, perhaps after a disagreement. Name two objects after the 'warring' parties and wrap them in a
cobweb. Place in the light of the Sun for 7 days.

Note that it is unlucky to kill a spider or to disturb it on its web, but
it is permitted to remove old, or unoccupied, webs.

"Remember,
the housework will always keep."

MAKING MAGICAL CANDLE HOLDERS

Making your own candle holders is relatively inexpensive and this technique can be used to create magically-enhanced ones specific to your spell.

You will need to buy some modelling clay which dries in the air or the oven, rather than the kind which requires a kiln. This is usually available from art shops and even some toy stores. You will also need a flat surface, or a baking tray if your clay is oven bake, covered with some aluminium foil. For each candle break off a lump about the size of an egg and roll it into a ball between your palms. Place it onto the foil firmly, so that it flattens on the base. Push your candle into the centre of the top to create a hole which is exactly the right size for your candle, removing the candle immediately.

At this point you can decorate the holder with symbols to represent the person you are working for, perhaps their Sun Sign, initials or even a sketch of them; symbols representing the nature of the spell; leaves and flowers for fertility; a book to represent successful study, and so on. Cocktail sticks are useful for making fine lines in the still moist clay. If the clay is air drying you could also press into it gemstones, feathers, leaves or seeds with the appropriate attributions to enhance the spell. Once the clay has been dried, following the instructions on the packet, you can paint your holder and perhaps even glue further additions on to it.

"Never say you can't, if you haven't tried."

WITCH NAMES

Many people like to take a magical or Witch name when they enter the Craft.

This is thought to originate from the time when Witches were persecuted, and it would have been safer if people could not give real names to the authorities. Although I find this dubious as people would have known one another anyway. The belief that knowing someone's true name will give you power over them is far more widespread and vastly predates the Witch Hunts. Many Witches feel that the giving or taking of a Craft name reflects the feeling that they are starting afresh, almost as a new person. In some traditions the Witch name is given as a part of the second degree Initiation Ritual; in others it is a separate Rite. In some traditions a person may select their own name, and in others the name is chosen for them. Many Solitary Witches also take a name of their choice, not to be confused in these days of the internet with a pen or email name.

Whilst there are no rules on the selection of a Witch name there are some fairly strong guidelines. Read up on your chosen name, as some deities, heroes or heroines demonstrate attributes you may not wish to invite into your life. For the sake of everyone's sanity, choose something spell-able and pronounceable! Try not to select one of the many overused names. And lastly, it is considered self-aggrandisement to take the name of one of the 'major' Goddesses or Gods, such as Isis or Herne.

"At all times be honest
with yourself."

ALL FOOLS' DAY

The practice of playing tricks on 1 April dates back to 15th-century France, when the New Year was moved from 25 March and the beginning of Spring, to 1 January

This was so unpopular that people began sending officials on 'fool's errands' in retaliation. However, this is a good day to consider the nature of the Fool and his associations with the Craft.

Fools have long been considered to be blessed by the Gods; indeed it used to be thought lucky to meet one on the way to work. The Fool is the first card in the Tarot where he represents the start of the magical journey and the step into the unknown. He is also still represented in decks of ordinary playing cards by the Joker or Jester. The Fool is also linked with the Jester in his role of storyteller, or Bard, who travelled around taking news from place to place. Not only that but with connotations of riotous frivolity he is associated with fertility festivals, and may appear as the Teaser in midsummer Rites. His staff or wand with bells relates back to the sticks which were used to beat fertility into the population at the festivals of Pan. Hence he is linked with the trickster Gods Puck and Loki.

To gain a greater understanding of the Fool, take this card from a Tarot deck and place one green and one red candle on either side. Light them and focus on the image before you. As you meditate on it, consider the journey of the Fool: where is he going? Who will he meet?

"Judge me not until you
have lived my life."

VIOLET

**Whilst some colours are fairly obvious to identify, red
for example, others are more difficult to define.**

Violet, mauve, lilac and lavender, and to a certain extent purple, fall into
the latter category. In the Craft, however, we mostly deal with just two
forms: purple; a relatively straightforward blend of red and blue; and violet, which covers those blends when white has been added.

Violet is the colour of peace, tranquillity, harmony and healing. Burn
violet candles to bring these attributes into your life and home, to reduce
conflict and resolve disagreements. Anoint them with lavender oil for use
in healing spells. Violet is also one of the colours of the Element of Spirit,
representing the balance of the Goddess and the God. Wear violet clothing or gemstones to enhance your spiritual awareness and to help you to
develop your psychic skills.

To create a spiritual meditation mandala, take a large sheet of stiff
paper and some white, red and blue paints, or chalks. Draw a large circle
on the paper and cover this with white using circular strokes. Then, using
the red and blue, draw spirals into and out of the centre, blending the
colours into shades of violet with your fingers. Work slowly and rhythmically, and whilst you do so let your inner focus drift. By all means
incorporate swirls and whorls, but avoid straight lines and hard edges.
When you are satisfied with your picture, let it dry and then hang it over
your bed to develop your spiritual understanding.

*"Everything you do should
be an act of honour to the Gods."*

CUCKOO

It said that the call of the Cuckoo is the herald of the real arrival of Spring.

There is a lot of folklore surrounding hearing the first call. See the bird before you hear it and you will uncover secrets in the season. Catching a Cuckoo and releasing it unharmed will bring great luck, but to bring one into the house invites misfortune. It is unlucky to hear the first Cuckoo before breakfast, so rise early at this time of year. If you are not active when you hear the call, you should dance a jig to be sure of having work. If you have money in your pocket, turn it over to avoid being penniless. It was thought that when you hear the call you can ask a question and the Cuckoo will answer it by the number of its calls, telling you how long before you wed, have a child, or die. Indeed it is held that the poor bird is so busy answering these questions that it has no time to raise its young, and has to foster them out in other birds' nests.

By the way, the bird is somewhat larger than most expect being around a foot (30cm) in length, and is often seen standing on posts in the manner of a hawk.

In Scotland the Cuckoo is known as the *eun sidhe*, the Bird of the Fairies, and is thought to winter inside Barrows or other entrances to the underworld. Elsewhere, it is thought that the Cailleach, pre-Celtic Goddess of Winter, released it from the underworld when she was finally ready to give way to Spring.

*"For an instant facelift,
try a big smile."*

WEATHER MAGIC

One of the older accusations levelled against Witches
was the raising of storms, especially with a view to
wrecking ships at sea. Sailors in some places will still
'buy the wind' from a Witch before setting out.

Many 'spells' are taught to children in an attempt to bring good weather. Probably the most common of these is the chant, "*Rain, rain, go away, come again another day*," although I was brought up with, "*Rain, rain, go away, come again at night, not day*," so as to maintain the balance of wet and dry. I have also come across, "*The clouds are sheep, the wind's a shepherd, shepherd take your sheep away*," which should be repeated three times, facing into the wind.

Whilst children may want to keep the rain away, lest it spoil their outdoor games, spells to produce rain are just as useful. Douse a cat in water and let it shake itself outside to bring showers. Similarly, douse a besom and shake it into the wind. Rain sticks can be bought or made for this. Ours is so effective that we keep it well out of reach unless really needed! To raise the wind, perhaps to dry your washing, stand with your back to the clothesline and whistle into whatever slight breeze there might be. Of course, the ability to 'whistle up the wind' has long been said to be a sure sign of a Witch.

To conjure sunshine place 7 orange candles in a circle with one gold one in the centre. Light the orange candles starting in the East, moving clockwise around the circle, lighting the central one last.

*"Laughter is the
wine of the Gods."*

QUARTER LIGHTS

Quarter lights are candles or lamps placed at the four Quarters of the Circle.

Their purpose is to define the Quarters and to help mark the boundary of the Circle. In outdoor locations they also serve the purpose of making sure people don't step off into holes, brambles, etc. It should not be necessary to have indoor Quarter lights, as you should be able to remember the Quarters, but many people still like to have them so that the candles can be lit as the Quarters are called.

Indoors, candles used as Quarter lights can be placed in any usual holders, or in special ones which have been decorated to indicate the Elements to which they refer. When used for big celebratory Rituals, such as Handfasting, these holders can be highly ornate, decorated with ribbons and flowers in the Element colours. In our Coven we have a set of tall holders which stand on the floor, onto which large candles are placed.

When used outside it is necessary to ensure that the flames are shielded and that they cannot damage the environment. One of the easiest ways of doing this is to place nightlights in small glass jars. As these will get very hot during use, it is a good idea to tie string around the top, prior to lighting the candles, so that you can carry them away after use. These glass jars can also be decorated, perhaps with glass paints in the colours of the Elements: yellow for Air, red for Fire, blue for Water and green for Earth. Whatever you use remember to clear it away afterwards.

"Fire burns so treat it with respect."

MALACHITE

**Malachite is a beautiful, deep-green stone,
sometimes with bands of darker greens and black.**

A stone of Venus, it has properties of protection, love, business success and drawing money. Malachite was thought to warn of impending danger, by spontaneously breaking when it was near. A round flat piece of malachite with a gold Sun painted on it was thought to bring great fortune if worn over the heart.

Malachite is a protective stone. It is carried by travellers, particularly on journeys over rough ground. Malachite bead necklaces are often given to children, or placed around their beds to protect them from negativity.

Worn next to the skin near the heart, Malachite improves your ability to love and draws love towards you. If worn together with Rose Quartz it helps to enhance self-respect and self-confidence. It is also used to dispel depression: lie down and smooth a piece of Malachite in circles on your forehead, or better still get someone else to do it for you.

For success in business place a piece of Malachite in the till to bring sales, or place a piece under the entrance to the business to bring customers. It also enhances business skills, so wear it whenever you need to negotiate any kind of agreement. In this respect it can be added to spells to resolve arguments. Place Malachite on the Altar to increase the power of spells for success in love and business.

*"Use magic to help your life,
not to replace it."*

FINDING A COVEN OR MENTOR

> Whilst it is possible to learn the Craft alone, using
> books, it is often easier and more pleasant to work
> with others, or at least to have someone to talk to.

However, finding the right person or group is not always easy; they need to be reputable, to practise the form of Craft you seek, and you should be willing to meet their requirements. The best way to locate the guidance you seek is to work a spell and ask the Goddess.

Ensure your aims are clear. Do you desire a Coven, meeting regularly and practising formal Rituals, or simply a contact for guidance? Are you prepared to travel, or content with letters, email and the phone? Would you prefer simple herbal 'Hedgewitch' magic, or are you after something more complex? When you are ready, cast your Circle with a large white candle in the centre. Raise energy by dancing, chanting, clapping, and as you do so visualize building a cone of energy over the Circle. When you feel this cone is ready, light the candle and call upon the Goddess, *"Gracious Mother, aid me to discover the one(s) who can guide me. Guide me in my choices, that I may select only those who will help me to follow your path. Blessed Be."* Now focus on the candle and send your energy as a beacon of white light rising into the sky to draw the right contacts to you. Using the same candle repeat this spell every day for 7 days. Remember to use your common sense and intuition when making any kind of contact.

> *"Time; you can't buy, steal, beg or borrow it,
> so don't waste it!"*

REMOVING A NUISANCE

It would be wonderful to be surrounded by people who were a pleasure to be with, but life isn't like that.

Occasionally there is someone who we would dearly love to be free of, like a persistent admirer, an irritating neighbour. However, to do so would go against the Rede, and negative magic invariably rebounds on the person performing it. It is always worth trying to resolve our differences: perhaps you were not firm enough when invited out, or your noisy parties caused a breakdown in communication. If, however, you can find no way of resolving the situation, and it really is making life a misery, then it is time to take steps.

First, rid yourself of all negative feelings towards this person. Take a bowl of rainwater to which you have added some sea salt and place the fingers of both hands into it. Visualize all your annoyance, pain and irritation flowing through your body, down your fingers and into the water. Repeat this on three separate nights, disposing of the water carefully each time. Set your Altar as usual. Take a black candle and inscribe the person's initials into it and pass it through each of the Elements saying, "*I pass this through Air, that their thoughts turn from me. I pass this over Water, that all their feelings turn away from me. I pass this over Salt, that they may move from me. I bring this to Fire, that they enjoy success and happiness elsewhere. Blessed Be.*" Light the candle and visualize the person turning physically, emotionally and mentally away from you.

"If you think people are driving you mad, how do you think the Goddess feels?"

MINT OR MENTHA

Legend says that the Goddess Proserpine was jealous of
her husband Pluto's love for a nymph, so she changed
that nymph into Mentha, or the plant we know as Mint.

An alternate version states that Mentha is in fact another facet of Proserpine
(or Persephone) and rules the Underworld with Pluto (or Hades).

Mint has a great many uses. It aids digestion and is greatly useful in
cases of stomach upsets: Mint cordial added to warm milk and sipped will
soothe even the most uncomfortable problems. Rub a leaf or two over the
temples in cases of headaches and migraines. In cases of travel sickness,
crush a couple of leaves and inhale, or suck mint sweets. Likewise the
scent of freshly-crushed Mint is a powerful mental stimulant and especially useful when studying.

Mint brings good fortune when grown in the garden, although it is
considered unlucky to give away the roots. It is said that Mint flourishes
in the gardens of those who will become wealthy. Mint should be grown
as a deterrent amongst plants which are being eaten by wildlife, and
placed along doorsteps to deter ants.

Magically it is used in spells for protection, lust, travel, exorcism and
money. Hang bunches of it in windows to deflect negative energies.
Carry leaves in your purse or wallet to draw money to you. Add Mint to
charm bags for physical and psychic protection when travelling. Place
Mint on the Altar and invoke Proserpine in spells to increase lust.

"When talking of others, consider: Is it good?
Is it true? Is it useful?"

TRAVEL PROTECTION

Whenever you or a loved one will be setting off on a journey then create a charm of protection to ensure a safe return.

Make a small bag from fabric containing the traveller's favourite colour, sewing it with yellow thread. Into this place some dried moss collected from as close to the house as possible, a few Mint leaves, a piece each of Moonstone, Malachite, Amethyst and Jet. Add a small feather and some salt crystals. Tie the neck of the bag tightly. This should be worn or carried by the traveller until their return. Note: these days it is best not to put this in luggage of any sort if it is likely to be scanned by a security machine, as it could lead to some awkward questions.

There are various ways of securing a traveller's safe return. Take a piece of chalk of the colour of the person's Elemental sign; red for Fire signs, blue for Water, etc, and as they get up on the morning of their journey, write their initials under their pillow and leave this in place until they return. Alternatively, bury a piece of Fig wood together with a silver coin under the traveller's doorstep. If you and your lover are to be parted by a journey, then exchange Aquamarines.

It has long been held that it is extremely bad luck to turn back once you have started a journey, not even to wave farewell. If something has been forgotten, then the traveller should return, sit down and perform some action such as looking at a book, or eating something, before setting out again.

"If you travel slowly you can enjoy the view."

FROGS AND TOADS

Frogs and toads feature quite largely in the lore of Witches.

They were also used in a number of folk cures, most of which we would not try today. In most cases the cure involved the torture and/or death of the unfortunate amphibian. It was said that swallowing live frogs would prevent tuberculosis and cure asthma. Spearing one and rubbing it on warts would cause them to disappear as the frog died. The bones of a frog or toad were used in healing charms. The heart of a toad was considered to prevent burglars from being caught. Having said that, in some parts frogs were thought to be the souls of dead children and hence it was unlucky to harm one. A frog coming into the house presaged a wedding, whilst for a toad to cross a bride's path on her way to her wedding would ensure the couple's happiness and prosperity.

Toads were definitely associated with Witchcraft, and several unfortunates were accused of Witchcraft because a toad was seen in their house or garden. It was held that carrying the breastbone of a toad would enable a person to practise Witchcraft safely. It was also believed that the toad carried a magic stone in its head which could confer great powers. Frog- or toad-shaped ornaments also have 'Witchy' connotations, it being thought that they attract the spirits of dead Witches who will help the living in their spells. I have met Witches who also believe that to place a spell in a frog-shaped box will cause it to have greater energy.

"Happiness is a gift, not a right."

PENTAGRAMS AND PENTACLES

A Pentagram is an equal-armed five-pointed star,
the points representing the five Elements of Air,
Fire, Water, Earth and Spirit.

The Pentacle is a Pentagram within a circle. The circle represents the Circle
which is the Sacred Space, as well as the circle of the fellowship of Witches.

The Pentagram is drawn in the air to invoke or banish the Elements.
Each Element has its own invoking and banishing Pentagrams, although
the Earth Pentagram is sometimes used for general invoking and banishing. A Pentagram drawn or engraved onto a metal, stone or wooden surface is also used on the Altar to represent the Element of Earth, although
one can also be drawn in salt for the same purpose or to act as a way of
magically cleansing or empowering an object or spell. Rarely, the
Pentacle is drawn on the ground to denote the Sacred Space although this
is more the domain of the Ritual Magician than the Witch.

In some traditions different Pentagrams are worn to denote different
degrees of initiation. The first degree is worn point upwards, the second
point down and the third is topped by a triangle. An alternative system
has the first as a triangle, the second as a Pentagram and the third as before.
Usually these symbols are only worn within the Craft, not as daily decoration. Having said that, both Pentagrams and Pentacles are worn by
Witches as a symbol of their Craft, but as they are also worn by others,
they are not a reliable indicator that a person is a Witch.

*"Strength in your convictions means
not needing others to share them."*

RIVER GODDESSES

Springs, wells, rivers and streams were all sites of reverence for ancient peoples.

Not only were they seen as entrances to the underworld, but water itself was the life blood of the land, for without water nothing will grow. To ancient peoples the presence of the Earth Goddess was closest at the junction of land and water, and offerings would be made to her there.

Today reverence is still paid to the Goddess at these locations. Well-Dressing Rituals can still be found in many places at differing times of the year, and many springs are sacred sites where petitions are made to the Old Gods by tying pieces of cloth, grass or hair to the trees which grow nearby.

As a Witch it is always a good idea to be aware of your local Goddesses and Gods. Whilst it may be easier to identify with more well-known deities, those who are local to your land will have a more immediate impact in your magics. In many places the only remaining clues to the names of local deities are the names of rivers, lakes and springs. Just some of these are: Banna of the Bann, Brigantia of the Briant, Clutoida of the Clyde, Devona of the Devon, Ganga of the Ganges, Matrona of the Marne, Sequana of the Seine, Sinann of the Shannon, Sabrina of the Severn, and Tacoma of the lake of the same name. In others, whilst the name of the body of water may have been changed the connection remains, like Belisama of the Mersey and Nahkeeta of Lake Sutherland.

"Learn to know your local deities,
for you are already known to them."

VEGETABLE MAGIC

We know that vegetables are good for us to eat, but they are also good for us to grow.

Working with your hands in the soil is one of the best ways of becoming closer to the land and of relating with the Goddesses and Gods of fertility. It can also be a form of meditation and magic in its own right. A seed can as easily become the focus of a spell as a candle.

Use seed magic for spells which involve growth for advancement, and for changes in direction. For long-term change, start at the moment you plant the seed, but in the case of slow growers (like vegetables) use seedlings from any stage of growth. When you plant the individual seed or seedling invoke the Mother Goddess and dedicate your spell to her, asking for what you need. As you nurture your plant so you are nurturing the spell. Use the colour of the intended crop as your guide to which plant will best advance your magic.

At this time of year, with the hours of daylight growing and Spring well and truly begun, plant vegetable seeds indoors. Even if you do not have a garden there are foods which can be grown in the corner of a room. Tomatoes are an obvious example, but you can also try peas, beans and others which fruit above the soil. Root crops are not suitable inside as, to provide a sufficient depth of soil, you need very large containers, which can put a strain on your floors as well as looking unsightly.

"There is nothing in all life which is not
of the Goddess and the God."

WILLOW MONTH

**Willow has always had many uses, from today's
baskets, chairs and fences to the wattle walls of the past.**

Willow's long, straight and pliable branches have been pollarded to provide the material to literally furnish our homes and lives. The bark of the
tree contains salicin, from which aspirin is made. The leaves can be boiled
and the solution used as a shampoo to reduce dandruff, as a gargle for sore
throats and on the skin to reduce blemishes. It used to be thought that
bathing the external genitals with this would improve sexual performance.

Willow prefers moist ground and is often found along riverbanks,
close to the boundary of the otherworld and has strong links to the earth-
water Goddesses. The pale colour of the wood is said to be similar to that
of a person who has left this life and is commencing a new life beyond the
veil. The Willow has often been associated with loss and grief; hence the
name weeping Willow, although in the Craft this refers to the ability to
let go of material things in order to free yourself to take on more spiritual attributes. In this the Willow can act as a guide. Visualize yourself
weaving a small boat from branches of Willow. Work carefully, and set
forth upon the waters in it. Let the wind and tides take you where they
will. The sights you see, the places you visit and the people you meet will
guide you on your spiritual path.

The Willow is used to make incenses for divination and otherworld
journeys and the traditional Witch's besom is tied with willow.

*"Always challenge assumptions,
for most are born of ignorance and prejudice."*

PRIMROSE

The Primrose is another spring flower which it
was felt unlucky to bring indoors in a quantity of
less than thirteen, for fear that less would limit
the number of eggs or chicks from poultry.

However, in larger bunches they were welcome. The flowers were said
to protect against evil spirits and Witches, although once again I can't say
my Craft has suffered in any way from Primroses!

Primroses have long been associated with children, it being said that
placing the dried flowers in a child's pillow would ensure their respect.
Keeping the plant in flower on the window sill is also said to encourage
their sleep and to guarantee pleasant dreams. The plant does have sedative properties and an infusion of the flowers can be used to calm the
nerves. The roots are infused as a headache cure, although as they can also
be used as an emetic it is wise to make the solution a weak one. Primroses
used to be used in cooking as well as medicine, the petals being added to
rice, floated on soup or crystallized as cake decorations.

Primroses in the garden are said to be protective, especially as they
are favoured by the fairies, who look kindly on those who grow them.
Wearing the flower is said to attract love, although in some places it used
to be considered the sign of a wanton.

The Primrose is used in spells to attract love, and for the protection
of a loved one. Place a pressed Primrose flower in the front of the car of
someone you care for to ensure safe journeys.

*"Beautiful people are those who
do beautiful things."*

THE TAROT

The first Tarot decks were produced in medieval times as gaming cards and sold by the monks who painted them.

It's no wonder that the church called them the devil's picture book! These days Tarot cards come in many different shapes and sizes, and there are over 200 decks available ranging in price from reasonable to ridiculous. A Tarot deck has 5 'suits', four of which make up the Minor Arcana: Wands or Staves, Swords, Cups, and Coins or Pentacles. These are similar to the suits in ordinary playing cards, except the Jack or Knave becomes the Prince and there is an extra 'royal' card, the Princess or Maiden. These suits correspond to the Elements of Air, Fire, Water, and Earth. The fifth suit is the Major Arcana and has 22 numbered and/or named cards, corresponding to the Element of Spirit. A full deck totals 78 cards. The two main kinds of deck are fully pictorial where every card has an illustration, and semi-pictorial where only the Major Arcana has illustrations; the other suits only having a literal design, e.g. the 3 of Wands will show only 3 wands.

Tarot cards are most often used for general divination readings and to answer questions, but they can also be used in meditation exercises and in spell work. There are several myths attached to the Tarot. It is sometimes said that it is unlucky to buy your own cards, although this may have something to do with people protecting their own interests as readers. It is also said to be unlucky to read using another person's deck, probably for the same reason.

"Optimism's good, but planning works better."

NETTLES

Nettles are greatly underestimated, and usually rooted out by most gardeners.

The young tops are good to eat and are rich in iron and other minerals. Once cooked or dried they lose their sting, and can be used in savoury dishes in much the same way as spinach, or made into soup. Baked with sugar, Nettles were reputed to enliven the spirits. Dried Nettles, so long as they retain their green colour, can be used as a harmless replacement for salt.

Nettle stings were used to relieve rheumatic pains and to reduce chills. Freshly-cut Nettles can be placed under the sick bed to hasten recovery. Nettle juice is helpful in stopping bleeding, being added to a dressing or even taken internally. It is also used in cases of asthma and other chest complaints. Cooked and cooled Nettles can be used as a face pack, and an infusion makes an excellent hair rinse.

Magically they are used in healing, defence and protection spells. Placed in a charm bag Nettles will keep negativity and fear at bay, and are said to remove curses by returning them to the sender. Sprinkle Nettles around the house for protection against negative thoughts and lightning. Nettles can also be added to the bath for added protection when working defensive magic, or prior to working on the Astral plane. Most people know that Nettle stings are eased by rubbing with a dock leaf, but to increase its efficacy you should recite the following spell: *"Dock in, nettle out, dock rub nettle out."* But it is not as well known that the juice of the nettle is even more effective than dock.

"Success is the best revenge."

READING THE TAROT

When you get a new deck of Tarot cards, take them from the box and, replacing any advertising cards and the little book, wrap them in a silk or cotton cloth.

Sleep with them under your pillow for three nights to make them yours. During the days shuffle them, examine them and familiarize yourself with their content. When you feel ready, start to use them. At this stage it is useful to have a notebook handy to help you analyze the cards.

Each evening, shuffle the deck whilst focusing on the following day. Take 3 cards and place them face down in front of you. Now turn over the first, which denotes the morning, note it in your book and write any thoughts and feelings which come to you. Repeat this with the second for the afternoon and the third for the evening. Place the 3 cards within the book until the end of the day. At this time look again at each of the cards and your notes: how did the cards relate to the events of the day? Were the notes you made appropriate? Now return the cards to the pack and repeat the exercise later in the week. If you are very keen you could do this every day, but be aware that it is easier to learn your cards if you do not overload your memory.

When you feel that you are beginning to know and understand your cards well, it is time to move on to more complex spreads, at least one of which will probably be in that little book you placed to one side in the beginning.

"Skills worth having
take time to acquire."

OLD BELTANE

**Beltane was traditionally celebrated when the
Hawthorn, also called the May, blossomed.**

A major fertility festival, it used to be traditional for the unattached to
dress in green to signify that they were available and seeking a partner.
These young people would then spend the night in the woods. Any child
born of such a union was considered especially blessed and to bring
good fortune to the village. As a result both mother and child would be
cared for by everyone. It is thought that one of the reasons why it is considered unlucky to bring May blossom into the house is because this
would have indicated an unsuccessful night! It is just as likely that the
flowers would have given away the fact that the people of the house followed the Old Gods.

When the Hawthorn is in blossom go and seek out a bush and, if you
can, lie down under it and meditate on the festival and its meaning.
Visualize the Goddess as Mother and the Horned God as her Consort,
for this is the time of their marriage. Gather enough flowers to weave into
a circlet. Most florists sell preformed wicker rings which are ideal for this.
Whilst you thread the flowers into the ring, focus on the meaning of the
festival. If you were not able to meditate under the Hawthorn you can
meditate wearing the circlet, otherwise use the circlet to decorate your
home for the festival. If you have an image of the Goddess in your home
it is nice to also create a smaller circlet for this.

*"Give thanks for the gifts of the Goddess,
lest She decide to take them back."*

SELF-CONFIDENCE SPELL

Whether it's for a job interview, meeting new
people or just because you feel the need for a
little bit more assertiveness, we all need to
boost our self-confidence from time to time.

This spell is in two parts: the first takes the form of a bath, whilst the second is something to carry with you.

Run a warm but not hot bath, and before getting in add a piece of gold (jewellery is fine, but remember to remove it before pulling the plug!), a Sunstone, 4 drops of Sandalwood oil and a small handful of Bergamot flowers. You might like to put the latter into a muslin bag to avoid a difficult cleaning job later. When you get into the bath submerge yourself completely 3 times, then relax and soak for at least 10 minutes whilst visualizing the energies of the Sun entering you. Allow yourself to dry naturally.

Now that you are cleansed and energized, take a gold candle and carve your initials into it towards the top. Rub a drop of Sandalwood oil into the letters and then light it. Whilst it burns create a small charm bag from gold fabric. Into this place the Sunstone you used in the bath together with a Tiger's Eye, a piece of Yarrow and half a teaspoon of green tea leaves. Let the candle burn all the way down to the last inch, then pinch it out. When it has cooled, add it to the bag and seal it tightly. Carry this with you at all times for a full Lunar month.

*"If you cannot learn to love yourself,
how will you learn to love others?"*

GEESE

*Whilst at first sight not the most magical of birds, the
Goose is a traditional staple of country life with many
tales surrounding it, and its plentiful fat is used as the
base for many remedies and beauty preparations.*

Geese were also kept as guardians as, when disturbed, their cries would give ample warning and the birds themselves would see off intruders.

A Goose flying around the house indicates a death in the family. When Geese are noisy and restless for no reason it means rain is on the way. If a flock of Geese walking away from home should turn back it indicates a stranger is coming. If the flock leaves home it portends a fire in the house. If the breastbone of a cooked Goose is white or bluish it indicates harsh weather is coming, or a hard winter later that year. It was also said that he who eats Goose on Michaelmas Day (29 September) will never lack the money to pay his debts.

Goose fat, or grease, which is almost liquid at room temperature, was rubbed on to treat strains, sprains, bruises and other knocks and aches. It was also used to treat baldness and burns. It was rubbed into the chest to cure coughs and colds. I can remember my father telling how his mother would smear goose fat onto the children's chests at the start of winter, and then sew them into their vests until spring! Young ladies wishing to improve the appearance of their hands should rub in Goose fat in the evening and wear cotton gloves overnight.

> *"As a rule of thumb the greater the advertising
> the less you need the item."*

DRAGONS AND DRAGON'S BLOOD

23 April is St George's Day.

The patron saint of England, St George is credited with having slain a fearsome dragon to save the life of a virgin. However, the Dragon means different things to different peoples. In some medieval traditions it is linked with the devil or Satan, hence the carvings and windows depicting St George, or sometimes St Michael, slaying one. But the Dragon has far older associations in which it represents the life force of the land. In the Craft we often refer to the Earth Dragon, a great coiled beast who sleeps within the Earth and who can be called upon to work healing for the planet. The Earth Dragon is often invoked in cases of potential ecological danger. King Arthur's father was named Uther Pendragon, and it is thought that his name shows that he was a defender of the land. The Dragon is a symbol of Wales and appears on the country's flag.

Dragon's blood is not the blood of some luckless lizard, but the resin of the palm *Calimus draco*. Magically it is used for spells of protection, exorcism and sexual potency. Added to incenses it increases their potency and drives away all negativity. On its own Dragon's blood can be burnt at an open window to secure a lover's return, and a piece of the resin placed under the mattress is said to cure impotence. In the past Dragon's Blood was used medicinally to cure diarrhoea, dysentery and even syphilis. Like many other resins it is also used to stop bleeding wounds.

"Meddle not in the affairs of Dragons,
for you are crunchy and taste good with ketchup!"

THE SUN IN TAURUS

The Sun has entered Taurus. As an Earth sign this
indicates a down-to-earth attitude, practicality,
resourcefulness and common sense. It is also a
Fixed sign, bringing qualities of persistence, reliability,
stability, strong reactions and stubbornness.

Those born under this Sun sign are generally self-restrained, intense, practical and steadfast. The typical Taurean is quiet, reflective, patient, forbearing, but very determined. They really need stability, security and reassurance. They are methodical but can be set in their ways and opinions. They are very affectionate and home loving with an appreciation of the good things in life. Once a Taurean has made up their mind it is almost impossible to change it. Being methodical they are ideally suited to work where patience and perseverance are needed. On the negative side they can be possessive, overpowering and self-centred. Their desire to avoid conflict can result in problems escalating rather than being resolved.

Taureans will find this period good for reflection and self-care. It is also a good time for any form of building or construction, especially DIY. However, in relationships they need to be careful not to be too cloying or clingy, and to give their partners enough room to breathe. They should ensure that they take extra care of their throats at this time. Others will find this a good time for all matters involving the physical realm: the home, the garden and the body. It is also a good time for tackling difficulties which require a methodical approach.

*"At least some of a nature based belief system
should be based in nature."*

WITCH BOTTLES

The term Witch Bottle is often used to describe a counterspell which is intended to hit back at the perpetrator of a harmful spell.

The 'victim' would place some of their hair, nail clippings and urine into a spherical glass bottle together with some pins or nails. The bottle would be sealed with a cork and wax and hidden in the house. This would result in the originator being plagued with sharp pains (hence the pins) and thus being persuaded to remove their spell. Sometimes the bottle was heated and it was said that this would induce the Witch to appear at the door. Many Witch Bottles have been found secreted in the rafters or under the floorboards of houses, as well as outbuildings. A similar bottle with the addition of iron filings placed under the doorstep was thought to prevent a Witch from entering the house. Later, people used Bellermine stone jars for the same purposes. Imported from Germany these are distinguishable by the bearded face, usually found on the neck.

However, the use of hidden bottles is not confined to counter-magic. Written spells are sometimes placed within a sealed bottle to preserve them, especially those for the protection of family or livestock. A more recent spell to create harmony in the house is to take powdered dragon's blood, mixed with sugar, salt and sweet wine, seal it in a Witch Bottle and place it where it cannot be found. Another version designed to keep the family together uses hair and nail clippings from all family members in sweet wine.

"Tell your parents you love them while you still can."

MUSIC AND MAGIC

Music and music-making are some of the earliest forms of magic.

The use of drumming to raise energies, either those of the spirit world or those of the participants to power the magic, is evident in almost all societies around the world. Likewise the use of vocal sounds to harmonize with the Elements and the divine is a very ancient tradition. This is not surprising when you think of the emotions and feelings that music can engender.

In today's Craft we use singing, dancing and chanting to raise energy for our spells and it has become traditional to 'drum up the Sun' at both the Summer and Winter Solstices. However, I would point out that out-of-time drumming on an out-of-tune drum is more likely to persuade the Sun to hide rather than to shine. Many Witches also like to have music as a part of their Rituals and workings, although if you are not personally musical this can be a problem as most CD and tape players seem to malfunction if placed within a cast Circle.

Another way you can use music is to find pieces which, to you, embody the essence of the Elements. Many people find that instrumental pieces are the most useful for this. Use your selected pieces to meditate on the Elements. If you are talented you can even create your own, as my partner has done for us. I have also found that tapes of wildlife, birds for example, and natural sounds, like the wind in the trees or the sea, are an excellent aid to meditation, and you can always record these yourself.

*"Try listening with your eyes
closed and you will hear more."*

THE DAYS OF THE WEEK

*Just as the phases of the Moon and
the seasons have their own magical energies,
so too do the days of the week.*

Therefore, if you can work your spells on the appropriate days then these energies will be in your favour. The following outline gives the planet influencing the day, its colour and the types of magic it is most beneficial for.

Sunday: The Sun. Gold, orange. Physical healing, health, vitality, confidence, hope, success, honour, glory. **Monday:** The Moon. Silver, white. Dreams, female fertility, divination, animal healing. **Tuesday:** Mars. Red. Courage, defence, conflict, endurance, physical strength, energy, surgery, male fertility. **Wednesday:** Mercury. Yellow. Knowledge, study, communication, writing, improving the mind, inspiration, mental healing. **Thursday:** Jupiter. Dark blue, purple. Luck, employment, business, wealth, riches, legal matters, improving magical skills, spiritual healing. **Friday:** Venus. Pink, green. Love, friendship, family, affection, partnerships, spiritual harmony, compassion, earth magic and earth healing. **Saturday:** Saturn. Black. Duty, responsibility, familiars, building, binding, banishing, meditation.

The above is by no means comprehensive and you may find that, with practice, you are able to add to, or even alter it. Of course there will be times when your magic cannot wait even a few days; in these cases do not worry that you are using the 'wrong' day, as the daily influences may add to your energies but they will not detract from them.

*"Look for the pleasure in each day,
for it will happen only once."*

THE GREEN MAN

The Green Man is most often depicted
as a head with leaves and branches issuing
from his mouth, nose and even eyes.

Some of these heads include vines and fruit, and several are actually Green Women. The face can be seen peeping out of wood and stone carvings in many older churches and places of worship all over Europe. The Green Man also appears in many traditional festivals and parades. These foliate masks and men represent the spirit of the life of the land, of nature and fertility, and some think they are images of Sylvanus, God of the woods. Today you can buy them in many stores and garden centres. Place one in your garden to encourage growth.

With a little patience you can make your own Green Man head for indoor use. Inflate a balloon to roughly head size. Stand it knot down in a cup or bowl. Using newspaper and an equal mix of PVA glue and water, papier maché the front of the balloon, using several layers to make a firm base. When you are happy with the shape, pop the balloon and trim the edges of your mask. Cut eye, nose and mouth holes and paint the whole in greens and browns. When this has dried, glue on leaves in an overlapping pattern so that the original shape is all but completely concealed. Make a discreet hole in the sides or top so that you can insert a thread to hang it from. As this will not be weatherproof, hang it indoors, perhaps looking out over your garden.

*"Take pride in your land
and use it caringly."*

April 29

TALISMAN OF DEFENCE

**Whilst you may not actually be going to war, there
are nevertheless times when you may need to defend
yourself, or your near and dear, against attack.**

In this day and age it could be verbal attack, rumour mongering, or perhaps bullying. The following Talisman gives an example of the use of a magic square. For best effect you should create this on parchment or hand-made paper using red ink.

Take the following 5 sequences of numbers and write them onto an equal-sided grid keeping the same order as here. Top row: 11, 24, 7, 20, 3; Next: 4, 12, 25, 8, 16; Next: 17, 5, 13, 21, 9; Next: 10, 18, 1, 14, 22; Bottom row: 23, 6, 19, 2, 15. This is the square of Mars. Now take the name of the person you wish to protect. This should be the name they most identify with, eg Sally-Ann Jones may be the full name but if she prefers to be known as Sally Jones that would be the name to use. Assigning numerological values to the letters of this name would give you: 19, 1, 12, 12, 25, 10, 15, 14, 5, 19. Again using red ink mark the numbers of this name over the square with a series of straight lines which join up the numbers in the order they appear in the name. The beginning and end of the line should be two small circles. Where two consecutive letters are the same, like the ls in Sally, make two points on this number linked by a short line. Consecrate this Talisman by passing it through the Elements and then ensure it is carried at all times.

*"If you reach for the stars
you might just attain the Moon."*

BELTANE EVE

*Beltane is the major fertility festival
in the Wheel of the Year, and there are
many traditions associated with this.*

The Goddess now changes her robes of Maiden for those of the Mother and the God stands by her side as partner and Consort. We celebrate the marriage of the Goddess and the God for the fertility of all. Many Witches also celebrate their own weddings, called Handfastings, at Beltane. The change of the Goddess from Maiden to Mother is echoed in many places by the selection of a May Queen. Beltane is also the festival of the solar God Bel and in times past the people would drive cattle between two fires to purify and protect them, and to induce fertility for the coming season. The people would jump the fires for fertility in their own lives.

Just one of the ways of celebrating Beltane is to organize a Fire Ritual. Take two fireproof bowls or vessels with nightlights inside and place them close enough to make it interesting but far enough apart to be safe! Loose or flowing clothes should be hitched up well out of the way. Organize a dance which takes each person around each 'fire' in turn. As they circle the first fire they should say something positive about themselves, and as they circle the second they should say something about the season or the festival. Once everyone has circled both 'fires' several times they should then jump through the gap between them, making a wish for the coming season. If the fire remains lit their wish will come true, but should their jump extinguish the flames it will not.

"True love doesn't hold grudges."

BELTANE

The festival of Beltane marks the onset of summer;
the Hawthorn is in blossom, as are many other plants;
wild animals and birds are busy raising their young.

All around us we can see the life of the land. This is the time to welcome the Mother Goddess in all her bounty, and the God her Consort as they come to bring fertility to the land and the crops.

Take a little wine or fruit juice, honey and fruit out into the woods. Find a well-grown, mature tree and make your offering under its branches. Then sit down, resting your back on the tree, and take several deep breaths to centre yourself. Look slowly and carefully all around you and observe all the signs of the season. Now close your eyes and visualize the Mother Goddess walking towards you. As you watch her approaching you become aware that walking towards you from the other direction is the God, a young man in the prime of life. Watch as they greet each other and then turn to smile at you. If you have a question for them you may ask it now. Wait until they say farewell and walk away together. Once they have gone, you can open your eyes. Once again look all around you and take in all the sights, sounds and scents of the season. Look carefully to see if there is anything special which catches your eye; a piece of wood, stone or whatever. If there is, you may take it with you as a reminder of the festival.

*"History is always written
by the winner."*

MAYPOLES

Until the advent of the Puritans it was common to see Maypoles on every village green.

A tall pole would be placed in the centre of an open space; at the top would be tied ribbons of many colours, the whole crowned by a garland of flowers. Children and young people would take the ribbons and dance around the pole, weaving in and out of one another, in such a way that the ribbons tightened and the garland was gracefully lowered down the pole, in unmistakeable symbolism of the union of male and female.

Whilst you may not wish to have a full-sized Maypole in your home or garden, you can, however, create a smaller version to celebrate the season. Take a stick or garden cane about 15 inches (42 cm) tall and place it in a pot full of earth or sand. Tie ribbons in the seasonal colours of red and green to the top. They will need to be approximately 3 times the length of the stick. Create a small circle of seasonal flowers and place it at the top. Weave the ribbons back and forth around the pole. Keep this in your garden, or with your pot plants to bring them fertility and growth. If you wish you can do a scaled-up version with friends, getting one to stand in the centre holding a broom handle or something similar above their head, whilst the others weave the ribbons. Maypoles are being revived in many places, so if you can, try to get along to a full-sized May dance.

"Strive ever towards your highest ideal,
let naught stop you nor turn you aside."
THE CHARGE OF THE GODDESS.

THE HORSE

*There are several associations between horses and
the Craft: a horse is said to be 'hag-ridden' if it is
found sweating and exhausted in the morning.*

In some countries a horseshoe is hung points upward on the outside of
the house or property to avert Witchcraft. However, in other places it is
felt that this position allows a Witch to sit in the curve so shoes are hung
points down. Horsebrasses were originally attached to harnesses to prevent a horse being bewitched, as it was thought Witches could prevent it
from working. Witches were also credited with knowing the Horseman's
Word, which could control a horse's behaviour. It is considered unlucky
to meet a red-haired woman (often a sign of a Witch) riding a white horse,
especially bareback. In some places it is thought unlucky to see a white
horse and lucky to see a black one, in other areas this is reversed. It is also
thought that white horses are called grey because of the ill luck attached
to a white one. Likewise white markings such as socks are held to be
unlucky, unless they are one at the front and back and on opposite sides.
A star on the forehead, however, is thought to be lucky.

The Horse is central to the legends of many Goddesses and Gods,
including: Aine, Apollo, Epona, Etain, Hecate, Hippia, Loki, Manannan
and Rhiannon. Its image has long been magical and can be seen carved
into the hillside at Uffington, as well as on Ritual items.

*"Learn to change that which is changeable,
and to set aside that which is not."*

HANDFASTING

A Handfasting is the Witches' form of wedding.

It differs from a conventional ceremony in a number of ways. Like any other Craft Ritual it can take place anywhere the couple wish, indoors or outside. Friends and family will gather in a circle and the Ritual takes place within it; usually this will be a cast Circle. Both parties enter the Circle as equals; no-one is 'given' to the other. The promises made by Bride and Groom are their own, there is no set form of words, so this can be as personal and individual as they like. The couple's hands are tied, with a cord or ribbon, during the Ritual, hence the term tying the knot. They jump a broomstick, to symbolize the leap from one life, as an individual, to another, as part of a couple, which gives us the term jumping the broom.

Witches may marry in any colour, not necessarily white, as the necessity for a woman to be 'pure for her husband' has no meaning in the Craft. Having said that, the non-Craft superstition of someone wearing green at a wedding being unlucky originates in the Beltane tradition of wearing green to show that you are actively seeking a mate.

Probably the largest difference lies in the fact that the couple can choose to be Handfasted for life, or for a year and a day. The latter option is sometimes taken up by couples who like the notion of renewing their vows annually, perhaps tailoring them to the practical aspects of life together.

"Treat your partner with the same politeness
and respect you would give a stranger."

SEA MAGIC

**The sea and the coastline give us many magical things:
stones and crystals for use in spells and charms;**

Holey stones which represent the Goddess; flat pebbles which can be made into Runes; driftwood which we can use to decorate our Altars, homes and gardens; sea water which can be used in spells for protection, energy and success. Visit the waterline often, especially after a storm, to see what the waters will yield. If you are fortunate enough to live near the coast, or other tidal water, then you can use the power of the tides in your magic.

To put something behind you, go to the beach just after the high tide. Write it, in one single line, onto a strip of paper in black ink. Kneeling at the water's edge burn the paper and cast the ashes into the retreating sea saying, *"Air, Fire, Water, Earth. Take this from me, no longer of worth. Blessed Be."*

To secure safe travel for you or a loved one, especially over water, cast a silver coin into the sea at high tide and say, *"This coin I freely give to thee, pray bring back my beloved safe to me. Blessed Be."*

For emotional healing go to the water's edge at low tide and write the name of the sufferer in the sand. Around it draw a Pentacle. Say; *"Waters pure and waters deep, heal these hurts that run so deep. Waters deep and waters pure, may the pain no longer endure. Blessed Be."* Say the sufferer's name three times, then sit and watch until the tide has completely taken your spell.

*"Magic is not conjuring,
give it time to work."*

HONEYSUCKLE

Honeysuckle is cleansing, antispasmodic,
diuretic and laxative. It has been used to relieve
cramps and speed the birthing process.

The flowers have decongestant properties and have long been infused as a cure for chest complaints, especially asthma. This is also used to lighten the skin, to reduce scars and remove blemishes.

It is lucky to have Honeysuckle growing near the home, and should it grow over the door it will keep fever and sickness away. It used to be thought that Honeysuckle flowers should not be brought into the house where an unmarried woman lived as they would induce erotic dreams! Certainly the scent of Honeysuckle used to be considered an aphrodisiac, particularly when mixed with that of Rose. It was also thought that bringing it indoors would mean a wedding would follow. Honeysuckle is used in spells for protection and money. Wearing the flowers over your brow will strengthen psychic powers. Place a dried flower and leaf in your purse or wallet to attract money. Honeysuckle grows wild in many places and it is said that if it grows thus around the home then it will bring money towards you, but planted Honeysuckle does not produce the same result.

Honeysuckle climbs upwards with a clockwise, or Deosil, spiral, whilst bindweed grows with the converse spiral. Where the two can be trained to meet over the door it is said there will always be love in the house. There is even a folk song which alludes to this.

"Coping is another way of saying
you're trying to do too much."

TAROT SPELLS

Whilst the Tarot is principally used for divination, it is also possible to use it to create spells.

Whilst you can use your reading deck for this, most Witches who use this form of spell-casting prefer to use a different deck. This is mainly because spell-casting can leave marks, both physical and psychic, on the cards which may interfere with subsequent readings. To create Tarot spells it is helpful if you are already very familiar with the cards and have fully developed your own interpretation of their meanings.

To create a spell, first break it down into a few steps, eg if you are seeking a mentor in the Craft you would want the following: the right place to look, locating a mentor, getting on well together, and establishing good channels of communication. This gives you four steps. The most effective spells will have between 3 and 10 steps in them. Now examine your cards and select those which you feel most closely represent each stage. Once you have chosen them place them in a row reading left to right, and light a candle of the appropriate colour in front of them. Whilst it burns visualize each step coming to pass. Now place the cards in their sequence in a place where you will see them each day, but not where others can touch them. Leave them like this for a full cycle of the Moon, 29 days, before returning them to your pack. Between spells the pack should be placed in the light of the Full Moon to clear old spells.

*"Find the time every day
to do something for yourself."*

RED

**Red is the colour of the Element of Fire,
and is ruled by Mars; hence it represents
all things associated with the passions.**

The colour of blood, it has always been associated with life and death, and in many cultures is considered sacred to the Gods. It is linked with bloodshed, war and violence, but also with sexual energy, procreation, birth and motherhood. Indeed, it is one of the colours of the Goddess as Mother, and therefore the Full Moon, as well as being a colour of the Solar God.

Red is used magically in spells for all the above as well as in defensive and protective magics. It is a positive and energizing colour, so wear red when you need extra energy or a 'lift', when you need courage, and when you want to make an impact on others. Red stones were used to draw out and drive away aggressive feelings and conflicts. They were also thought to guard against fire and lightning. Because it is the colour of blood they are also used to heal wounds and burns, reduce inflammation, stem bleeding and prevent miscarriage. Red thread was tied to children and livestock for protection as well as around the appropriate part of the body to heal it. It used to be thought that a red thread around the neck prevented drowning. Red hair in a woman has long been thought to be a sign of a Witch, whilst a red birthmark indicates a person with special powers. Red lighting, as well as being the sign of a house of ill-repute, causes sexual energy to rise.

*"It's hard to be enlightened
when the truth is poorly lit."*

BLESSING AND CONSECRATING

We usually Bless and Consecrate items before
we use them in our Craft and our spells. This
dedicates their use to the Gods and for our magic.

Working tools such as the Athame, Chalice, Censer, etc should be consecrated after cleansing, but before use, whereas the objects we use in spells will be consecrated after the spell has been constructed, eg all the objects added to a charm bag, or the candle engraved.

Probably the most common way of doing this is through the Elements. You will need some incense, a candle, some water and some salt on your Altar. Take your object and pass it through the incense smoke and say, *"I do Bless and Consecrate this ... (name it) with incense that it be inspired by Air. Blessed Be."* Pass it briefly through the candle flame, or over it if it's likely to burn, and say, *"I do Bless and Consecrate this ... (name it) with flame that it be impassioned by Fire. Blessed Be."* Sprinkle a few drops of water on it and say, *"I do Bless and Consecrate this ... (name it) with Water, that it have true feeling. Blessed Be."* Sprinkle it with a little salt and say, *"I do Bless and Consecrate this ... (name it) with salt that it be rooted in earth. Blessed Be."* Now hold your object up over the Altar and, visualizing the Goddess and the God, say, *"I call upon the Goddess and God to Bless and Consecrate this ... (name it) I ask that they guard, guide and protect its use. Blessed Be."* Your object is now ready for use.

"Hasty magic leaves
plenty of time for regret."

VISUALIZATION

Visualization is a key technique of the Craft.

It means being able to 'see' things within your head so well that it is as good as being there. Once you have mastered the technique you will find that you can smell, taste, hear and feel the things you visualize. It resembles a form of controlled daydreaming, where you can guide events. It is a very important skill to master, and whilst for some it comes easily, others really have to work at it. Visualization contains elements of memory and imagination. The former is necessary to recall and use experiences such as the scents of a summer field and the feeling of the warm Sun on your skin. The latter is useful because you may need to visualize things you have not experienced. As a result it is a good idea to practise these skills individually as well as the technique itself. Start with recalling recent events and take your time to explore them in all their detail; strengthen your imagination by listening to your favourite programmes with your eyes shut, opening them to check how you are doing.

Visualization is important in magic because by seeing the steps in our spell taking place we are actually focusing our intent and will to make the change we seek. If you can visualize the white blood cells moving to a source of infection, fighting it and killing it off, then your healing will be that much more effective. The ability to visualize is also important in meditation and pathworking, where we follow a storyline to seek answers.

"Technology brings us together
in an isolated way."

Legend, Triple Aspect

EAGLE

The high-flying and far-sighted eagle is a truly majestic bird and is sometimes called the King of birds.

But it is as well to remember the claim to that title of the Wren, who when all the birds were competing to see who could fly the highest, sat upon the Eagle's back and thereby won the competition. An example to all that might can be overcome by intellect. The Eagle is sacred in many belief systems. The ancient Egyptians believed the Eagle was a messenger of Ra and therefore a Royal bird whose appearance was essential to confirm the title of Pharaoh. The Greeks associated it with the God Zeus and the Romans with Jove, or Jupiter, who shared many of Zeus' attributes. From both of these, and in many other pantheons, the Eagle is associated with thunder, due to a belief that its appearance heralded storms. The Eagle has been used as a symbol of authority from ancient Egypt and Greece to today's America.

The Eagle is protected by law in most parts of the world today, but it has long been believed that to steal an Eagle's eggs will bring a lifetime of grief. It was also held to be a portent of death if seen circling.

The Eagle stone or Aetite is a form of geode: round, hollow stones which contain crystals, in which the crystals are loose and hence will rattle when the geode is shaken. It was believed that such stones came from Eagles' nests. They were strapped to a woman's left arm to prevent miscarriage and then to her thigh to ensure a quick and easy birth.

"Practise random acts
of spontaneous kindness."

BEL

The festival of Beltane is dedicated to the God Bel,
in whose honour we light the Bel fires.

Worship of Bel originated in Sumeria where he is identified with Enlil son of Anu the father of the Gods. He is also seen as the Babylonian Marduk and the Phoenician Baal. Indeed in Babylonia and Assyria the term Bel means Lord and was attributed to all great Gods. The Romans saw him as Belenus who was linked to Apollo, both a Sun God and a God of Healing. In Europe he is the Celtic God Beli, and also Balor, grandfather of Lugh.

Bel is a God of light and fire, of health and prosperity. Not only did the Bel fires purify but they also invoked fertility. Hearth fires were extinguished at Beltane and new ones rekindled from the great fires, which would have been like beacons across the land. Indeed, beacon fires are being revived today for moments of great celebration. Lugh, another fire and light God, gives his name to the Sabbat of Lughnasadh. As a descendant of Balor, his tale reminds us that as the old King dies so a new one ascends to the crown. Balor, by the way, was credited with having a great 'poisoned eye' which took three men to lift its lid. This eye dealt death to any it looked upon, and is the origin of the expression 'a baleful stare'. Bel presides over much of the year, being in the ascendant from his festival at Beltane through to that at Lughnasadh, but also making his appearance at the other Sabbats.

> *"Look out for the good things,*
> *but guard against the bad."*

HAWTHORN MONTH

The Hawthorn is a tree of defence and protection, its
sharp spear-like thorns making an impenetrable fence.
It is one of the three trees most sacred to Witches,
together with Oak and Ash.

It is said that where the tree appears on an earthen mound it has been
planted by the fairies as a warning to stay away, lest disaster be visited
upon the disturber. The Hawthorn has many folk names. Whitethorn
relates to it being a tree of the White Goddess, distinguishing it from the
Blackthorn or Sloe which flowers earlier and is sacred to the Dark
Goddess. It is also called the May, which indicates its month of flowering
and it is the tree, not the month, which is referred to in the saying, *"Ne'er
cast a clout till May is out"*. Another name, Hagthorn, shows its links to
Witches and the Craft.

Hawthorn berries were used as a cardiac tonic, to ease sore throats,
asthma and aching joints. They also make a very fine liqueur which light-
ens the spirits. At one time it was thought Witches could transform themselves into the tree and few Witches would have had a garden without at
least one Hawthorn tree. Hawthorn blossom is used to decorate
Maypoles and in the celebrations around this time. It protects the house
from lightning and evil spirits, and was placed in the cradle to keep the
child safe from spells or being taken by the fairies. Magically, Hawthorn
is used in spells for fertility and, conversely, chastity, to increase a fishing
catch and to promote happiness and remove depression.

*"Whatever you make by hand will hold a
little piece of your Spirit within it."*

AMBER

**Amber has been considered special for at least ten
thousand years, beads being found in graves of that date.**

The fossilized resin of pine trees, it is warm to the touch and is sometimes found with pieces of plant or insect which have been trapped inside for millions of years. Because of these attributes it has long been thought to contain life.

Amber is protective and is used in magic relating to luck, healing, strength, beauty and love. It is used in amulets to defend against negativity and an Amber bead is often placed around the neck of a child to guard against disease. Powdered Amber is burnt during childbirth to protect both mother and child, and rubbing a piece of Amber over a newborn child was thought to protect them in the dangerous early days. Three Amber beads hung on a thread in the window will deflect the negative thoughts of others. Amber is worn and used in spells to enhance beauty and attractiveness. It also promotes happiness and draws love to it.

Witches wear Amber to honour the Goddess as Mother and to enhance and strengthen their magic. An Amber ring is often given as an Initiation present, and a necklace of Amber and jet is worn by the High Priestess. A piece of Amber placed on the Altar empowers both Ritual and spell casting. To enhance meditation roll a smooth piece between your fingers. As with other gems it is as well to be cautious when buying it; there are fakes around as well as 'reconstituted' Amber, which is nowhere near as effective.

"The most important things are people."

THE BESOM

The besom or broomstick is made from many twigs,
usually birch or heather, about 3 feet (90 cm) in length,
tied in place around a pole of Willow, Ash or Hazel.

The ties are made of willow. As the besom is a fertility symbol, the pole
being the male principal and the twigs into which it is inserted being the
female, it was popular to carve the hidden end of the pole in a phallic
shape. Like some other tools of the Craft it is best to make your own.

Popular images of the Witch show her riding a broomstick, or besom.
Whilst this is not a form of transport, many Witches will have one for
other reasons. The besom is an ideal garden broom, as it can sweep leaves
off flowerbeds and lawns in a way no other garden tool can. It is useful for
sweeping indoors, and in some ways it is superior to a vacuum. Magically
we use it to sweep the Circle or to sweep away negative influences
and energies. For a Handfasting Ritual it will be decorated with ribbons,
flowers and even bells. It is held across the Circle for the couple to jump,
signifying their leap into a new life together, often being slightly raised
during the leap to add to the fun. The besom was once used as an indicator as to whether visitors were permitted to call at a house. Bristles
upwards would mean that callers were not welcome, whilst bristles down
indicated that you could expect a welcome.

*"Just because you can send an email instantly
doesn't mean it is a good idea."*

BASIL

Basil is a greatly under-appreciated herb;
in addition to enhancing the flavour of food,
it has many medicinal and magical properties.
Indeed one of its folk names is Witches' Herb.

It has long been inhaled to relieve headaches, head and sinus congestion. Today we would put the oil in a vaporizer but snuff was once made from the dried leaves. It clears the mind, reduces mental exhaustion and aids concentration and memory. A tea of the leaves reduces temperature and alleviates many symptoms of the common cold.

Basil is used in spells for love, protection and wealth. In much of Europe it is associated with love, where it is said that any boy will love the maiden from whom he accepts a sprig of the plant. Magically it is added to love sachets and incenses. To resolve arguments a couple should rub the leaves on their skin and sit with their foreheads together and a leaf between. To discover if a relationship will work, place two leaves on a live coal, or charcoal disc; if they lie together and burn the relationship will be good, but if there is spitting and crackling the amount will indicate the degree of strife to come. To see if a lover will be faithful place a fresh leaf on their hand. If it withers before the day is out they will soon seek another partner. Basil is carried in the pocket to draw wealth. If the leaves are powdered and sprinkled about the home no evil will be able to enter. They are also burned in incenses of purification and protection.

*"Share things with your
friends, but not your germs."*

MAGICAL IMAGES

There are times when it is useful to have a picture
or image of the person you are working for, more
so when you don't know the person.

Whilst it is possible to work on a healing for a stranger using their name, date of birth, Sun sign, etc it is much easier to maintain your visualization if you have their picture in front of you. Obviously photographs are the most useful for this, but a drawing can be just as useful. Whilst you may not be able to get a 'good likeness', you can represent details which a photograph may not capture, like the person's favourite colour or the fact that they like gardening. You could even represent aspects such as the fact that they have had their hair coloured and style changed. It is a good idea to practise this skill before you need it. Try sketching a close friend and then adding other personal details to create an image of them and their life.

Likewise, the creation of an image, sometimes called a fith-fath or poppet, can help you to visualize the healing process for, say, a broken limb. Fith-faths are also frequently used in fertility spells where you can create the image of pregnancy as part of your magical working. The image can be made of wax, clay, straw or any other medium. You can even add pieces of hair if the subject gives them. Of course it is possible to create an image with a photograph and a sketch containing other details if you really need the extra help in your spell.

"Everyone has a self destruct button,
but try not to press it."

CHILLI PEPPERS

Chillies have long been used to stimulate the digestion,
especially where it is sluggish. A small pinch of Chilli
in a pint of water is used as a gargle for sore throats.
Chilli powder used to be added to ointment in the
case of aching joints, but it is worth testing first to
see if you are sensitive.

Added to food it helps to relieve chills and is thought to reduce a fiery
temperament.

Magically Chilli is used to break hexes, being placed in sachets to
carry, or scattered around the outside of the house. To ensure fidelity,
take two dried Chillies, tie them together with pink ribbon and place this
under your partner's pillow. Chilli is also used to enhance spells related
to the Sun and to Mars; those for prosperity, defence, courage, strength
and energy.

Unless you are very fond of hot and spicy foods you will only need
a few Chilli peppers, so why not grow your own? As the plants are relatively small they are easy to grow indoors and this is the time of year to
plant up a few seeds. Place 3 or 4 into some moist seed compost and cover
with their own depth of soil. Cover the pots with plastic bags to keep
warmth and moisture in until the seedlings have a few leaves and then
remove the bags and place them in good, indirect light and keep them relatively warm. When young, pinch out the tops to encourage bushy
growth. If you don't want to use them as soon as they ripen, they can be
dried, pickled in vinegar or frozen.

"Seek balance in all things."

ARTEMIS

The Greek Goddess Artemis is most often pictured as
a huntress carrying a bow with a quiver full of arrows,
but she was, and is, much more than that. She
represents womanhood throughout all its stages of life.

She was the 'Most Beloved' of Greece. She is the Virgin (Maiden) whose
rites embrace sexuality. She is the Mother who protects her young and the
young of all life. She oversees the passage from life to death: the Crone.
As Lady of the Beasts she carries her bow and quiver to despatch the old
and the sick, and yet to protect the pregnant, the young and their carers.
It was said that she would kill any man who harmed a pregnant animal or
who looked upon her without leave. Like woman she can seem contra-
dictory: she hunts yet protects animals, she is the virgin lover. But if we
look at her more closely we see that each of these attributes has its time,
just as there is the need for a woman to have differing roles at different
times in her life. Artemis is the Mistress of natural law, that which gov-
erns life, death and rebirth. She is represented by the Moon, and called
Huntress of the Moon. One of her symbols is the bear, and she gives her
name to the plant Artemisia or Wormwood.

Astateia, Goddess of the Amazons, is thought to be another form of
Artemis having also the role of Goddess of warrior women. Artemis is
sometimes confused with the Roman Diana, whose form was assimilated
into the Greek Artemis.

*"Look and listen to the rhythms of the land,
for they give timing to our lives."*

PATHWORKING

Pathworking, or interactive guided visualization,
is a technique which we can use to meet with the
Goddess and the God, to seek answers to our
questions or to access inner knowledge.

A Pathworking is a form of story where you visualize yourself as the central character: you walk through the tale, using your abilities to visualize
to create a complete scene. But it is a story with a purpose and usually
you will be heading to a place, perhaps to meet a person or deity with a
view to seeking your answer. As a result the story will have a break where
you can ask your question. Whilst the answer may come in the form of
words in your visualization, it is just as likely to come in terms of seeing
a symbol, or being given an object. Often these signs will need interpretation of their own.

In group Pathworkings the 'story' is usually narrated by one of the
people, but there are many examples of written Pathworkings where you
need to assimilate the story in order to be able to play it back in your
mind. You can also construct your own Pathworking to suit your needs.
First, you select the Goddess or God that you wish to meet; then determine the kind of environment that would most suit them and construct
your tale. Do not be disappointed if this does not work first time as it is
a difficult technique; indeed many people find that it is best to write the
'story' and, when they feel it is right, record it, so that they can relax into
the Pathworking.

*"Place your trust in your instincts,
not in strangers."*

A WEALTH PURSE

There are many reasons to be cautious in working magic for money, indeed it is far better to work for the opportunity to earn money.

However, one exception to this is when you wish to work a spell to help someone else. If you have a friend or loved one who needs a little magical assistance then you can create a Wealth Purse, but do ensure that you are working altruistically and not to benefit yourself.

Take a circle of green cloth 5 inches (12 cm) in diameter and hem it all around using silver or silver-coloured thread. In the middle place a pinch of dried Basil leaves, 3 Honesty seeds, 7 Pomegranate seeds and a small roundish piece of coal. Gather together the outer edge of the circle and secure it with 9 turns of the silver thread and then, using the ends of the thread, attach a coin with a hole in it. Tie this on with 9 knots. Bless the purse through the Elements at the waxing Moon and give it to your friend.

If your friend is not magical then a similar, although far slower, effect can be obtained by growing and giving them a money plant. Honesty, also called Silver Dollar and the Money Plant, is excellent for this. Plant seeds in the spring, just after the New Moon, and give the plant when it is several inches high at a Full Moon. The proper name of Honesty is Lunaria, and, as well as drawing money, it is sacred to the Moon. It is perfectly OK to grow it in your own garden to attract wealth.

> *"Try to fix the problem, not affix the blame."*

COAL

It is in some ways easy to understand why Coal should be imbued with magical significance; it burns and gives heat and, to a lesser extent, light.

Found in the Earth, it is a giver of Fire and hence life. Some miners believed that the Coal seam had a living presence and should be 'paid' regularly, with an offering of food, lest its spirit caused a disaster. Likewise to whistle underground was thought to annoy the spirits.

Coal has long been held to be lucky. Should you find a piece of Coal you should spit on it, toss it over your left shoulder and walk on without looking back to ensure good fortune. A piece of Coal washed up on the shore will protect a sailor from drowning. Coal is given as a good luck present to newlyweds and when a person moves into a new home. It is part of the traditional gifts of the 'first footer', the first person to enter a house after New Year. Indeed this may well predate the modern calendar, as it is also a customary gift at Samhain celebrations. A piece of Coal in the purse or pocket is said to draw money to it, and is still part of the more effective money spells.

Coal has been carved to create good luck amulets and into various images for good fortune. Like its harder 'cousins', Cannel coal and Jet, Coal has also been used to create jewellery. This is not as messy as it at sounds, as Coal can be washed, dried and then polished to prevent it soiling.

"A person whose every sentence begins with 'I' has little room for others."

SUN IN GEMINI

*The Sun has now entered the sign of Gemini,
an Air sign. As such it indicates the world of thought,
ideas and communication. It is also a mutable
sign adding flexibility and problem solving.*

Those born when the Sun is in this sign are generally adaptable, versatile and good at communication. The typical Geminian is mentally alert, inquisitive and constantly on the go. They are talkative, sociable, dexterous, mentally agile, interested in new experiences, good at adjusting to circumstances, and they make excellent communicators in all fields. Whilst they have a lot of nervous energy they tend to squander this by over-committing to too many people or projects at one time. Geminians are better at superficial relationships than they are with their near and dear, to whom they may appear cool and unaffectionate. They are, however, very alert and aware and good at picking up hidden signs and signals from others and from their environment. On the negative side they can be devious, inconsistent and variable, moving rapidly from one idea to another.

For Geminians this period is good for work with an intellectual bias so long as they prioritize, apply themselves and do not let themselves be distracted by new and more exciting things that come along. In relationships they need to be aware that others may need more open signs of affection than they do themselves. Non-Geminians should use the energy of this time to pursue intellectual pursuits and to work on all aspects of communication.

"Let yourself accept praise with grace."

MANDRAKE

**The Mandrake, or *Mandragora officinarum*,
can grow in most temperate climates.**

The brown root, up to 3 or 4 feet (90 cm to 1.2 m) long, often branches
in such a way as to give a human image. Mandrakes are thought to come
in both male and female forms. The leaves are large, dark green, and have
a distinctive, slightly unpleasant smell. The white flowers on long stalks
are followed by yellow, apple-sized fruit which give it the folk name,
Satan's Apple. The plant was reputed to grow under gallows and it was
thought that its scream, when pulled from the ground, could kill or drive
a person mad.

Use of the Mandrake goes back thousands of years. The root provides a powerful emetic and purgative, but has been used to treat rheumatism. The fruit was used to bring sleep and even as an anaesthetic. The
leaves are cooling and can be made into a poultice to treat ulcers.
Magically, the root was decorated to increase its human appearance, by
placing seeds for eyes and keeping some leaves in place that they might
look like hair when it dried. A Mandrake poppet was considered protective and brought good luck if placed on the mantelpiece. It was used to
expel demons, to counter curses and in defensive magic. Mandrake is used
in money spells and as a fertility poppet. It is hung over the bed to induce
sleep, attract love and to prevent nightmares.

White Bryony root, which is poisonous, is often used as a substitute
in magical working as it has a similar appearance.

*"Good advice makes sense,
even though it may be uncomfortable."*

VISIT THE CRYSTAL FOUNTAIN

The Crystal Fountain is a place of peace and
tranquillity you can visit whenever you feel
stressed or tired. Here you can ask a question
and seek the answer in the waters.

Lie down comfortably, with your arms by your sides and your legs
uncrossed, close your eyes and take several deep breaths. Visualize yourself walking through the woods on a Summer's evening. The trees along
each side of the path are Oak and Ash and Elm, and they move softly in
the gentle night breeze. The air moving through their branches seems to
whisper a welcome. The ground beneath your feet is soft and mossy,
and cool. You slip off your shoes to make contact with the earth. Above
you the sky is a deepening blue and the Full Moon lights your way. As you
walk, you hear the sound of running water, and through the trees
you glimpse a small stream, tumbling over rocks and making music
which complements the night. Turning a bend, you see a small waterfall
descending into a pool almost at your feet. Take a step towards it and
kneel at its edge. Reflected in the rippling waters you see the face of the
Moon and below the surface stones and crystals of differing colours.
Gazing at the Moon's reflection you ask your question and then, dipping
your hand into the waters, you withdraw a stone. Look carefully at this
stone and remember it. Now give your thanks to the Moon and the
waters, and return to the here and now. Remember the stone and seek the
answer to your question through its meaning.

"Everyone deserves at least some time off."

DIVINING WITH THE TAROT

There are times in life when we seek to know when
something will take place, like the arrival of information,
a reply to a letter or even the birth of a child.

First, you need to select three time periods suitable to your event. This is usually days, weeks and months, but it could be hours, days, weeks and so on. Shuffle the deck thoroughly whilst focusing on your question. Now deal the cards into a pile, stopping when you get to an ace or thirteen cards, whichever comes first. Then deal a second and third pile in the same way. Your first pile indicates the number of days, or the smallest time interval; the second the weeks; the third the months. Where a pile has thirteen cards and no ace this indicates a zero, but if none of the piles has an ace then the question is unanswered.

Once you have established your time interval look at the suits of the aces, or at the thirteenth cards. These will give you an indication of the nature of events surrounding your question. Swords indicate difficulties or conflict may be encountered. Wands indicate that you need to think carefully and proceed with caution. Cups tell you that this will be an emotional time, but that support will be available if you ask for it. Coins tell you that success will be achieved, but there may be a price. Where your 13th card(s) are of the major Arcana, examine them carefully to analyze their meaning. These cards will also relate to the time intervals you originally decided upon.

"Organizing Witches can be like herding cats;
exciting but hard work."

CENTRING, EARTHING AND GROUNDING

*There are techniques which it is best to
perform before and after meditation,
visualization, ritual, acts of magic and spells.*

Those performed before have the effect of preparing you physically, mentally and psychically for the work you are about to perform. Those you carry out after are designed to ensure that you are truly back down to earth before you go on with daily life.

Centre yourself by taking several deep breaths and focus on the Earth beneath you, the Air you are breathing, the light and heat of the Sun and your heartbeat, and the Water and blood which flow within your veins. It is essential to balance the Elements before starting magical work.

Earthing and Grounding are both techniques to use after working. Earthing involves much the same as Centring in that you visualize the Elements within. It is assisted by actually placing your hands and feet on the earth, if you are outside, to allow residual energies to transfer to the ground. When indoors you may find that it helps to rub your arms and legs briskly, again dissipating left-over energy. Grounding is most easily achieved by having something to eat and drink: this encourages your body to focus on the physical realm. Earthing is used to disperse residual energy whilst Grounding helps to replenish the body's physical resources. If you can, perform both after any act of magic.

*"Conversation is supposed to
be a two-way process."*

PINK

**Pink is one of the colours of Venus. It is the colour
of friendship, affection, romantic love, respect.**

It is also a colour of the self and is used to bring self-understanding and acceptance, thereby to develop self-respect, self-esteem and hence self-confidence. It is used in all kinds of emotional healing, and to bring peace and harmony. Pink is calming, soothing and removes physical and mental stress. It is used to strengthen relationships of the heart, whether with family, friends or a loved one, and can help to resolve difficulties in long-standing relationships. Pink also positively stimulates the emotions, attracting friends and bringing laughter and happiness.

Pinks are often used in places where it is felt needful to reduce tension, aggression, stress, concern or worry, such as prisons, hospitals and so on. The tradition of surrounding female infants in pink is done to enhance the gentle qualities of love, respect and affection, whilst dressing boys in blue is intended to encourage a more outgoing personality.

Use pink lighting, the very pastel pinkish-white light bulbs are ideal, to encourage a more harmonious atmosphere at home. Wear pink, especially on your top half, if you feel you may need to calm those around you. Pink stones, especially Rose Quartz, can be worn to attract friendship and love. Use it in spells to bring emotional healing for others. To bring self-acceptance and understanding burn a pink candle surrounded by small pieces of Rose Quartz.

*"Learn to love yourself, faults and all, and you
will understand the secrets of true love."*

MAZES AND SPIRALS

Today's Mazes with their high hedges, twists, turns
and dead ends, created with straight lines, are not
representative of their predecessors.

The older mazes are made from curves and spirals, and usually from a single line which leads you in and then out again. Many, cut into rock, date back thousands of years. These are possibly the earliest form of maze. Some are simple single spirals, others are more complex groupings, often of three. Some are small and can be covered by a hand; others are huge and can be walked. The spiral path was thought to lead into the underworld and hence was a symbol of rebirth, for you walked inwards to death, then outwards to life again. There used to be many mazes which could be walked, but they have mostly gone. Perhaps one of the largest still available to us today is the spiral path which winds up Glastonbury Tor. Walking one of these mazes can have a profound effect and opens the inner eye to the spiritual plane.

Today we sometimes create spirals from cut turf, or by using flour or sawdust as a marker, and we use them as meditations or in Rites of Passage. The spiral is sacred to the Goddess in her aspect of Crone and by walking the spiral we can draw closer to understanding her and seek her wisdom. In my garden I have a spiral made of slate paving which can be walked Widdershins (anti-clockwise) on the way in, to cast off negatives, and then retraced Deosil, clockwise, to take on new ideas and feelings.

*"Hindsight is always better
than that at the time."*

WICCAN RULES

Unlike other belief systems the Craft does not have a
long list of things you should not do or eat, or other
prohibitions. What it looks to are two simple 'rules':
The Wiccan Rede and the Law of Threefold Return.

The Wiccan Rede simply states, *"An it harm none, do what you will."*
Whilst at first it may appear simple, on examination it is far from an easy
ideal. If taken as an absolute 'command' it would be impossible to live up
to, but if looked at with sense it is easier to interpret. The key word is
'will'. It is not 'wish' or 'want' but 'will', as in the focusing of your energies in the magical context, the magical harnessing of your willpower. The
Rede is there to guide us and to encourage us to consider the results of
our workings: will our magic cause harm, whether deliberate or accidental, to others?

The Law of Threefold Return does not actually originate in the Craft
but is derived from older, eastern beliefs. Again it needs to be taken in
context, as this instruction is not confined to Witches, or to the working
of magic. It is derived from the belief in Karma, with its emphasis on
wrongdoing catching you up in this life or the next. It is as well to
remember that this is not just a magical rule, but a life rule.

Interestingly, I first came across these rules through a verse: *"Eight
words the Wiccan Rede fulfil, an it harm none do what you Will. Lest in
thine own defence it be, ever mind the Rule of Three."*

"Anytime is good for a fresh start."

PLANETARY HOURS

Different days of the week have different planetary influences which can help us in our magic.

Likewise different hours of the day and night can also aid us. To make the most of these we have to do some maths. Day and night are not the same length all year round, but they each have the same number of planetary hours, 12, whatever the season. Hence in Winter the planetary hours in daylight will be shorter and those at night longer, and vice versa in Summer.

Having chosen the best day for your working, you will need the exact time of sunrise and sunset. Decide whether you will be working in the day or the night and divide that period by 12 to get the planetary hour length. Assign the planets to the planetary hours keeping the following sequence at all times: Sun, Venus, Mercury, Moon, Saturn, Jupiter, Mars. If you intend to make much use of planetary hours it is a good idea to draw up a table for reference.

The sequence of planetary hours starts with a different planet for each day and night of the week, but otherwise they proceed in the same order. The starting planet for daytime is the planet of that day:

Sunday daylight: Sun, Venus, Mercury, Moon, Saturn, Jupiter, Mars, Sun, Venus, Mercury, Moon, Saturn.

Sunday night: Jupiter, Mars, Sun, Venus, Mercury, Moon, Saturn, Jupiter, Mars, Sun, Venus, Mercury.

The other daytimes start with: Monday the Moon, Tuesday Mars, Wednesday Mercury, Thursday Jupiter, Friday Venus, Saturday Saturn and Sunday the Sun.

"Practise laughter, it's good for you."

SUNFLOWERS

Sunflowers have been the flowers of the Sun since early civilizations.

Their flowers turn to follow the passage of the Sun across the sky. The Priestesses of the Aztecs wore crowns of Sunflowers in rituals to honour the Sun. In the Craft we often find Sunflowers on the Altar or marking the entrance to the Circle in Summer Rituals and when working magic with the Sun.

Sunflowers are grown commercially for their oil and for animal feeds. The flowers yield a yellow dye and the stems make paper and animal bedding. The leaves are used in herb tobaccos and incense. The seeds are expectorant and can be added to home-made cough remedies. A tincture of seeds was used to treat fevers and was held to be as useful as quinine. The seeds are also edible and can be dried by placing the whole head into a luke-warm oven overnight. They are ripe as soon as they can be easily removed from the heads. They can be roasted, with or without spices, and make a nutritious snack. Ground, they are added to flour and used in bread and pastry making.

Sunflowers have long been associated with good luck. Not only do the seed heads attract birds, bees and other useful creatures which remove pests from the garden, but their presence is believed to draw the Sun's energy into the home and garden. Cut a Sunflower at sunset and make a wish and, if it is small enough, it will come to pass before the next sunset. Place a sachet of seeds under your pillow and you will learn the truth of a matter.

*"The truth is useful,
but not always helpful."*

INSECT REPELLENTS

As Summer approaches, we want to open our windows to let the warm air flow through our homes to cleanse and freshen them.

When it is fine enough we like to sit outside, take walks, go camping or have barbeques and picnics. All these activities can be made uncomfortable by the presence of flies and other insects. The warmer weather is also a signal to fleas and other beasties to hatch and assail our pets.

There are many ways of addressing the problem without using toxic chemicals. To keep flies from the home hang bundles of strongly-scented herbs in the windows. Try Basil, Bay, Chilli, Garlic, Lavender, or Marjoram. Grow small pots of other aromatic herbs such as Mint, Oregano, Rue, Sage and Thyme on windowsills. Place small pots of freshly picked herbs in water in the bedrooms. Dried herbs and powdered cayenne pepper can also be scattered on the carpets.

To protect your skin add a couple of drops of oil of Geranium, Rosemary, Lavender and Citronella to some body lotion and, after testing it to see if you react to it, rub it into the skin. Place Bay leaves, dried Lavender or Rosemary sachets amongst your summer clothing as well to deter biting insects. Pets can be helped by making an infusion of Wormwood, Fleabane and Sage. Rub a little of this into their coat two or three times a week. When camping, burn small amounts of any of the above herbs outside your tent to deter insects. Burning old or unwanted incenses will also help to keep them at bay, and use them up.

"Magic works, whether
you believe in it or not."

GREEN

Green is the colour of nature, life, growth and fertility.

It is a colour of the Goddess Venus and linked to fortune, prosperity, money and good luck. It is also a colour of the God. Dark greens relate to the Holly King and light ones to the Oak King. Associated with the Element of Earth, it is a colour of the physical realm.

Green is used magically for all of the above and also in spells relating to maintaining or improving good health, for balancing and for grounding. Wear green when you need to focus on the practical and keep your feet on the ground. Green stones are said to draw money and are often carried or placed in a till. Likewise green candles are burned to bring the opportunity to earn. Empower green stones and place them around your plants to encourage growth. Wear green stones, or sleep with them under your pillow to strengthen your eyesight and reduce headaches caused by eyestrain. Interestingly, it has been found that using a pale green background to your computer screen will help to reduce eyestrain, headaches and other related ills.

Green fell out of favour around the 18th century when it was sometimes said to be the colour of fairies, and therefore to wear it would bring their wrath. Likewise it was associated with Witches and again considered an unlucky colour, especially at weddings, but this probably relates to its earlier use as a colour to advertise sexual availability! Green eyes were also held to be the sign of a Witch.

*"Raise the cup of life to the
Horned God and the Ancient Ones."*

LEGEND, TRIPLE ASPECT

DOWSING

Dowsing is a divination technique usually used to find things.

Despite the scepticism of some, dowsing is actually used professionally to locate water, oil and other substances. Dowsing is usually performed with a single forked stick, sometimes called a dowsing fork, or a pair of dowsing rods. The former is usually made of Hazel, or Rowan, but other woods such as Willow are also used. The stick has to be of a size that the operator can comfortably hold one of the forked ends in each hand, leaving the main 'stem' free to move. Dowsing rods are usually a pair of metal rods bent at right angles about a quarter of the way along. The shorter ends are held, enclosed in loose sleeves allowing the rods to move freely. Some people maintain that copper is the best metal for dowsing, but others say that any kind will work so long as they are balanced in the hand.

The fork or rods should be held lightly in the hands so they may move freely. The operator focuses on the substance they are seeking and walks up and down the designated area waiting for movement. Many dowsers can give additional information, such as the depth of the substance they are looking for, or the direction of flow of an underground stream. Experienced dowsers can use maps to locate what they are seeking. Some dowsers say they feel a tingling in their hands when they make a find. If you want to try dowsing, and don't wish to start digging holes in the landscape, then check your finds using a map.

> *"It is not so very long ago that electricity was considered magical."*

PINS

Pins have long been credited with magical abilities.
Most of us are familiar with the saying, *"See a pin
and pick it up and all day long you'll have good luck."*

However, the pin must point away, for to pick it up when it is towards you, or by the point, will bring disappointment. It was also thought unlucky to lend a pin, and the lender would turn their back so as not to see it being taken. Unmarried women would remove all the pins from the Bride's costume to enhance their chances of marrying within the year. The Bride was given a pin immediately after her wedding so that she would have control in the house. Pins were closely associated with Witches, and accepting a pin from a Witch was thought to place you in her power. Of course they were also stuck into images as a curse.

Magically, pins are placed in a candle to signify the point at which the magic is sent forth. We use them in time-specific spells to 'pin' the magic to a date. They are, and have always been, cast into wells as an offering, and placed under doorsteps or in doorframes to protect the house.

Today we see pins as being of little value, but this was not the case in the past. The humble pin held things together: clothes, wrapping and even small wooden items. Hence it had much value and pins were always kept safely. Moreover the term pin could mean anything from the object we recognize, to fairly sturdy tacks, fine nails, or even a brooch.

*"Practise the things you enjoy,
even if you're not very good at them."*

SAGE

Sage, as its name suggests, is good for the mind,
as it strengthens the memory, brings clear
thinking and enhances the senses.

But it is also one of those herbs which have been traditionally used to treat a number of ills. A tea made from the leaves is said to aid the digestion, help the liver and kidneys, help treat ulcers, reduce aches and pains. It makes a good gargle to reduce sore throats, mouth ulcers and bleeding gums. Mixed with sugar and lime juice it is used to reduce fevers, delirium, nervous problems and cure headaches. The leaves can be used to create an antiseptic wound dressing or a poultice for aches, strains and sprains. Dried leaves make a snuff which is used in the treatment of asthma and chest infections. In ancient Greece and Rome it was considered to prolong life and youthfulness if it was eaten regularly.

Sage should be planted alongside Rue, both to protect the Sage from pests and to encourage its vigour. Indeed it is held to be unlucky for sage to be the only plant in the bed. It is said that where Sage grows well then the business will thrive, and also that strong Sage plants indicate a woman of strong will.

Magically Sage is used in spells for wisdom, knowledge and protection. Inhale freshly cut Sage leaves or the oil to enhance visualization. When someone dear to you travels away, hang a sprig in the kitchen: so long as it is healthy they will be happy in their travels. Burn freshly cut Sage wood to bring about a change in fortune.

"Youth may not last,
but beauty lies in wisdom."

STUDY SUCCESS

For many this is the season of revision and stress.

Whether these are yours or those of your loved ones, there are several ways to help. Having said that, magic will only enable you to maximize your potential, it will not make up for a lack of knowledge or application!

Make yourself a study success charm from yellow fabric containing a few leaves each of Rosemary, Basil and Mint, add a piece of Sunstone and a piece of Aventurine and a small piece of Rowan wood, or leaf. Bless this through the Elements and keep it by you both when studying and during any tests.

When you have a heavy study period ahead make a tea of Rosemary and sip this throughout the day, and put Basil on your food whenever you can. Both these will help your brain to become more effective and to absorb information. Have yellow around you at your desk, to stimulate thought, and if you are at home burn a yellow candle which has been anointed with oil of Rosemary. Keep a sprig of fresh Rosemary beside you whilst you work and inhale its scent whenever you need inspiration. At the end of each study session, ensure that you retain your knowledge by spending a few moments holding a piece of Haematite in your hands. Visualize it 'fixing' in your mind all that you have learned, and keep this stone by you when working. Be sure to rest your mind by taking a bath with a piece of Sunstone and a couple of sprigs of Lavender in the water.

"Watch and listen and
you may find wisdom."

TAROT PATHWORKING READING

The Tarot can be used for many things: reading,
meditation, pathworking, and to give greater
understanding of the subconscious mind. A Tarot
Pathworking reading works well for the latter. In this,
only the cards of the major Arcana are used, and it
helps if the subject is unfamiliar with the deck.

The cards are placed face upwards on a surface and the person seeking
knowledge picks 3 cards. The first is the card which appeals to them
most, the second is the one they most dislike and the third is the one they
find most intriguing or mysterious. The chosen 3 are then examined in
turn, first the most liked, secondly the least liked and lastly the most
intriguing. For each card the subject constructs a sort of story which covers the following. What is happening in the picture? How did this come
to be? What happened before, to make this happen? What is likely to
come next? It is a good idea to make rough notes. When you have dealt with
each of the cards in this way, go back through your notes. Where you are
doing this for yourself you need to be careful not to look for the answers
you wish. If it is for another, then you can help them by asking questions,
such as: Which part of the picture draws your eyes? Why is this?

    The first card and its story represent the subject's life and aspirations
at present. The second refers to the outside influences around the issue.
The third indicates the problems or potential problems that are perceived
by the subject.

"The longer the journey,
the greater the discovery."

STRAWBERRIES

Now is the time when cultivated strawberries appear
in the shops, although I would recommend growing
your own wild strawberries in a pot.

These delicious fruits have long been associated with love, and whatever
your age it is romantic to dip them in sugar and feed your partner. But
they also have other uses and associations. The fruit is an excellent source
of vitamins and as it is easily digested it is helpful in treating a number of
digestive ills. It has been used to reduce fever and diarrhoea. The roots are
used in cases of diarrhoea and even to cure dysentery. A tea made from
the leaves is held to ease the pain of rheumatic gout. Strawberries can be
used to reduce sunburn: in mild cases rub a Strawberry over the face just
after washing with tepid water; in more severe cases rub the juice well in
and leave half an hour before rinsing off. Strawberries can also be rubbed
over the teeth and gums, and the juice left on for 5 minutes, before brushing with bicarbonate of soda, to make the teeth whiter.

Strawberries contain many volatile oils and some people actually give
off the scent after eating them, which is held to be attractive to the opposite gender. In the past the leaves were used to fragrance the skin, the
scent being compared to Musk-rose and Violet. Strawberries are used
magically in spells for love and luck. Carry 3 of the leaves to attract good
fortune. Rub a deep pink candle with a Strawberry and light it to make
your beloved think of you.

*"If you give nothing of yourself,
you will get nothing in return."*

OAK MONTH

The Oak is the King of Trees and sacred to the Celts and Druids.

It has long been considered bad luck to cut it down or to take the living wood. Since early times it has been associated with Herne who was thought to have practised magic under one, and with the stag, symbol of the Horned God. It is also sacred to Thor and acorns are said to protect a house from storms and lightning. It was sacred to the ancient Greeks and the Romans dedicated it to Jupiter, and King Arthur's round table was said to have been made of a single slice of Oak. The Oak is strongly associated with the Element of Earth and the physical realm. The Oak represents the sacrifice of personal freedom in order to take up magical work.

The Oak is slow-growing and capable of living well over a hundred years. Its hard wood was used to build ships, and burnt to provide charcoal for metalwork. The bark was used in leather making and to create dyes of purple, black, yellow and browns. The young wood is used to make furniture. Acorns have long been noted for their antiseptic properties and used in folk medicine to dress wounds. They have also been used to make flour and a form of coffee. The inner bark makes a gargle for throat and sinus problems. The leaves make a soothing dressing for sore eyes.

To protect your home from all manner of ills, make an equal-armed cross, bound with red thread, of two pieces of Oak. To bring prosperity, plant an acorn the day before the New Moon.

"Things endure which grow slowly."

TREE KNOWLEDGE

*Trees are magical entities; each species having different
properties and being used in different ways.*

Every person has one or more tress that are special to them, even though
they may not have found them yet. In the Craft a personal tree becomes
a Sacred Space in its own right, as well as a place where we can draw on
the energies of the Elements in a very direct way. These personal trees
may change over time just as we change as we go through life.

First, you need to select a tree. Take your time and look at many different kinds and specimens. When you feel you have found the type of
tree you feel at home with, it will pay to spend a little time with several
examples of its kind. Sit beneath each with your eyes closed; look on the
ground for any signs which may indicate that it has chosen you. One
such would be to catch a falling leaf, or to find a twig with leaves and perhaps the 'fruit' of the tree. When you have chosen your tree, or it has chosen you, create a plait of several of your hairs and bury it beneath the tree,
taking away a small piece of wood, fruit or leaves. These provide a link
between you and the tree. Also place an offering of honey and raisins
beneath its boughs.

Get to know your tree, making regular visits and spending time in
meditation and contemplation under it. Take photographs or make
sketches and drawings of it. Learn to see it in all its moods and seasons.

*"Everyone is entitled to their own opinion,
however wrong you may think it."*

HOLED STONES

Stones with holes through them,
whether naturally occurring or caused by
erosion, are much prized in magical working.

They are also known in folklore as Holey Flints, Holey Stones, and even
Odin Stones after the tale in the Eddas. They are a symbol of the Great
Mother and the Element of Earth and are used in magic for fertility, pro-
tection, and to improve health.

Some such Holey Stones are large enough for a person to pass
through, and have been used as sites of worship and magic for thousands
of years, like the Men-an-Tol near Lanyon in Cornwall. A woman would
be passed through the hole in order to aid conception. Children were
passed through them to prevent or cure diseases such as rickets, whooping cough, epilepsy, consumption and boils. Lovers would hold hands
through the stone and make their promises of commitment. In some
Rites a person would be passed through as part of the process of rebirth.

Smaller Holed Stones were used to protect against negative influences and Witches. On a trip to California we stayed in a hotel which
boasted Holed Stones in every chamber to guard against Witches! They
were also placed on stables and barns to protect horses and livestock.
Some fishermen still carry them to prevent drowning, and many people
wear them to cure disease. Such a stone, if discovered by chance or given
as a gift, is said to bring great luck. It is also said that if you take a Holed
Stone to a wild place on a moonlit night and look through it you will be
able to see spirits and visions.

"It's never too late to learn a new skill."

FREYA

In the Craft the Norse pantheon seems to be less
often called upon than some others, which is in some
ways surprising when you consider that their deities
gave their names to at least three days of the week:
Wodin gave his name to Wednesday, Thor gave his to
Thursday, and Freya, or Frigg, gave hers to Friday.

Amongst scholars there is some discussion as to whether Freya is the
mother of Frigg or whether they are different aspects of the same
Goddess. Moreover, there is also some dispute as to which name is actually the origin of Friday. However, they do have different attributes.
Freya is mistress of all the Gods and ruler of death. She is most beautiful
of the Gods and wears a magical Amber necklace and a feathered cloak.
She rides through the skies in a chariot drawn by cats or on a great
boar. Freya was Goddess of love and sexuality. In her other aspects
she was Mardol, the beauty of light on water; Horn, the linen woman; Syr
the sow, and Gefn the generous one. Frigg was the White Lady of
Midsummer, a Mother Goddess known as the 'bearer'. She too wore the
plumage of birds; in her case hawks and falcons, and her other aspects
include Eir the physician, Saga the wise, Gefjon the virgin and others.
Frigg was the mother of Baldur who was killed because of the deceit of
Loki. She is thought by many to be a northern form of Ishtar or Cybele.
Whilst Freya was the favourite of the Norse Gods, Frigg was undisputed
ruler of Asgard, the home of the Gods.

"Unsought advice is a waste of breath."

NAMING OBJECTS

Sometimes when working magic for a person we want to physically represent them in the Circle.

To do this we can use a picture, poppet or fith-fath, or even an object such as a stone or a candle, and its effectiveness will be greatly increased if it is formally 'named' for the person. This is best done through the Elements in much the same way as an object is consecrated. The name that you use should preferably be the one which the person uses, which could be a shortened form, rather than necessarily their given name. On your Altar you will need incense, salt, water and a lighted candle to represent the Elements.

Take your object and pass it through the smoke of the incense and say, "*Through the Element of Air, I do name this ... (name of the person). As is my will so mote it be. Blessed Be.*" Pass it swiftly through the flame of the candle and say, "*Through the Element of Fire, I do name this ... (name). As is my will so mote it be. Blessed Be.*" Sprinkle it lightly with water and say, "*Through the Element of Water, I do name this ... (name). As is my will so mote it be. Blessed Be.*" Sprinkle it with salt and say, "*Through the Element of Earth, I do name this ... (name). As is my will so mote it be. Blessed Be.*" Now hold it up over the Altar and say, "*I call upon the Goddess and the God to witness that, through the power of the Elements, this is ... (name). As is your will so mote it be. Blessed Be.*"

> "*Craft every spell with as much care as though it were for you.*"

GOATS

**To many the Goat was symbolic of the Witch's
so-called 'pact with the devil', as the devil was thought
to disguise himself as one in order to pass unnoticed.**

During the Witch Hunts this was a convenient link for the authorities as the mostly poor and elderly women who were accused would often have been too poor to have a cow, having only a Goat to provide milk. This association is almost certainly derived from the image of Pan, the Goat-Foot God, who is a significant deity to many Witches. Indeed the archetypical devil probably has cloven hooves because of this image.

In some places it is still said that you will never see a Goat the whole day through as it will have to slip away at some time to visit Satan its master, and have its beard combed! Having said that, carrying a Goat's foot or hairs from its beard was also thought to keep the devil away. Sailors would pin a Goat's skin to the mast to ensure calm wind, and pieces of skin were placed on horse collars to avert evil. Goats were used to take away sickness, being encouraged to graze near a sick person's room and then driven away to take the disease with them. Male Goats were grazed with cattle to prevent them aborting, and Goats were generally felt to bring general good health and calmness to the herd and to horses. They were also said to kill adders. Drinking Goat's milk was said to make a maiden barren but was also thought to be a cure for consumption (tuberculosis).

*"Good friends will also tell you the
things you don't want to hear."*

SUNSTONES

There are at least three kinds of stone which are
referred to as Sunstones: an Indian Feldspar which
resembles an orange Opal with a fiery flash; a form of
translucent orange Quartz; and a deep orange stone
with Mica inclusions giving it a glittery appearance.

Of the three, the Indian stone is the one which was originally used for
magical work. However, I have found that any of the three will work
equally well, especially if appropriately charged by placing it in full
Sunlight for a few hours. This can be done well in advance of magical use,
which is useful if, like me, you get sunshine only rarely for large parts of
the year! Once charged, the stones should be wrapped in gold tissue or
fabric until they are needed.

Sunstones are used in magic for protection, energy, health and all
things associated with the energies of the Sun. Wear a Sunstone whenever you need extra energy or if you are approaching a difficult or trying
time. Worn in Circle they will increase the ability to raise power and to
focus it. Added to charms they will increase their strength. To protect the
home, hang one in a south-facing window, where Sunlight can bounce off
it. Sunstones have long been carried to attract prosperity, and are felt to
be especially potent if an image of the Sun is inscribed on one side. Worn
near the genital region they are said to increase sexual energy and fertility. To find a Sunstone is said to bring great fortune and to protect the
finder from all kinds of disaster.

*"Expand your horizons and you'll
be surprised what you find."*

TO DRAW LOVE INTO YOUR LIFE

*It is never a good idea to work magic
to make a particular person love you.*

First, because it interferes with that person's freedom of will, and is thus against the Wiccan Rede. Secondly, because you will never know if they love you for yourself or because of your magic, which, in the long term, will be self-destructive. It is, however, perfectly all right to work to bring love into your life.

This spell is most effective when worked on a Friday when the energies of Venus are strongest: Take a pink candle and carefully inscribe your initials into it about half way down. Surround the letters with 7 carefully engraved hearts. Anoint this with 7 drops of Rose oil and place it in a secure holder surrounded by 7 small pieces of Rose Quartz. Many rock and gemstone suppliers sell bags of mixed stone chips, and if you know your stones, these are excellent for working spells. Before you light it, close your eyes and visualize the Goddess Venus standing before you, ask her to bring love to you and then light the candle. Keep it close to you whilst it burns. Ensure you have enough time to let it burn all the way down, without having to leave it unattended. When your candle has burnt all the way down take the pieces of Rose Quartz and anoint each with one drop of Rose oil and wrap them in a pink cloth. Tie this tightly with gold thread and carry it with you for a full cycle of the Moon, 29 days.

*"Happiness makes up in height
for what it may lack in length."*

PLANT SPELLS

Not only do we use herbs and other plants in our spells but we can also use them as the spells themselves.

This is a good method to use when working for long-term change, like prosperity, health or protection, and also for use when crafting the spell for another, as a potted plant makes an attractive gift in its own right. Whilst you could set the spell in action at the stage of planting seeds, it is often better to start it off when actually potting up a small plant so that you can ensure that you actually have a healthy plant.

Select your plant according to its magical uses and with the person in mind, as there's little point in giving them something which you know they dislike. For protection try Hydrangea, Hyacinth, Lavender or Primrose. For prosperity try Basil, Honesty or Violet. Geranium, Marjoram and Tansy are all good for bringing good health, and there are many other examples in this and other books. If you can, select a container in an appropriate colour, like green for prosperity. Plant the spell at the New Moon and water it in with collected rainwater. Once you have done this ask the Goddess and the God to give their blessings on both plant and spell. Give it at least a week to settle into its new container before giving it to another. If they are not skilled at plant care, also give them some simple directions to tend it, as a dead plant has no magic.

"It's better to be there to pick up the pieces, than to try to change people."

THREE DEGREES

Many Craft traditions have an initiatory system which consists of three degrees or levels. These are not, as sometimes supposed, levels of authority but rather levels of understanding and development.

Each degree has its own initiation ceremony or Ritual and reflects different aspects of the Craft. There are no set periods between initiations, as each should take place when the individual is ready for it. Having said that, initiations will not normally take place with less than a year and a day between them.

The First Degree is the beginning of the journey into the Craft. The Ritual centres on the candidate's personal commitment to the Goddess and the God. It is the level in which the Initiate learns to learn. In a good training Coven the Initiate will have fairly formal instruction which should give an idea of the breadth of Craft knowledge. The First Degree reflects the Maiden aspect of the Goddess.

The Second Degree is the level at which the Initiate learns to teach, and in this and other aspects it reflects the nurturing of the Mother Goddess. In this degree instruction is far less formal, as the Initiate should be able to direct their study.

The Third Degree is given when it is felt that the Initiate is now ready and able to run their own Coven. This degree reflects the wisdom of the Crone. The Third Degree does not indicate that the time of learning is over; indeed, in the Craft, you never stop learning.

*"Speak out against injustice
before it happens to you."*

SUMMER SOLSTICE RITE

The Summer Solstice, also called Litha, marks the longest day and shortest night.

The Sun is at the height of its power and is now beginning to decline. In common with the other Solstice and the Equinoxes the date of this festival will vary from year to year, taking place between the 20th and 23rd of the month. Also in common with the other Sabbats it would have been traditional for celebrations to have taken place over several days.

If you have a group of people it can be great fun to enact the battle of the Oak and Holly Kings. At this time Lord Oak, who presides over the waxing year, gives way to Lord Holly, who will rule until the Winter Solstice. Select two combatants to wrestle or fight with staves until the one playing the Oak King gives way to the other. It is a good idea for them to practise in advance so that they do not harm one another, but still give a good 'show' so that the rest of your assembly can cheer and encourage the battle. Before the battle the Lord Holly should challenge the Oak King with taunts and insults, for Oak's time is over. Make Oak and Holly crowns; the Oak one being worn before the battle and the Holly one after. We usually stage this as a family event with the youngest person present being given the honour of presenting the crown. We also follow the battle with a barbeque, the best pieces being given to the Holly King who is allowed to preside over any subsequent games.

"Personal responsibility includes knowing when to mind your own business."

LITHA

**If you possibly can, on the day of the Solstice
go to the seashore, and at the low tide draw
a solar image in the sand.**

Make it as large and ornate as you can, for this is in honour of the Sun. In the centre place 3 stones or pieces of wood for 3 things you would like to change in your life. Position yourself where you can watch the incoming tide slowly erasing your image. As this happens, visualize the waters taking away the old and bringing in the new.

If you are unable to get to the shore then gather flower petals in reds and oranges and perform the same spell at the top of the highest hill you can reach. Try to time your arrival so that the Sun is at its zenith just after you have created your image in petals. Let the wind take them in the same way as the tide above. If it is a very still day you may need to leave the pattern after your visualization, but rest assured that the magic will still work.

Whichever of these you choose to perform, follow it by taking a walk. As you go, take care to notice the seasonal changes around you. The Solstice marks the start of Summer proper. This is the season when the crops are ripening and the trees and bushes are starting to produce fruit. It is also the time when we should look at our own lives and give thanks to the Gods for those things which have borne, or are bearing, fruit.

*"Sometimes it's more
helpful to step back."*

FIRE MEDITATION

Fire, in the form of a candle flame, is often used as a meditation aid.

Staring at a flame is a way of learning to enter a meditative state and, with practice, it becomes possible to work without the flame being physically present. It is used as a tool for practising magical skills, where the student works on changing the flame by willpower alone. It is also important to gain understanding of the Element in all its forms; the light and heat of the Sun, the power of the volcano, and the warmth of a Summer's day.

On a really hot day find somewhere to lie in the Sun. It is not necessary to risk sunburn, so wear a hat and/or sunscreen. Take a few deep breaths and close your eyes. Feel the heat of the Sun penetrating your skin as a scattering of golden particles, glowing and glittering and gathering inside you. Feel them filling your blood and circulating around your body. Continue to absorb these particles until you feel them combining to become a pure golden light. Visualize it going deeper into your body until it is soaking right through your bones into your very essence. Visualize it driving out your cares and worries and replacing them with peace and energy. Visualize it driving out aches, pains and illness and replacing them with health and well-being. Visualize it soothing away the stresses of life and feel yourself being filled with the light and energy of the Sun. When you feel completely refreshed open your eyes, rub your arms and legs and keep this memory for times of need.

"The Craft can be learnt but not taught."

SUN IN CANCER

*Cancer is a Water sign indicating the emotions
and feelings. It is also a Cardinal sign bringing
eagerness, impatience, action and anxiety.*

Those born with the Sun in Cancer generally appear to be self-assured, even tough, whereas underneath they can be highly sensitive and easily hurt. They are home makers and clannish, protective and defensive of their families. Cancerians require a secure shelter from the outside world into which they can retreat to recover from their wounds both real and imagined. They are usually shrewd and intuitive and have a good memory, making them good students, but are apt to let their emotions colour their lives and actions. They are good at caring for others and nurturing all manner of living things. They tend to be romantic, sentimental and tender although often appearing clingy. They are also very protective and have strong parenting instincts. They are prone to psychic influences and both pick up and emanate strong psychic energies. On the negative side they are moody, touchy and inclined to self-pity. They are easily flattered and can find themselves easily taken in by a barely plausible tale.

Cancerians' emotions will be very much to the fore at this time; they should be careful in any financial or business dealings. They should also be aware of the danger of emotionally suffocating their loved ones. It is, however, a good time for attending to practical domestic details, for decorating or otherwise tending to the home front. Others should be aware that this is a good time to focus on home and domestic matters. Use the energies of the period to consolidate relationships.

"If uncertain of the wisdom of an action, don't!"

ST JOHN'S WORT

This plant is inextricably linked to the Summer
Solstice, and is said to be named after John
the Baptist, whose birthday was supposed to
be 24 June, the red spots on its leaves being
supposedly caused by drops of his blood.

Placed in the window on the Saint's day it was thought to protect against
ghosts and Witches, as well as fire and lightning. However, to tread on it
was to risk being taken by the fairies. Outside of Christian mythology
the plant was known as *Sol Terrestis* and was considered to be sacred to
the Sun as it grew where the Sun had touched the earth. Its Greek name
hypericum means 'over the apparition', reflecting its use to deter evil spirits. Certainly one of its main uses today is to alleviate depression which
used to be thought to be caused by evil energies.

St John's Wort has many healing properties, being used to cure bed-
wetting in children, menstrual cramps, cold sores, eczema, rheumatism,
insect bites and all manner of aches and pains. In the past it was also
thought to cure chest and bladder complaints.

Magically it is worn to protect against colds and flu, to bring strength
in battle and to attract love. If it is gathered by a maiden on midsummer's
eve and is still fresh in the morning it indicates that she will marry within the year. Gathered on a Friday it will protect against madness. It is also
used in spells for health, protection and happiness. Plant St John's Wort
at midsummer to honour the Sun and to protect the home and family.

*"Remember, email communication
is about as secure as skywriting."*

SEAGULLS

Seagulls, like other seabirds, have long been considered birds of omen.

To see 3 flying close together foretells a death. In some places they are thought to be the souls of drowned sailors returning to give the living warnings of impending storms. Certainly they tend to flock inland when conditions at sea are very rough. Should one fly against the window of a house where someone is at sea it is thought that person will be in great danger. And if they fly around the house of a sailor who is intending to set sail he should not leave. It is also said that you should not look a Seagull in the eyes as, should your ship go down, it will return to peck them out, leaving you to drown. Several places also say that you should not feed Seagulls as attracting their attention in this way will make them return to bring you harm.

Despite all the above, Seagull feathers can be helpful in magic. Like other feathers they can be used to represent the Element of Air, but unlike others they can also be used to represent Water. As a result they can be used in spells where you wish to combine both elements. Hang a pair of Seagull feathers over your bed when you need to balance thought and emotion, especially if you have concerns about a relationship. If you wish to hear from a loved one, burn a Seagull feather outside and let the wind carry the ashes away. Seagull feathers can also be carried to bring safe travel, or placed inside a car to ensure safe journeys. Only use completely clean seagull feathers as they can carry disease.

"Sleep is the most effective beauty treatment."

THOR

Thor is another Scandinavian or Norse God.

The son of Odin, and second only to him, his mother was giantess Fjorgynn, Jord or Hlodyn. Thor was seen as red-bearded and immensely strong. He epitomized bravery, strength and endurance, but also boasting and brutality. He was depicted as riding a chariot drawn by goats, wearing iron gauntlets, a belt of power called Megingjardir and carrying a magic hammer called Mjolnir or Destroyer. Thor was the God of sailors, farmers and the lower classes, unlike his father who was God of Kings and warriors. He made his home in a mansion called Bilskinir. It is probably his appeal to the working classes which enabled his survival well into the onset of Christianity. Thor was sometimes depicted as a blacksmith and his day, Thursday, was considered the best for funerals, marriages and other contracts. This is still celebrated in the term 'married on the hammer', or 'married over the anvil', a tradition which still survives at Gretna Green, Scotland.

Thor's Hammer was traditionally said to break the ice of winter each year and was also thought to be the source of thunder in storms. Indeed he is close to the northern European thunder God Donar. One of the tales is of Mjolnir being stolen by the giant Thrym. Loki disguises Thor as Freya in order to trick Thrym into giving 'her' the Hammer as a wedding present. At this point Thor throws off his disguise and defeats the giants. Shaped like the letter 'T', Thor's Hammer is often worn as a symbol by today's followers of the Northern traditions.

*"Gossip is the sign of
an empty life."*

RUE

Rue is one of the oldest garden plants.

It has many medicinal uses, indeed its name comes from the Greek *reuo*, meaning 'to set free'. It is used to improve eyesight and relieve eyestrain. The juice alleviates earache, and a tea made from the leaves will ease coughs. The leaves are placed on the forehead to relieve headache and can be crushed and rubbed on to alleviate the pain of sciatica. They can also be used in salads and chewed to relieve stress, anxiety and nervous indigestion. Sprinkled around the house the plant will drive away fleas and other biting insects. The Greeks wore it around the neck to prevent epilepsy and vertigo. Even comparatively recently a posy containing Rue was carried by judges to guard against pestilence (plague) and gaol fevers.

Like many other plants used in magic, Rue was thought to defend against Witches and their spells, and would be planted by the gate or door to ensure the household's protection. It was also thought to bring second sight. Rue is protective, defensive, healing, strengthens mental powers, and used in love magic. Inhaling fresh Rue brings mental clarity, especially in affairs of the heart. Add it to baths to break hexes or curses and hang it in windows to defend against the same. Place it in travel sachets to protect your loved ones. When fresh Rue is used as an Asperger it drives away all negative feelings.

The expression 'rue the day' come from the old practice of throwing rue at someone who has wronged you with the curse, *"May you rue this day as long as you live."*

*"The most precious gift you
can give is time."*

MOTHER OF PEARL

The lustrous and opalescent internal surface
of many molluscs is called Mother of Pearl.

Some forms, such as Abalone, are highly prized in jewellery making, but all have their magical uses. Mother of Pearl and other shells were often used as currency in many parts of the world. Mother of Pearl is associated with the fifth Element of Spirit and relates to hidden depths and the unknown. It is used in magic of protection and wealth as well as to enhance power.

Mother of Pearl is worn, interlaced or mounted with silver, as Ritual jewellery and to empower the worker. It is also said to increase personal confidence and enhance beauty. It used to be placed on newborn babies to protect them from the perils of life, or alternatively powdered and a little rubbed into the top of the head and the soles of the feet. To increase your wealth, collect some Mother of Pearl and place it with a piece of silver in sea water in a clear glass jar. Leave this overnight in the light of the Full Moon. Then take the silver and the Mother of Pearl, wrap them in a small-denomination note and carry this with you for a full Lunar month.

It is best if you collect your Mother of Pearl yourself from the seashore as that sold is often obtained by killing the creature within. It will also have been cleansed and empowered by the action of the Moon on the tides and the sea water. Whilst you are doing this, you might also like to collect some sea water for use in other spells.

"Thinking before speaking
beats apologizing later."

WICCANING

Wiccaning is the name given to the Ritual which welcomes a new child to the world.

Its purpose is not to dedicate the child to the Gods but rather to invoke their protection and to welcome it to the larger family of the Craft. Whilst Wiccaning can be performed soon after birth, it is also performed for older children who express an interest in the Craft but who are still too young and inexperienced to undertake formal Ritual or Initiation.

The key points of the Ritual are the presentation of the child to the Elements and the Goddess and the God. In some cases individuals from the group will represent these and will then give the child their blessing. There is also the formal Naming of the Child, and older children will sometimes choose to take a special Craft name at this time. Finally, there is the presentation of the newly-named child to the gathering of friends and family.

Some groups like to supplement these basic elements with the addition of the nomination of Sponsors; people who are chosen to instruct the child in various practical or life skills, rather than the Christian Godparents who are there to guard a child's spiritual development. Like other Craft Rituals, Wiccaning may take place anywhere; in the home of the parents or perhaps outside to be closer to the Elements in their natural form. The most important difference between this and other Rites of welcoming is that there is no commitment made on the child's behalf to any particular path or beliefs.

*"Even wonderful people
need time for fun."*

FUN AND GAMES

The Craft is not a staid belief system; we encourage joy and laughter in our Rites and Rituals.

Most Sabbat Rituals include games of one sort or another. Whilst these can be related to the season or the legends of the Goddess and the God it is good to consider some which are just for fun. In our Coven we have many, of which a few appear here. We often select, by choosing lots, a Fool or games-master to preside over these, to hand out forfeits the losers, in the event of cheating, or just if she or he feels like it!

A good 'ice-breaker' is to arrange several sheets of newspaper on the floor and, like in musical chairs, to remove one each time the music stops. The difference is that several people can stand on a sheet together if they hold on tight. Those who do not fit are out. Another good game for getting to know one another is to line up several teams in rows. They must pass a balloon from one end of the line to the other and back again without using hands or letting it touch the floor. We also play games which test our knowledge, like the Elements game. An experienced Witch asks questions to which the answer is an Element, the others rush to the appropriate Quarter of the room, the last to arrive being out. One which causes a lot of mirth when people know each other fairly well is to pick two people and ask the first what animal, plant, fruit, etc the other would be and why.

"In mirth and reverence."
THE CHARGE OF THE GODDESS

DOGS

Dogs are linked to the Craft in a number of ways.

Many Gods and Goddesses have been credited with having, or being given, dog characteristics including the Jackal-headed Anubis; Nehalennia, Celtic dog-Goddess of sea traders; Ninkharak, dog-Goddess of healing; Turrean, the Irish wolfhound Goddess who gave birth to two half-human dogs Bran and Sgeolan. Cerridwen transformed herself into a greyhound when chasing Gwion; and Hecate is accompanied by a black dog and horse. Dogs have long been thought to have second sight and the ability to sense death. Certainly, to hear the household dog howling when someone was ill evoked dread right into modern times. Dogs are also credited with being able to detect a person with bad intentions towards its 'family'.

Despite these links to the Craft, dogs have not, generally speaking, been given the bad reputation that other animals were thought to have. Dog hair was thought to cure whooping cough, and even rabies. To be followed home by a strange dog was considered good luck, although a dog walking between a courting couple would indicate that a quarrel would soon take place.

Supernatural dogs, usually black, are said to haunt places in many parts of the world, and to see one is usually a bad omen. Where I live Black Shuck, a giant-sized dog, is said to appear to warn of impending disaster, although some locals may now be confused as we actually have an enormous black dog of our own! Further south a black dog is said to appear in the car of lone drivers who are in danger of an accident.

"The signs are always with us,
whether we take notice or not."

AMETHYST

**Amethyst is a beautiful purple Quartz which
has long been prized for its magical associations.**

Regrettably these days it is also one of those stones which are artificially
'enhanced' to 'improve' the colour, so when buying Amethyst be sure to
ask if it is completely natural. A good clue is that natural Amethyst usually has a graduated colour and is rarely a very deep purple.

Amethyst is a balancing stone, so when worn it prevents excesses,
and placed under the pillow it induces restful sleep whilst ensuring that
you do not oversleep. It is also worn to calm fears, raise the spirits and to
prevent self-deception. It is a spiritual stone, being used in meditation and
to enhance psychic powers. Many Witches will keep a piece with their
tools of divination. Place a circle of small Amethyst stones around a candle and bathe by its light to open your psychic centres before commencing magical work.

Amethyst enhances the mind and improves the memory so it is a
good stone to wear during tests and examinations, when involved in legal
dealings and for business success. It was said to protect against thieves
and was worn as a charm against sorrow and distress. When life is getting
on top of you, sit and hold a piece of Amethyst and visualize all the
stresses and strains of life being absorbed by the stone. Bury it in a small
pot of earth for 3 days to cleanse it afterwards. Amethyst used to be worn
by a man to attract the love of a pure woman, and was thought to encourage constancy if exchanged by lovers.

"Aim for moderation in all things."

TRADITIONAL

ISIS AND OSIRIS

Isis, Osiris, Nepthys and Set were the children of the
great God Ra, and four of the main Gods in the
Egyptian pantheon. Whilst parts of their story
are well known other bits have been omitted in
modern telling, so here is a fuller version.

The aged Ra would not pass on his throne so Isis tricked him into revealing his secret name which enabled her to gain power over him and to kill
him. Isis and Osiris then took over the throne of Egypt. Nepthys and Set
were left out. Partly in revenge at her sister and partly because she could
not bear a child by Set, Nepthys used magic to disguise herself as Isis and
became pregnant by Osiris. The child was the God Anubis. Set became
angry at this and, playing on Osiris' love of fine things, trapped him in an
elaborate golden chest which he cast into the Nile. Isis eventually found
her husband, but this time Set killed his brother and scattered his body in
13 pieces over the lands. Isis was distraught, but with the help of Nepthys
and Anubis she gathered 12 of the pieces. The phallus could not be found,
so Nepthys fashioned a replacement from wood and, using her magic,
restored Osiris to life for long enough for Isis to become pregnant. In this
version we see that the Gods are subject to the same kind of complex
emotions as people, and are not all good or all bad. Osiris develops into
a dying and rising God, Isis a symbol of beauty, Nepthys a Goddess of
Witchcraft and healing and Set a God of vengeance.

"People can, and do,
tell lies on the internet."

CURSE BREAKING

It is worth pointing out that real curses and hexes
are extremely rare as Witches are mindful of the
Wiccan Rede and the law of Threefold Return.

Whilst it may be easier to blame things on outside influences, many misfortunes are down to our own actions or inactions and some are just plain bad luck. Having said that, it is possible to be affected by negative energies from others, even if they are not actually intended. Indeed, negative energies can leave traces, which is why it is a good idea to cleanse a new home.

There are several techniques and spells to deflect anything from general negativity to a genuine directed curse. Placing a mirror in a window on each side of your home, facing outwards, will reflect negativity back to the sender. Likewise hanging a Witch Ball, a polished glass globe, in the window will absorb and return negative energy. Many herbs and plants can be grown and hung in the windows or scattered on windowsills and doorways to prevent ill will from entering. Chilli, Hydrangea, Thistle and Vetivert are all good examples. Protect your car or other vehicle with a sprig of any of these or with Rosemary, which has the additional advantage of keeping you alert to more mundane dangers. Wear Onyx or Sapphire, or carry a small piece of Lava or Pumice to defend yourself on the move. In rare cases when you are sure of who has cursed you, take a new pin and drive it into the ground where they are sure to pass, to break the spell.

*"You will never understand how another feels,
but you should try."*

LEMONS

Lemons might seem an unlikely addition to
the Witch's armoury but they have a good
many uses both medicinally and magically.

Lemons have long been prized for their high vitamin content, and lemon juice is still carried at sea to prevent scurvy. The juice makes an excellent gargle for sore throats and, when diluted, can be applied to reduce itching. It is recommended for rheumatic pain and can even be used to counteract some poisons. A teaspoon undiluted will cure even the most stubborn hiccoughs. If you make your own lemonade you won't want to touch the fizzy stuff again. Mix the juice of one lemon and a tablespoonful of caster sugar in ½ pint of cold water and drink for the most refreshing and cooling drink.

Lemon juice in water can be used to cleanse magical objects and is particularly good at shining up silverware. Lemon charms were often made and given to bring blessings and luck, especially in a new home. Take a small lemon and tie it with red ribbon to hang it up. Into the remaining skin press as many new pins as you can. Hang it in the central room of the house. An alternative version of this was sometimes made by pressing cloves into the skin. Grow a lemon from seed if you wish to attract love, and if the tree bears fruit, however small, give it to your lover to seal your relationship. Thinly slice a lemon crossways and carefully dry the slices. Arrange and glue these in a crescent moon and place above your altar as a gift to the Goddess.

*"Without the sour we would
never taste the sweet."*

CENSERS AND THURIBLES

**Witches burn incense to represent the
Element of Air and to scent the air in
preparation for the Goddess and the God.**

Incense is also used to enhance meditations and Pathworkings and even just to sweeten the air. Whilst you can use incense cones or sticks many prefer to use loose incense, often home-made to tailor it to the Ritual or magic. Loose incense requires a source of heat to make it burn, usually commercially-made charcoal blocks. As these generate a lot of heat they must be placed in a heat-proof vessel.

The two main kinds of holder used are the Censer and the Thurible. The former is usually a lidded metal dish which hangs from chains. It can be hung over the Altar, in the Eastern Quarter, or swung to distribute the incense throughout the Circle. Some Covens light the incense as the Element of Air is invoked and then, moving Deosil, take the Censer around the Circle, before placing it in the East. The Thurible is a dish which may be metal, stone or ceramic. It may or may not have a cover, but has no chains. It is not designed to be carried around the Circle as the ignited charcoal will make it far too hot to handle. Whichever you select for your use it is a good idea to clean it as soon as possible after use as many residues harden and become almost impossible to remove. Note also that 'self-igniting' charcoal is best handled with tongs to avoid burnt fingers, dropped charcoal and singed carpets!

*"As the incense rises on the air,
so should we rise above our failings."*

A.E.

CELANDINE

The true Celandine is the Greater Celandine *Chelidonium majus*, and not to be confused with the Lesser Celandine, a different species.

The 4-petal Celandine is related to the poppy. A fleshy plant, it 'bleeds' a bright orange juice with an unpleasant smell and nauseous taste, which probably gives rise to its folk name, Devil's milk. The juice was used to remove films from the surface of the eye, and to treat festering wounds. In the middle ages the juice was taken to treat jaundice, scurvy and diseases of the liver. The undiluted juice is applied to cure warts, ringworm and corns, although should not be allowed to touch other parts of the skin because of its irritant properties. It is also added to compresses to relieve toothache.

Magically the Celandine is used for protection, freedom and escape. Worn next to the skin, the flower helps to avoid pitfalls and traps, both emotional and physical. If you are in a relationship with a controlling personality wear or carry a Celandine flower close to your heart to prevent them overpowering your intuition. If you are feeling trapped in any way carry 4 of the fresh or dried flowers, changing them every 3 days. Dry the leaves and add to incense to drive away those who would take control of you. Celandine brings freedom of thought and expression, and brings joy and youthful feelings. It can also be worn to win favour and acceptance. Wear gloves and take care when handling Celandine as the juice stains and is a powerful irritant.

"The perfect garden is one you have time to enjoy."

HOLLY MONTH

*We tend to associate the Holly with winter, when its
red berries are brought in to decorate the house, but its
place in the Celtic tree cycle is far earlier, soon after the
Summer Solstice when the Holly Lord takes his crown.*

Magically, Holly and Oak are linked and their energies are seen as complimentary to one another. If you can find a site where they grow together, or even better entwined, this is ideal for magical workings, especially otherworld meditations. If you can find such a place, meditate there at dusk to see spirits and visions. Left to its own devices the Holly can grow as high as 60 feet, but most are trimmed to bushes or hedges these days. Well-seasoned Holly makes an excellent staff, although it is nowadays rare to find a tree high enough to provide the length required. It is said that a staff of Holly twisted around Oak will protect both the traveller and his home from danger. The Holly is a tree which links, so it can be used to strengthen relationships and also as a magical pathway. Carve pieces into charms of protection and give them to friends to make your relationship endure.

The berries, whilst poisonous, used to be given in cases of poisoning, being highly emetic and purgative, although I would not recommend this myself. Dried and powdered they were used to stem haemorrhaging. A solution of the leaves was drunk to reduce fevers and has been used as a tea substitute. The bark and leaves were made into poultices to help the setting and healing of broken bones.

*"Your destiny is yours;
use all your power to fulfil it."*

CHANGING RELATIONSHIPS

*Sometimes our relationships with others are
not all they could be and whilst we do not want
to change the person as such, we may want to
change aspects of our dealings with them.*

This could be on a personal level, perhaps after a quarrel or disagreement. It could happen in your relationship with employers, co-workers, teachers; perhaps you are not receiving the appreciation you deserve or are being misunderstood. In such cases it is a part of the relationship you wish to change, rather than the whole. Before starting it is good to be honest with yourself and make sure that you address any impact your behaviour may have contributed to the situation. Magic will work to resolve problems but not if you go and aggravate them again.

On a night when the Moon is full, place a mirror in such a way that you can see yourself and the Moon reflected over your shoulder. On the mirror write, in soft pencil or crayon, the nature of your problems: being unappreciated, lack of communication, etc. Go into as much detail as you can, as you will need it to make the spell work. Next, focus on each aspect. Give each about 5 minutes of contemplation, see if you can understand the reasons behind it and identify any practical steps you can take to resolve it. Once you have truly dealt with it, erase the word or symbol from the mirror. When the whole mirror is blank, thank the Goddess and the God. Go outside and make a small offering and then retire to bed.

*"It is better to be alone, than with
someone who belittles you."*

PURPLE AND INDIGO

Describing any colour in words is not easy, let alone those shades which result as a mix of red and blue.

But if you consider purple to be a straight mix of blue and red, with no white included, then indigo is a darker and bluer colour, as close to black as the deepest blue of the night sky. Purple stones include dark Amethyst and Suglite, whereas Indigo is represented by Sodalite. Both colours represent the Element of Spirit and are associated with spiritual and psychic development. However, whilst purple is also associated with magic for healing, indigo is more useful in money and success spells. Purple, because of the difficulty in creating it from plant dyes, has long been associated with royalty and high office in male-dominated systems, whereas indigo is more often associated with Wise women and more matriarchal belief systems such as the Craft. This subtle difference means that the two colours are very good in enabling us to access, and hence balance, our male and female aspects.

To create a balancing meditation aid, draw and colour in a purple circle inside an indigo square. Make it as large as you can. Place it upright in a place where you can comfortably sit and contemplate it. Burn a purple candle on the right and an indigo one on the left. Extinguish all other lighting and focus on the image. Do this every evening for a full week for at least 10 minutes per time. Alternatively, create a necklace of alternating purple and indigo beads, with an equal number of each, and wear this under your clothing next to your skin.

"Every scar is a badge of courage."

READING THE TEA LEAVES

**Tea leaf divination was very popular but
largely died out with the advent of the teabag.**

However, now that herbal teas are becoming more popular it could be
due for a revival. The technique is simple and requires no expensive tools,
just loose tea, hot water, a teapot and a cup and saucer. Make the tea and
let it stand for a few moments before pouring. Do not use a tea strainer!
Add milk and sugar to taste if required, stir and let it rest a moment so
the leaves sink to the bottom of the cup and do not end up in your mouth.
Drink down to the last ½ cm of tea. Now swirl the cup three times to re-
suspend the tea leaves in the liquid, and quickly turn it upside down onto
a saucer to catch any spills.

What you should have left are groups of tea leaves around the cup.
Examine these carefully: you may find it helps to half-close your eyes,
and look for shapes in the leaves. Those images on the right, as you hold
the cup in your strong hand, are coming and those on the left are depart-
ing. Images of Air shapes are to do with communication. Fire indicates
passions and urgency. Water images link to your emotional life and to
travel. Earth images are linked to the physical. Many shapes are easy to
interpret: birds mean messages, mountains indicate obstacles, and so on.
When you cannot easily interpret the shapes you see, it is a good idea to
make a quick sketch of them and then come back to it later.

*"When analyzing yourself,
remember to give credit for trying."*

THE POPPY

There are several varieties of Poppy;
some are poisonous, and some are illegal
to grow in some parts of the world.

From a magical perspective it is not important which you use, but if you are intending to consume the seeds it is best to purchase those which are sold for baking rather than gathering your own. Poppy syrup, made from the petals, used to be given as a treatment for coughs and as a sedative for children. It used to be said to be unlucky to bring blooms into the house, and to stare into them was thought to induce blindness. Both these tales may well have come about because of the narcotic properties of some species. Having said that, cut Poppies do not make good decorative flowers as they do not last in water. When gathering poppies for magical use, make an offering to the land before you cut them to avoid bringing misfortune into the house.

Poppies are used in spells for luck, love and fertility. Add Poppy seeds to food to induce love. Placed secretly in the pocket they are said to ensure that the person will never run short of coins. Gilded Poppy heads have long been said to bring good fortune, and can still be found in some stores selling dried flowers. Pressed Poppy flowers should be hung above the bed of a couple who are trying to start a family. There should be one flower for each hoped-for addition to the family as well as one each for the couple. Steep Poppy seeds in strong wine for a month to charge it for Ritual use.

*"Laughter is infectious,
spread it about liberally."*

HANDS

The hand of a corpse, preferably a hanged criminal, was long thought to contain powerful magic.

A candle made from such a hand was thought to render the carrier invisible, or to cause everyone in the house to sleep until it was extinguished. It was thought that this was used by thieves to conceal their activities. This was called the Hand of Glory. Another version of this legend called for the hand to be used as a candlestick for the same purpose. The hands of the dead were also thought to be able to effect a cure when rested on a sick person. A dead man's hand removed by the woman of the house would also enable her to create better butter than her neighbours.

Whilst we do not, in the Craft, use real hands we do use wooden or ceramic ones. The former, carved so that it seems to beckon from the knuckle side and warn from the palm side, would be stood upright in the window to indicate whether it was safe for other Witches to call. These are very similar in appearance to the ones sold as 'ring stands' these days. Ceramic hands are often made and given as Handfasting gifts to ensure a long and happy relationship. Making a cast of a baby or young child's hand is thought by some to ensure that the child will grow up to be successful. If you feel tempted to do this please ensure that you create a mould from each side of the hand separately, rather than encasing the whole in plaster which may shrink and cause distress, and possibly damage.

*"Self-forgiveness is the
most effective kind."*

SUMMER MEDITATION

On a warm day go out into the countryside or a park.

Take a blanket or something else to lie on. If things are noisy it may be a good idea to shield your ears with a set of headphones, so take a personal cassette player so that you do not look odd! Remove your footwear and lie down so that the palms of your hands and the soles of your feet are in contact with the earth.

Close your eyes and take a few deep breaths to help you relax. As you do so, be aware of the different scents all around you. With your hands and feet feel your contact with the earth, and focus until you can feel the pulse of the land. Now reach out with your mind into the earth, allowing it to travel and be one with the land. Feel the roots of plants and trees reaching down into the soil and follow them up into the leaves and branches so that you can feel the effects of Sun and Air. Now follow the roots into the soil again until you can detect the underground streams and rivers. Follow these with your mind, from their sources high in the mountains to the depths of the oceans. Feel and notice the different kinds of earth, soil, stones, rocks and even the particles of sand. As you let your mind travel, look at the varieties of life: the fish, animals, insects, birds and people. When you are ready, sit up and rub your arms and legs to ground yourself. On your return write down your experience to help you remember it.

*"Instead of waiting for the
phone to ring, make the call."*

BOOK OF SHADOWS

A Book of Shadows is the individual Witch's record
of the Rituals they perform and the Spells they work.

It may also include notes on divinations, meditations, dreams and even recipes. Books of Shadows are not to be confused with what has become known as *The Book of Shadows*. This is actually the record of Gerald Gardner's Coven, and in reality is no more valid than the record of any other group.

Many Covens require the keeping of a Book of Shadows to demonstrate commitment on the part of each person, and because it is a useful record of which workings have been done. Indeed, many Witches find that, however arduous it may have been to complete in the early days, it soon becomes an invaluable reference. It is helpful if the record includes details of when and where workings took place, including day, time and phase of the Moon. It should also include information on how the individual felt and the results of workings. What it should not include are details of other members of the group which would enable them to be identified should it fall into the hands of a non-member. Many Covens also insist that Books of Shadows should be kept in the almost forgotten art of handwriting. This is partly because bitter experience has taught some of us that the computer is not a reliable way of storing information. Even if you don't have the bad luck to experience problems caused by viruses or a crash, as software is upgraded you can easily find that your hard work becomes inaccessible.

"Your feelings are your feelings;
don't let anyone try to tell you otherwise."

FLINT

Flint has long been regarded as a valuable stone.

Early man crafted tools from it and used it as a medium of exchange and currency. It was also thought of as being highly protective. Flint amulets were worn around the neck to protect the individual or placed above the door to defend the house. In Ireland they were often mounted in silver, which is the metal associated with this stone as well as being sacred to the Goddess. Flint has long been associated with fairies and elves, being also known as Elf Shot and Elf Arrow.

    If you can find some flint, take the time to learn to knap it yourself, wearing glasses or goggles to protect your eyes. Take three pieces: one to use as a base, one to use as a hammer, the third being the one you intend to Craft. You may find it takes several tries to develop the skill, but do persevere. A handcrafted flint arrowhead is a powerful addition to the Altar and, if used to inscribe candles, will give them extra energy and focus. If you find that you have a talent for this, create a larger blade and securely fix it into a handle made of the wood of your choice and use this as your Athame. But please make sure that blade and handle cannot come adrift! The slivers of Flint created by working can be used in magic for protection, healing and divination. Tying pieces of flint over a swelling will help to reduce the pain, although be careful that they cannot move and cut the skin.

"State your case,
don't lose it!"

THE CROW

All the members of the Crow family; the Jay, Magpie, Jackdaw, Raven, Rook, Hooded and Carrion Crows, have significance within the Craft and a long tradition as birds of omen.

Crows are roughly the same size as Magpies, being around 47cm or 18 inches, although having shorter tail feathers. They can be distinguished from the Rook by their feathered, not bald, faces.

As scavengers and eaters of carrion, Crows have long been thought to indicate death, and associated with Gods and Goddesses of battle. Whereas the Raven is the form of the Morrighan, the Crow is the form of her aspect as battle Goddess Badb. Macha was visualized as a Hooded Crow and Nemain, another form of the Morrighan, was also thought to fly as a Crow. Crows sitting on a barn were thought to herald the death or disease of the livestock, and those sitting on a roof the death of an inhabitant. Crows were also thought to carry disease, not unreasonably since they will feed on the corpses of other animals. White Crows were also considered birds of ill omen, it being thought that any they followed would soon die. However Branwen, a Welsh Goddess of love, sent a trained Crow as a messenger to call her brothers to her aid, and her name is often translated as White Crow. In common with other creatures of omen it was thought unlucky to disturb their roosting places, as any area they abandoned was likely to come upon hard times. Many Witches find that Crows and other members of the family become their Totem animals.

"Being equal does not mean you have to be the same."

CHESTNUTS

Whilst not trees of the Celtic tree calendar, the two forms of Chestnut have their uses in the Craft.

The Horse Chestnut, which is not edible, and the Sweet Chestnut which is, are not actually related but do bear fruit which are housed in similar looking spiny cases. The Horse Chestnut fruits in the late Summer and the nuts are widely prized by young children for playing games of conkers. The Sweet Chestnut fruit ripen in the Autumn and these can be cooked and eaten; they even taste good raw. Being a sweet-tasting nut they are most often used in desserts and stuffing.

The bark of the Horse Chestnut was used to soothe fevers and applied to heal ulcers. The nuts used to be carried to relieve the pain of rheumatism, backache and arthritis. They are also carried to deflect the 'evil eye', or to protect against being over-looked by another. A nut placed in each window can prevent other Witches from astrally projecting into your house. The nuts are also used in divination; if two are placed together on a fire and burn steadily then a relationship will likewise be steady, but if they burst or fly apart then there will sparks between the couple.

Sweet Chestnuts have been used to make a form of flour which has been used as starch and to bleach linen. Dried Sweet Chestnut leaves can be infused to make a cough syrup, which was even said to relieve whooping cough. Sweet Chestnuts used to be cooked, crystallized and given as a token of love.

"Thank the Goddess for small mercies,
before you need large ones."

WILD FLOWERS

At this time of year the fields, hedgerows and woods
are full of flowers, and it is a good idea to take a good
field guide and go out to identify some of these.

Almost every plant has medicinal qualities as well as magical attributes
and the easiest time to identify them is when they are in flower. Please do
not go out picking wild flowers. Whilst they may seem plentiful in your
area it does not mean that they do not need as much protection as possible. Not only that, but in many places it is also illegal. Having said that,
you can always grow your own, as many garden centres sell the seeds. A
newer 'invention' is the seed mat. These are pre-seeded sheets of growing
medium which can be simply laid in place and watered to produce an
instant area of wildflowers or of flowers designed to attract bees, butterflies, etc. Some can even be laid on roofs or cut and placed on windowsills. An alternative is to look for flower shows; many of these now
include wild and semi-wild displays. Some even encourage the picking of
flowers, as the gardens themselves are temporary, but do ask first!

If you do manage to collect wild flowers, try to make sure you get
a leaf or two alongside. Press these and place them in a book with notes
which will help you to identify them as well as notes on their properties. In this way you can build up your own guide for use in your
recipes and spells.

*"Touch the earth with your hands
and it may touch your life."*

STRESS

Our lives are so full of conflicting
demands that almost everyone is under
some kind of stress most of the time.

This was no different for our ancient ancestors; the prospect of searching for food versus the possibility of meeting something that might eat you must be stressful! Whilst the strains on our lives today are not so acute, it is the accumulation which wears us down. We each have several different personas: parent to our children, child to our parents, student to our teachers, employee to our boss, and so on. When we allow the demands of each role to change the way we behave, as is usual in civilized life, we have to divide the facets of our personality. This is all right so long as we retain a central part of our lives where we can really be who we truly are; for many the home and/or the Craft fulfil this need. But for this to work we must learn to accept and forgive ourselves. We also need to make sure that, in our hectic schedules, we make time to actually be ourselves.

Try to ensure that every day you have at least half an hour of special time for you alone. This can be used for exercises in personal development, but only if you really want to; ideally you would set aside a separate time slot for this. It will be just as beneficial, if not more so, to use this time to do something which really pleases you, like reading a book, having a long, scented bath or taking a gentle walk.

*"Coping is just another way of saying
you're trying to do too much."*

OLD LUGHNASADH

Lughnasadh is the festival of the Celtic Sun God Lugh.
It is also known as Lammas from the old Hlafmas
or Loafmas, a name which comes from the fact that
it is also the festival of the first of the harvest.

It used to be the case that everyone would put aside their usual occupations and join together in the harvest. The first bread baked from this became the main part of the celebratory feast. It was considered unlucky to gather the last of the harvest and so everyone would gather around the last stems and, hurling the scythes, would work together to cut them down. Because of the way the crops were harvested many small animals would be driven from the corn and these would also make their contribution to the feast. Regrettably today they are often slaughtered indiscriminately as the great harvesting machines clear all before them.

Seek out a place where crops are being grown and see if you can pick just one or two ripe stems. If you look along the edges of fields you will often see some 'strays' which avoids any need for trespass or walking on the crop, neither of which benefits the land nor will endear you to the farmer. Take these home and place them on your Altar. If you can find enough, weave a circle of corn to honour the season. You may also find that you can purchase ripened dried corn stalks from your florist. Whether you find or buy your corn, remember to make an offering of thanks to the land for the harvest.

"The easiest way to find love
is to stop looking for it."

BREAD MAKING

Bread has long been one of the staple foods; indeed it holds a place in most belief systems.

Making your own bread might seem laborious but it really is worth the effort. Not only does it taste considerably better than the mass-produced version, but it is much healthier to eat. Making bread can also be an act of magic in itself. As you add the ingredients think about the bounty of the Goddess and the God and the land they have come from. Dedicate your work to the Old Gods as an offering of your own.

There is not enough space here to discuss recipes, but select a fairly simple one to start with. As the best bread is that which is allowed to rise really slowly it can be best to start the process the evening before you want to cook it. In this way you will also reduce the time pressure on yourself. If you have access to a bread machine, use it to make the basic dough but then go on to knead it and shape it yourself. Bread making has been described as a good way of relieving stress, so make the most of this by not setting yourself impractical deadlines! Once the bread has risen and been kneaded a first time it can be shaped and decorated with seeds, nuts and other additions. At this time of the year a harvest loaf can be the centrepiece of your Altar as well as the focus of your feast. You can create it in the shape of a wheatsheaf, a plait or, if you are feeling ambitious, a corn man.

"Bread and life both need warmth and time."

SUN IN LEO

**Leo is another Fire sign, bringing enthusiasm,
spontaneity and energy. It is also a Fixed sign
emphasizing the senses, desires, and intense reactions.**

Leo's symbol is the lion, the King of Beasts, and this gives a good indication of those born at this time. The key phrase for Leos is *"I will"*. Those born when the Sun is in Leo are generally extroverts. They will be self-assertive and self-controlling. Whilst usually generous and warm hearted they will also know how to use power and to control others. They are high achievers and their commanding personalities make them good leaders unless they allow themselves to become overbearing and dominating. Leos are good organizers and, being outgoing, make good spokespeople, speakers and actors. They are usually highly principled and forthright but tend to acquire very fixed opinions, sometimes despite evidence to the contrary. In relationships Leos are wholehearted, sincere, very sensual and pleasure loving. On the negative side they can be overwhelming, intolerant and autocratic. They sometimes seem to be bossy and boastful.

At this time those born with the Sun in Leo should be careful to exercise their self-restraint, as the Sun's energy will emphasize any failings. They should also be aware of their tendency to dominate any group of people, whether deliberately or not, and be prepared to step back and let others have their say. Non-Leos can utilize the energy of this time to become more self-assertive and to look towards claiming what is due to them. Magically this is a good time for learning new skills or improving talents.

"You are the sum of all your memories."

PRESSED FLOWER MAGIC

The art of pressing flowers has largely dropped out of favour, which is a pity as pressed flowers can be used to decorate any number of objects.

They can also be used to give spells to those around you in a way which is useful rather than overtly 'Witchy', perhaps as a picture or bookmark. Another use is to select one plant for each Sabbat and affix them around a circular board or stone to create your own Wheel of the Year Altar symbol.

Pressing flowers, whilst sometimes a bit fiddly, is not as difficult as it may appear. You could buy a proper flower press, but you can just as easily improvise with some kitchen paper and a pile of heavy books. First, you need to collect flowers, with their stems and some leaves, which are in good condition. At first it is best to use smaller flowers rather than ones with thick blooms or stems which will have a lot of moisture in them. Take them straight home and arrange them between sheets of kitchen paper, one or two thicknesses unless you have chosen something really fleshy. Then place them on a flat surface and pile heavy books on top. Leave in a dry place for a week or so and you will have pressed flowers. Take great care when freeing them as many become quite fragile.

The following are just a few suggestions for pressed flower spells. Love and friendship: Sweet Pea, Periwinkle and Rose petals. Household harmony: Lavender, Passionflower and Morning Glory. To enhance magical working: Crocus, Honeysuckle, St John's Wort and Witch Grass.

"Scary monsters lurk inside,
but only if from them you hide."

EXTINGUISHING CANDLES

Probably the first deliberate act of magic anyone
ever performs is blowing out the candles on a
birthday cake: make a wish and if you blow
them all out together the wish will come true.

Those wanting to foster a belief in magic in their young are advised not to play tricks with non-extinguishable candles! This would seem to originate from the ancient Greeks who believed that the candles symbolized the years of your life and by blowing them out you indicated that you have completed the time passed and were ready for the time to come. But there are other beliefs associated with the putting out of candles. Should a candle be accidentally extinguished, or go out of its own accord, the household will be either one fewer, or one greater, by the morning. If a candle burns down one side, but not the other, someone will betray you.

In the Craft it is said that a candle may be pinched out with the fingers (moistened if you are sensitive), or snuffed with a snuffer, but should never be blown out. Some people add that to blow it out is disrespectful to the Element of Fire, or even to the Salamanders which are the creatures of Fire. Whether you agree with this or not it is certain that to blow out a candle spell will prevent it from working. Indeed most candle spells require that the candle should burn all the way down. It is certainly true that to blow out any candle will risk blowing hot wax all over the surface it is standing on!

"Plan for success,
failure doesn't need the help."

CLOCKS

When working in Circle
we always remove our watches.

There are several reasons for this. We cast the Circle as a 'time out of time', so it's rather pointless for everyone to be bristling with timepieces. Also, people in Circle really shouldn't want or need to keep an eye on the time; if they need to be somewhere else then perhaps that's where they should have gone in the first place! Secondly, mechanical and electrical things are often affected by the energies in Circle and your watch may stop. Lastly and personally, in this digital and electronic age, I have a loathing of things that ping, bleep or otherwise make noises!

Outside of the Craft there are many beliefs associated with watches and clocks. Should the clock strike 13 it was believed that someone had just died, or in some places, that the spirits of the dead would visit. There is also a strongly-held belief that everyone has a 'personal' timepiece which will stop at the moment of their death. Of course this originates from a time when most clocks were quite temperamental and sometimes only their owner knew how to keep them working. It used to be thought that all the clocks in the house should be stopped when a person died, and should not be restarted until the corpse had been removed, lest Death should think his job was not completed and take another person. One of the reasons why weddings used to be scheduled to commence on the hour was the belief that it was unlucky for a clock to strike during the ceremony.

"If I'd known then what I know now,
I'd have been older, sooner."

IRON

*Iron has long been considered magical,
perhaps because pure iron was only ever
found in meteorites, which were thought
of as being stones from the skies or heaven.*

As the working of iron became more frequent, and its practical uses so highly prized, it fell out of favour for Ritual and Magical uses. Neither Greek nor Roman priests allowed it in temples, and you will find that many belief systems around the world proscribe its use.

Despite this, iron is still considered to have great properties and the Blacksmiths who worked it were considered to be magical practitioners. Its primary use was protective, particularly against Witches, it being as much the metal itself as the horseshoe which was used to protect the people, livestock and buildings. There are still some Witches who do not allow iron tools or implements into the Circle because of this. I have done experiments with iron and have found that its use does not hinder magic although where pure iron is used to cast the Circle it can make it harder to release any energy raised. Iron is also grounding, and touching iron after Ritual will help bring you back to yourself. Similarly, wearing iron can make meditation somewhat more difficult. However, if working defensive magic then wear iron to increase the power of your spell. A circle of iron filings placed around the house has been used to protect against Witches and conversely to protect them against discovery. To find iron, especially the nails from a horseshoe, has long been considered good luck and these nails were often driven into walls to protect the house.

"Emulate only the worthy parts of your heroes."

MIRRORS

Mirrors feature strongly in magic and superstition.

Witches place mirrors in windows to deflect negative thoughts and energies. By placing a picture of someone between two mirrors we can prevent them working negative spells and magic. Mirrors are also often used to bring the face and light of the Moon into the house to enhance spells or for Divination.

It has long been considered that to accidentally break a mirror will bring 7 years' bad luck. In England, to avoid this we take all the pieces and place them in running water to wash the bad luck away. In America it is said that you should make the sign of the cross over a gold piece or a $5 bill. To deliberately break a mirror will sever a friendship, and sometimes this is used as a way of terminating a relationship. Many Europeans consider it bad luck to see yourself in a mirror by candlelight, although this is probably a result of the uses to which Witches put this. Some think that mirrors offer a window into another world or to the psychic plane. Mirrors used to be covered after the death of someone in the house, to prevent their spirit becoming confused and returning. Indeed I know several Witches who prefer not to have mirrors in the house as it allows others a means of access which bypasses any protections placed on doors and windows. Should this be a concern to you, place a Holey Stone or holed shell collected from the shore, or a Peacock's tail feather, onto the mirror as a guardian of this particular portal.

"Sometimes your skin is the
only thing holding it all together!"

FAMILIARS

**In medieval times it was believed
that Witches had familiars.**

These were thought to be demons who assisted the Witch in her (they usually were women) evil ways and took on animal form to avoid discovery. Indeed, having an animal in the house was often sufficient to raise suspicion. However, the keeping of animals has a far longer history; many of the old or lonely would have animals they had taken pity on and raised, healed or simply given a home to. Cats in particular have long been welcome in the home for their ability to keep rats and mice at bay, so it is fairly certain that these animals were nothing more than useful or friendly companions.

Having said that, as every pet owner knows, animals do have a greater range of perception than people, and some are more psychically attuned than others. As someone who has lived with many cats over the years I can attest that some seem to be quite mystical whilst others have not a psychic bone in their bodies! One of the more familiar cats would always lie on an Athame or Book of Shadows, whether mine or not, and I was sufficiently in tune with him to be wary if he did not show such an interest in a newcomer's equipment. You may be fortunate and find that your companion animal is likewise attuned. Observe them and learn their ways, and you may well find that they can show you things you might otherwise miss. However, if they are not inclined, there is no way of enticing them to take an interest in the Craft.

"Sometimes tears are the seasoning of life."

MAKING A CORN KING

The Corn King is such a key part of the festival of Lughnasadh that, even if you only do it once, it's worth having a go.

You will need to obtain, with permission of course, a reasonably large bundle of ripened corn. It is best to work outside as it can be messy.

Divide your bundle into four even sections: two will be kept mostly together for the body and legs, one will be divided and reunited to make the arms and one will be made into the head. Unless you are confident enough to tie the bundles with corn, you will need some similar-coloured thread. Take two bundles and tie them together so that the two thirds from the cut ends are reunited to make one bundle. Below this, towards the grains, divide the bundle into two for the legs and tie these with thread. You should have a sort of A shape with grains at the bottom to represent the feet. Take one of the remaining bundles and add it to the cut ends, folding it over to create a head shape, with the grains sticking up as hair. This usually takes a bit of trial and error. When you are happy with the result tie this in place. Now take the fourth quarter, divide it into two and lay the halves along each other so that there is grain at both ends, for the hands. Tie this across the 'body' to represent the arms. You will now have a fairly primitive 'man shape'. Decorate the head with flowers: dark ones for the eyes, red for the mouth and perhaps a crown of yellow.

"Build bridges, not walls."

LUGHNASADH RITE

**Not only is this the festival of the first of the harvest
but it is also the feast of the Sacrificial King.**

There are many things which can be symbolically 'slain' at this time: a
harvest loaf, which can be broken up, or a Corn King which can have
stalks, or bunches of stalks, removed until he is no more. If you are
working alone, a gold candle can take the place of a more complex sacrifice. As with all the Sabbats it is important to reflect balance in your
Rites, so you should also make an offering of wine in thanks to the Old
Gods and the land.

   If it is at all possible, perform your Rites outside. Start by thinking
of all the things that have been given to you in the past season, and for
each take a part of your sacrificial 'victim' and say, "*I give thanks to the
Old Gods for ... (name it). Blessed Be.*" If there is a group of you, take it
in turns. Where you are using a candle, it may be as well to place a pin
into the candle for each, so that as it burns they fall away one by one.
When the victim is dismembered, or all the pins have dropped, make your
offering: Hold the wine up and say, "*I give thanks to the Old Gods who
bring life and light, death and rest, rebirth and renewal. May they accept
this offering. Blessed Be.*" Take a sip of the wine and then pour the rest
onto the ground, remain and meditate for a short while.

> *"Before you work hard for an answer,
> check it isn't obvious."*

LUGHNASADH GARDEN RITE

At the height of the growing season it can be hard to
remember that all aspects of the cycles of life, death
and rebirth are still taking place around us. Even at
the height of the season of growth there are things
which have passed their peak and are dying
back to allow other plants their turn.

Go into your garden and cut back those things which have finished their
growing cycle. This represents the sacrifice of the God. Unless you are
able to have a bonfire, select a token amount of this and, in a fireproof
container, burn them until you have only ashes. When these are cool hold
them high in your hands and allow the wind to scatter them to all parts
of the garden, so that the ash can return and empower the land, to represent sacrifice for the benefit of the land. Lastly take a few seeds and plant
them where some of the ash has fallen, that the God might rise again and
bring new growth. If possible get your family and friends to share this
with you. If you do not have a garden of your own then go out to a wild
place and collect your dead plants from there. Burn them carefully at
home and put the ash into some soil in a pot and plant your seeds there.

Some people like to add some of the dead vegetation to a barbeque
fire, eating the barbequed food in celebration of sacrifice and in honour
of the God. Whichever your choice, try to include traditional harvest
recipes in your feasting.

"The impossible we do now,
miracles take a little longer."

TRADITIONAL

LUGH

**A Sun God, Lugh comes from the Celtic pantheon
and gave his name to the festival of Lughnasadh.
There are many legends surrounding him.**

He was son of Cian of the Tuatha De Danann and Eithne, daughter of Balor, King of the Fomor. Commander of the Tuatha, Lugh slew his grandfather Balor in battle, although some tales say he only blinded him, thus becoming the Young God who supplants the Old. He carried a great sword and a spear, both of which form part of the treasures of the Tuatha, and was accompanied by a mighty hound. Lugh is hence a God of Light and Fire, and of warriors and battle.

Another legend tells of Lugh's betrayal on his marriage night by his wife, and his slaying by her lover. He returns as an eagle and is later restored to power by his uncle Gwion. This is in keeping with the tradition of the Sacrificial King, who mates with the Goddess, dies and is reborn for the sake of the land. The theme of sacrificial mating may seem farfetched today, unless we recall that in giving ourselves totally to another we are in fact experiencing a form of death, and it is only when we do this that we can be reborn. The theme of the King as the sacred personification of the people, representing earthly power, uniting with the Goddess, representing spiritual power, is a strong one and can be found in many beliefs. It is a theme we celebrate in the Craft for it is an integral part of the cycle of life, death and rebirth.

*"When the light is at its brightest
there will still be shadows."*

A BRIEF HISTORY OF THE GODS!

People have always
worshipped Gods and Goddesses.

They saw their effects in the Sun, the Moon and the Stars. They found their paths in the Elements of Earth, Air, Fire and Water. They sought for them in every aspect of life and the land. And as they came to understand them, they interpreted their stories in the words and ways of mankind, and passed these tales from one generation to another.

As different peoples migrated and scattered they took their Gods with them and they found the same or similar Gods under new names. Sometimes incoming Gods were added to the local culture, and sometimes incomers would worship their own Gods but by the new names of the locality. The stories of the Gods, passed by word of mouth, likewise changed and altered, although often remaining the same at their core. There were invaders who would likewise bring their beliefs, sometimes to overlay the beliefs of the indigenous people. This might result in new combined beliefs or in beliefs being driven underground, but still the Old Gods lived on.

Thus today we find recurring themes through the differing groupings of Gods, and their stories have been told and retold in many forms. For us in the Craft today, this occasionally disjointed history is where we have come from and forms the underlying basis of our beliefs. This is why we study the old tales of the Gods as well as why we seek to meet them in meditation, visualization and through working with the Elements and the land.

"Every tale has something to offer, if only we can find it."

THE FOXGLOVE

The Foxglove has many folk names:
Dead Men's Bells, Fairy Thimbles, Fairy Weed,
Fox Bells, Goblin's Thimbles, Witches' Bells,
Witches' Gloves and Witches' Thimble

The folk names indicate that it has long had a place in folklore and healing. Having said that, the Foxglove is poisonous, and the poison can build up within the body. It contains three powerful heart stimulants and one heart depressant, and should therefore be handled with the greatest of care. Foxglove was used to cure dropsy and today it is commercially processed to provide heart medications. The leaves can be processed to make a black dye which was used to darken lines on stone floors. At first this was done to protect the house from evil entering but later it became fashionable, and there were cases of staff in larger houses becoming poisoned through the use of Foxglove stain.

Foxglove is strongly protective and is grown in the garden to protect it from disease and pests as well as to protect the house and its inhabitants. Dried Foxglove leaves can be added to incense for house cleansing, but make sure that you open the windows first. Place Foxglove over the door lintel to prevent enemies from entering, or circle the house with them to prevent them finding you.

Should you decide to grow and/or use Foxglove, please take the greatest of care that you do not get any onto open wounds or into your eyes or mouth. If you have young children it is safer not to keep this plant, as the flower which fits so neatly over the fingers can be an irresistible toy!

"Take a moment to thank yourself every day."

HAZEL MONTH

In Celtic lore Hazel is referred to as Fair Wood and Sweet Wood.

It is coppiced and used in much the same way as Willow, and has been so since ancient times. Hazel wood is much favoured for dowsing, and the nuts are mineral rich and highly nutritious. The nuts can be ground and used as flour, and the whole shell, husk and skin were powdered and added to a drink to ease heavy menstruation.

The Hazel features in the tales of many of the Gods. It is said that when Lugh severed Balor's head, he placed it in a Hazel but the dripping blood poisoned the tree until Manannan felled it. Later Fionn used the wood to make his shield Dripping Ancient Hazel. It was said to be a tree of keening (a form of weeping) over death and sacred to Brighid, the Goddess who first used this form of grief over the death of her son, Ruadhan. The Hazel is also sacred to her in her role of Goddess of Wisdom and Inspiration, as some of the nuts are said to contain her wisdom. It also features in the tales of Artemis, Diana, Mercury and Thor.

Today we use the Hazel in spells for luck, protection, wishes and fertility. Eat the fresh nuts in season prior to Rituals for divination and burn them in a fire when seeking the knowledge of Brighid. Weave Hazel wood around your hat to make your wishes come true. Hazel Wands were also the symbol of the herald, and sometimes used in Covens to mark the office of Summoner.

> *"Why wait to be given flowers*
> *when you can grow your own."*

PAINTING MAGIC

One of the oldest forms of magic involves creating pictorial images.

Whilst some of these were carved, many were painted, and some can still be seen in the caves of our forebears. Some of these are simply a form of sympathetic magic, where the artist or Shaman would create an image of what he, or she, intended to come to pass. Others are more complex and use spirals and other patterns which we still use to access the subconscious mind. You do not need a huge artistic talent in order to create magic through pictures; after all, it's not as though you're trying to sell them! You just need to be able to create an image which has meaning for you and which is imbued with your own personal energy. Having said that, if you are not accustomed to working in this way, it is a good idea to experiment to see which medium, eg paint, pencil, crayon, chalk, you prefer, before trying to produce a spell. You may also want to experiment with the form of art you create, whether it is to be literal, abstract or some other.

When painting protective and defensive spells create them on circular paper, or ensure that your spell is surrounded by a circle. Oblong paper in the horizontal or landscape direction is best for spells intended to draw things towards you, whilst in the upright or portrait position it is best for spells referring to an individual. Use square paper for spells relating to personal development and balance. Spells relating to movement, or action, should not be confined by any lines.

"A little of what you fancy does you good."

SWANS

Swans are now protected birds,
but it has long been thought unlucky to kill one.

In some places it is said that anyone who kills a swan will meet their own death within the year. It used to be thought that Swans' eggs would only hatch during a storm. As a royal bird it was thought unlucky to bring their feathers into the home, probably because of their associations with the worship of the Old Gods.

They appear in several of the stories of the Gods. Zeus was thought to have taken the form of a swan to seduce Leda, from which she bore an egg which produced two sets of twins, one pair the mortal Clytemnestra and Pollux and the other pair the immortal Helen and Castor, after which Leda became the Goddess Nemesis. The Swan is dedicated to Apollo the Greek God of music and it is perhaps from this that they are thought to sing as they die: the origin of the term swansong. In Ireland there is the Caer: the Swan Maiden who lured the God of poetry Aengus to her lake where he too became a swan. Their song was said to lull whole towns to sleep. Likewise Germanic/Scandinavian legend includes the Swan Maidens as a form of Valkyrie. Wayland the Smith, under his Norse name of Volund, together with his brothers Egil and Slagfid, married Swan Maidens, who departed to their homes after nine years. In the Celtic tradition the children of Llyr, a King of the Tuatha, were turned into swans in an act of jealousy by his second wife.

> *"Every cloud has a silver lining,*
> *even if it's well hidden."*

CARNELIAN

Carnelian is a red/orange stone which has very strong associations with the Craft.

It is used in spells for courage, healing, peace, protection and to enhance sexual energy. It relates directly to the base Chakra and therefore can also be used to ensure that your personal energy flows are linked to the earth. Roll a piece of the stone over your whole body to give your energy flow a gentle boost.

Traditionally Carnelian was used to treat bleeding and blood disorders, especially for menstrual problems. It was also thought to guard against skin disease and to increase sexual appetite. Wear Carnelian when entering any environment which makes you feel nervous, like a job interview, or when speaking publicly. Wear it also to conceal your thoughts and feelings. The Egyptians used it to dispel anger, jealousy and hatred. It was thought to bring harmony and drive away negatives. Hang one over the bed of a child to drive away nightmares. Carnelians are worn to increase psychic ability and to enable astral projection. Place a piece over your third eye and visualize its energy being absorbed. Allow the energy to move throughout your body until it has permeated your whole being.

Although the Carnelian is often worn by Witches, you should be cautious about accepting one from a Witch, as it is sometimes given to invoke the law of Threefold Return on a person who has done them, or those near to them, a disservice.

"Anything you say in confidence is almost certain to be overheard."

FENNEL

Fennel was used as an anti-Witch plant and
hung over doors to protect the household from
enchantment; it was supposed to be most
effective if this was done at midsummer
and the herb then left in place all year.

However, it was also thought that to sow Fennel was to sow trouble in
the house, so it was always sought from the wild.

Fennel stimulates the production of breast milk in nursing mothers,
and it is said that children thus fed will suffer far less from wind. A tea
made from the seeds is a great digestive, relieving indigestion and flatulence, and has long been used as an aid to losing weight. Fennel tea is also
a cure for hiccoughs. Chewing the seed, on its own or in food, is also said
to alleviate coughs and to speed recovery after illness. It used to be
thought that Fennel would also cleanse the body and remove obstructions
to the liver, spleen and gall bladder. It was used to treat jaundice, gout,
cramp and all kinds of urinary problems. It was also used to treat snake
bite and mushroom poisoning. Compresses of Fennel alleviate inflamed or
sore eyes and it can be added to honey to make a facial which removes
wrinkles. Rubbing Fennel on the skin can help to prevent insect bites.
A small amount of Fennel tea added to food was thought to induce love.

Magically, Fennel is often incorporated in baths for purification and is
added to incenses for protection during spell working. Fennel seeds are
sometimes included in spells to attract money and are carried for protection.

"If you sit on the fence
long enough, you'll get splinters."

RITUAL CLOTHING

Some Witches, especially those of the Gardnerian tradition, work their Rites and Rituals skyclad, or without clothing.

Some wear Robes or clothing set aside for such work, and yet others wear their everyday clothes. There are many reasons. Those who work skyclad believe that they should appear naked before the Goddess and the God, as implied in the Charge; that we should be comfortable in our skin; and that it marks us all as equal and allows a greater flow of energy.

Those who wear Robes feel that their uniformity also marks us all as equal and that a layer of fabric will not interfere with the flow of energy. The putting on of Robes defines the change between the mundane and magical worlds. They also feel that Robes are more practical for outside work where the weather is not always temperate and where you may be observed by outsiders. Robes are usually worn by those who work in non-Gardnerian Covens, and sometimes the colour of the cord or belt indicates the level of attainment of the individual.

The use of special clothing like Robes, but less uniform, is often preferred by Solitary Witches. These garments are sometimes also worn when attending social events within the Craft, such as conferences.

Of course there is no reason why you should not work magic and Ritual in your everyday clothes and many Witches do so, especially those whose magic involves working in the garden and kitchen and where flowing draperies would be more of a hindrance than a help!

"It may be easier to judge by appearances,
but it's not reliable."

ORANGE

Orange is the colour of the Sun and Solar power.

It is linked to the time of the ripening harvest. It is also associated with the Element of Fire but in a more gentle and personal way than red. Orange is created through blending red and yellow which indicate the effects of Fire, or the passions, being tempered by those of Air, or thought. Orange is an energizing colour, bringing inner illumination, increased energy, personal power and growth.

Wear orange to increase your sense of self-worth and when working on personal development. Wear it in Solar Rituals to attract the energy of the Sun to your magic. As orange is protective, wear it when you feel negative outside influences affecting you. Use orange stones such as Orange Calcite, Citrine, Amber and light Carnelians to help you access your personal power. Take one in each hand and open your mind to feel the flow of power between them. Then focus on this as it awakens your inner resources. Add the power of the stones to your personal power. This can be used prior to working magic to enhance your energy, or afterwards to recharge your inner levels. If you are feeling particularly low take an orange stone and hold it in your right hand, fold your left over it and project all your negativity into it. When you feel that it has absorbed all it can hold, take it and cast it into running water. Collect orange leaves and place them on the Altar for Autumn Rituals or use them in spells for personal enhancement at this time.

"Your future is ahead of you,
so stop looking back."

DEVELOPING THE SENSES

*In order to develop our sixth sense we first
need to maximize and balance the use of the
other 5: sight, smell, taste, touch and hearing.*

Our senses are constantly bombarded by sights, sounds and smells which can lead to confusion, if not actual overload. To test this for yourself, sit quietly and listen. What can you hear? You will probably start to identify many sounds; perhaps passing traffic, people in the distance, aircraft passing overhead and the wind in the trees. Underlying this you may also detect the hum of the refrigerator, the tick of a clock, and other sounds.

To understand and improve our senses it is often best to try limiting the amount of input they receive. As sight is, for humans, the dominant sense, try closing your eyes to allow you to focus on another. Close your eyes and listen, and after a few minutes you will find that you are hearing sounds you would otherwise have missed. Take a selection of items, perhaps flowers or herbs, close your eyes and spend a few minutes smelling each; you will find that there is a greater depth to the scents. This is especially useful when choosing ingredients for incense. Do likewise with things you can taste and with different textures to examine the sense of feeling. Sight can often be enhanced by blocking off hearing, so try watching people at a distance to see what you can learn about them. If you practise really using each of your 5 senses regularly you will soon find that your sixth sense is enhanced.

*"Know that you will never know everything,
but every tiny increase in knowledge will benefit you."*

SHEEP

Watching sheep, or remembering their reputation for stupidity, you would be forgiven for thinking they are probably one of the more un-magical animals!

However, in common with much of the livestock on which life depended, there are many traditions associated with them.

When sheep graze peacefully then the weather will be good, but if they huddle at the edges of a field then rain will follow. Sheep that are unusually active are said to presage a storm. It is considered good luck to meet a flock of sheep when on a journey, it being said that you will soon achieve your heart's desire. Another tradition says that when you see the first lamb of the year you should note which way it is looking for this will tell you where you will live. A black sheep, despite it being used as a term for a maverick, is said to bring good luck to the owner and to protect the flock.

Sheep are associated with the festival of Imbolg, as the word Oimelc from which it derives is interpreted to mean 'Ewe's milk'. Collect sheep's wool from the fences around their pasture to place on the Altar at this time or to give to those seeking to become pregnant. It is thought that the wool of a new mother sheep, or a blanket including the same, placed under the bottom sheet will bring children to the couple who lie on it. The three Fates, who spin, weave and cut the web of life, are sometimes said to create it from the wool of a sheep.

"Making mistakes proves you're trying."

DEMETER AND PERSEPHONE

The story of Demeter and Persephone has, like many
other Goddess tales, changed through time. Probably
the nearest we can come to the original is as follows:

Demeter, Goddess of the Earth is working in the fields. She cautions
her daughter Persephone to stay nearby who, being youthful, doesn't.
Hades, Lord of the Underworld, comes by in his chariot and persuades
Persephone to go with him and become his Queen. Demeter travels the
earth searching for her daughter. As she goes she tears her clothes and the
dropped rags become the flowers of the fields. As Demeter is in mourning the plants begin to shrivel and wilt. The Goddess wanders the dying
Earth, at one point taking a job as nursemaid to the Queen of Eleusis,
Metanira. One day by the well, Demeter meets Baubo the Queen's daughter. To cheer up the Goddess, Baubo exposes herself, causing Demeter to
smile, and a few brave shoots spring through the barren land. Soon after
this Demeter meets Hecate who tells her where Persephone is. Seeking
her daughter's return Demeter discovers that Persephone has accepted a
gift from Hades, of 6 Pomegranate seeds, and hence will only be allowed
to return to the surface for 6 months of the year. The other 6 she will
preside over the underworld with Hades.

This story, which has many echoes for our lives today, sees
Persephone, Demeter and Hecate as Maiden, Mother and Crone. We also
see that Persephone is her mother's younger carefree self, whilst Hecate
is her older persona who knows the truth of what occurs.

> *"To make your dreams come true,*
> *first take them out of the bedroom."*

EYES

The eyes are considered significant in many
cultures and for many reasons. In some parts of
the world the Eye of Osiris, an ancient Egyptian
symbol of good fortune, is still painted on the prows
of boats, on walls and doors to ward off evil.

The colour, shape, size and distance between the eyes have all been given
significance. Dark blue eyes indicate a refined and/or magical person.
Light blue or grey are the sign of someone strong and healthy, green are
said to indicate hardiness, and hazel a deep thinker. In America it is said
that a black-eyed woman will be deceitful and a grey-eyed person greedy.
Eyes which are too close together, or eyebrows which meet in the middle
are said to indicate untrustworthiness, or even a werewolf! An itch in the
right eye means good luck, whilst one in the left means the opposite. My
practical self would suggest that both eyes itching is probably a sign of
hay-fever or overtiredness! Eyes are often referred to as the windows of
the soul and certainly a person who will not meet your eye is likely to be
concealing something.

It was long thought that some people, whether Witches or not, were
able to give the evil eye. This includes those with crossed eyes, odd-coloured
eyes, a double iris and those with dark marks on the iris. These people were
also credited with being able to 'over-look' a person, a reference to Astral
travel. Many Witches today assert that you can in fact tell another Witch by
their eyes, but that the signs are not so much physical but in the depths.

"Clairvoyance means clear sight,
so practise looking."

THE PEACOCK

Like the swan, the peacock is considered a royal bird, probably because it was originally imported by royalty and the very rich.

It is seen as being only partly domesticated, like the cat, and therefore treated with suspicion; any creature which is only tame to some individuals was likely to bring the accusation of Witchcraft or trading with devils on those who did have the skill to handle it.

It is said that it is unlucky to bring peacock feathers into the house, probably because of the 'eyes' in the tail which are associated with the evil eye. This may have originated from Ancient Greece where they were temple birds and to even touch one was punishable by death. This superstition is still so strong that many people will not even allow a picture of a peacock in the house. Having said that, some people believe that if a peacock drops a tail feather in front of you it indicates a windfall is coming. In some places the cry of the peacock is said to be the cry of souls in purgatory, whilst in others it is thought to signal rain. However, as peacocks are very vocal creatures this would seem to indicate either that it never stops raining or that purgatory is very overcrowded!

In the Craft we sometimes use peacock feathers in protection and defensive magic. Place one before a mirror to prevent it being used as an Astral access or against you, or place one in the window to deflect negative thoughts and intentions.

"People who seem to sail gracefully through life are usually paddling frantically under the water."

SOUL MATES

Most witches believe in reincarnation; the spirit continues through many lives, being different people and learning different lessons.

An adjunct to this belief is the hope that we may meet those we have loved in previous lives in this, and future ones. We call these people, who we are drawn to lifetime after lifetime, Soul Mates. There are misunderstandings about who Soul Mates are likely to be. This is mainly caused by the ways in which we use the word 'love'. Love is not only confined to the relationship between a couple, it is also the feeling we have for close friends and family. Whilst your Soul Mate could be your partner or lover, they are just as likely to be someone else. They do not need to be of the opposite gender, nor will you necessarily have only one in this lifetime, for we love our parents, children, other relatives and friends. Sometimes we even have ties of closeness to those with whom we have, or have had, an antagonistic relationship. So a Soul Mate may be the love of your life, or anyone with whom you have close ties, shared thoughts and feelings, and an enduring relationship. Quite often we find that a Soul Mate is in our lives, but not yet recognized as such.

To find and identify the Soul Mates in your life light a purple and a gold candle every night for a week during the waxing Moon. Take all the stubs and bury them under an Oak tree and your Soul Mate will be revealed to you.

"Labels are for luggage, not people."

BRASS

Brass has long been used as a magical substitute for gold. Whilst not as powerful as gold it is very effective in money spells.

At dawn place 8 green candles in the sunlight on a square of gold paper, and in the centre place a brass ring: a brass curtain ring is fine. Ring a brass bell three times over each candle, whilst visualizing money coming to you. When the candles have burnt all the way down fold the paper and place it, together with the brass ring, in your wallet or purse and carry it with you.

Brass keys used to be dropped down the back to relieve nose bleeds and it is said that wearing a brass ring will prevent stomach cramps. Horse brasses used to be said to bring good fortune and to protect the home from evil spirits, and, of course, Witches. To be effective they had to be polished once a week. The preferred symbols on them were Acorns, Birds, Beasts, Flowers and Hearts.

A good number of items of Altar equipment are made from brass, and well kept and polished it can look really magnificent by candlelight, Sun- and Moonlight. But allowed to tarnish and become dull it looks cheap and quite nasty. If you want your magic to work and the Goddess and God to grace your Rituals, keep any brassware at its best! If you empower your brassware, Ritual and otherwise, by placing it overnight in the light of the Full Moon, and place it in your windows, it will protect your household and return any negativity to the sender.

"Stepping into even verbal crossfire
is a good way of getting hurt."

SNAKES

Even before the Bible snakes were connected to evil
and demons, which is not surprising given the venomous
bites of many species. The myth of St Patrick driving all
the snakes from Ireland is thought to be a reference to
the church ridding the country of Pagans.

As a result it is not surprising that snakes were despised, reviled and
thought to bring ill fortune. A snake in the house foretold death. It was
said that you should always the kill the first snake you see in the year to
rid yourself of your enemies. It was also thought that a snake, however
badly injured, would not die until sunset. To keep snakes away from the
house you should scatter Ash leaves on the floors. Should you come
across a sleeping snake then draw a circle around it with an Ash twig to
cause it to die, although I think it's safer all round to just leave it be! It
used to be thought that eating a snake would keep you young. Relatively
recently in Wales it was thought that eating the flesh of a white snake
would enable you to understand the language of beasts, birds and reptiles.
The snake's skin was said to cure a headache if placed around the head.
The freshly-shed skin of the Adder hung from the ceiling was thought to
protect the house from fire, and to bring good fortune.

If you are lucky enough to obtain a shed snakeskin, carry it to
increase eloquence. To conceal things which you wish to keep hidden,
write them on snakeskin and bury this at the Dark of the Moon.

*"Ignoring antagonists
really gets on their nerves."*

CATNIP

Some cats go wild for Catnip. They, chew it,
eat it, roll in it, becoming excited, and it seems
to have an almost narcotic effect upon them.

As a result it can be hard to grow if you have cats, although a hanging
basket can be the solution! The other difficulty is that although Catmint
is one of the other names for Catnip, it is also a name given to some other
plants. So when buying it, ensure that you get *Nepeta cataria*.

Catnip is one of the 16 healing plants of Druid lore, where it is recommended for use in fevers, headaches, bronchitis and digestive and
stomach complaints, including diarrhoea and cramps. Catnip tea is balancing, being calming for those who are excitable and quarrelsome, yet
stimulating for those who are overexerted or who need courage. It is also
useful in treating troublesome menstruation. Added to preserves it is useful in treating nightmares in children.

Magically it is used in spells for love, beauty, friendship and happiness.
Rub Catnip on your palm before holding the hand of someone whose
friendship you wish to secure. Place the pressed leaves in your Book of
Shadows to protect it from prying eyes. Float a few leaves in the bath and
meditate there to enhance beauty and attract love. Put the flower tops
under your pillow to secure a good night's sleep and for prophetic dreams.
Drink Catnip tea last thing at night to promote healing. Grow Catnip by
the door or window to attract good spirits. To create a psychic bond with
your cat, drink Catnip tea at the same time as giving them Catnip.

*"Loud voices do not make
sound arguments."*

FAIRIES

It is only in recent times that fairies have been visualized as cute, winsome figures.

Prior to the 19th century they were considered to be complex and frequently mischievous creatures. They were thought to steal good children and replace them with naughty ones, and abduct unwary travellers who fell asleep in the wrong place. If slighted they would sour milk and prevent butter from being churned. They could cause food to spoil and prevent bread from rising. Of course if they were kindly disposed to you and treated with respect they would bring good luck and fortune.

Fairies are believed to be encouraged to look kindly on people who grow certain plants: Ash, Bluebells, Red Carnations, Clover, Cowslips, Elder, Hawthorn, Hollyhocks, Lilac, Lobelia, Oak, Pansies, Blue and Red Primroses, Roses and Shamrock. They are said to live in Foxgloves and straw. Fairies are thought to gather at midsummer wherever Oak, Ash and Hawthorn grow together. At dawn or dusk sit quietly amongst these plants whilst wearing Thyme and you should be able to see Fairies. Alternatively, place 7 grains of Wheat onto a four-leafed Clover as an offering, and Fairies will come. Fairies are also thought to dance in Fairy rings: circles of mushrooms which are found in some fields.

If, however, you feel you need to defend your home from the attentions of Fairies then plant Dill, Morning Glory, Gorse and Rosemary. To protect children from being stolen by the Fairies tie Peonies around their neck. Otherwise, carve beads from Peony root and string these together as a necklace which will guard against all kinds of spirits.

"Become richer, by buying only what you need."

RITES OF WITHDRAWAL

Witches believe that, after death, we pass on to the
Summerlands, the place beyond the veil of life where
we go between lives. Here we may meet with those
we love who have already passed on, and here we
choose the lessons we will learn in our next life.

We have a number of Rites which we can hold when a loved one passes
from this life. Collectively these are called Rites of Withdrawal, although
this encompasses a variety of quite different Rituals. A Rite of
Withdrawal can take place as a person dies, in which case it will serve to
give them peace as they commence their journey. A Witch may even create their own meditation Rite to take them through the veil. There are
Rites which may take place at the same time as a burial or cremation, if
this is not likely to offend or upset other mourners. Or there may be
Rites which are a celebration of life which take place some time after the
remains have been committed. These latter may take place more than
once, with a person being remembered on several occasions by different
groups of friends or family.

Whenever they are held, Rites of Withdrawal serve two main purposes: they allow us to celebrate the life and achievements of our loved ones,
and they allow us to remember them as the people they really were, faults
and all. Whilst we do feel grief at our own loss, we emphasize the celebration of a person's life with shared experiences and tales of the times we
enjoyed together.

"People live forever in the memories they leave."

THE SUN IN VIRGO

*Virgo is an Earth sign bringing qualities of
resourcefulness, practicality and skill. It is
also a Mutable sign which brings flexibility,
problem-solving and skills as an intermediary.*

Virgo is symbolized as a female holding an ear of wheat and is identified as the Earth Goddess: Isis, Ishtar, Persephone or Ceres. Virgos are usually analytical, critical and seek efficiency and perfection, although they are also practical, adaptable and variable. They tend to be restrained, passive and prefer to avoid confrontation. Intelligent and discerning, they can appear to be critical. Their attention to detail is often seen as fussiness and fault finding, but makes them effective where precision is needful. In relationships and love they tend to be reserved, conventional and even-tempered. Although they can sometimes seem quite cool, they do need the reassurance which they rarely seek. They are self-analytical, often self-critical and apt to worry. Virgos often find themselves counselling and advising others, sometimes to the detriment of those close to them, as their ability to unravel problems, analyse information and get to the root of the matter is much sought after.

At this time of the year Virgoans should take care to slow down, remembering to ask for, rather than give, advice. In relationships they should by all means seek the reassurance they crave, but be wary of appearing too needy. Non-Virgoans will find this is a good time for undertaking any kind of self-analysis and personal exploration. Work involving attention to detail, numbers and memorizing things will be enhanced.

"Tackle big things a step at a time."

RABBITS

Like their cousins the hares, rabbits are associated with
luck and fortune and sometimes with the Craft.
However, whereas hares are considered to be the symbol
of the Goddess, rabbits are sacred to the Moon God.

To see a white rabbit means the death of someone who is ill, as the rabbit is the sign of the person's soul leaving their body. In Devon it is thought unlucky to harm a black rabbit as it may be a Witch in disguise. This is contrary to many other beliefs where animals were more likely to be persecuted because they might be Witches. A rabbit seen running up the street indicates there will be a fire in one of the houses. In many places it is thought that the first person to say *"White Rabbits"* on the first of the month would have luck all that month. In other places it is thought that you should say *"Rabbits"* last thing on the last of the month, and *"Hares"* first thing in the morning. Some say that the first person to do this will have a wish come true. When I was young, *"White Rabbits"* was also said to avoid being 'pinched and punched' on the first of the month, or to call a halt to any kind of rough and tumble.

A rabbit's foot has long been carried to attract good fortune. Indeed it was estimated in the 1970s that Americans were buying about 10 million rabbit feet every year, and the Europeans a further 5 million. None of which strikes me as lucky for rabbits!

> *"If a person speaks ill of others,*
> *what will they say about you?"*

MERLIN

**The legends of King Arthur, his court,
knights, the round table and his 'sorcerer'
Merlin have come down to us over the years.**

However, they have come to us piecemeal through surviving fragments, such as the song of Taliesin, only being 'united' by Geoffrey of Monmouth whose romantic tales were written centuries after the events they depict. As a result, whilst we can be reasonably sure that there was a leader called Arthur (or Artor) and a sage called Merlin (or Myrddin), there is little else we can be sure of.

However, both Merlin and Arthur have become important archetypes. Whilst Arthur was the face of the Celtic warrior, Merlin represented the mystical aspect. Merlin nurtured Arthur and gave him the test of taking the sword from the stone, to confirm his kingship. It seems that although Merlin spent much of his time at court as advisor, he also wandered the land, and was very much free to do as he saw fit. From the surviving records it would seem that Merlin existed for more than a hundred years and indeed Welsh history has it that Taliesin was Merlin reincarnated. This has given rise to the suggestion that Merlin was a title held by several individuals.

From the perspective of the Craft it is well to remember that in addition to the above, Merlin was almost certainly a Druid or Druid-type leader, not a Witch. However, today there are many in the Craft who have taken the name Merlin in honour of the tales of the skills of the original.

*"Be generous with your smiles,
after all they're free."*

FEATHERS

*Feathers symbolize the Element of Air, and
therefore represent thought, communication and
travel. I know several Witches who have one or
more feathers in the car to ensure safe driving.*

The feathers of different birds can be used to work magic directly related
to the attributes or associations of that bird. For example, a spell connected with the eyes might include a Hawk feather; a spell for knowledge that
of an Owl; or if performing a meditation to the Morrighan you might use
the feathers of a Raven. A good many Witches have collections of feathers which they keep to use in different spells. It goes without saying that
these feathers should be fallen, not taken from a live or even dead bird.
When you find a feather take it home and place it in a hot place, preferably in direct sunlight, for a couple of days. This has the effect of killing
off any germs it may harbour.

Feathers can also be used in house cleansing and protection spells.
Burn a feather and take it around every room in the house to drive out
all negative energies. Open the windows first as it will give off a powerful smell. For general household protection place one or two feathers in
each window. A small bundle of feathers tied with red and green thread
can be hung in the room of a baby or small child to bring long life and
good fortune. To be reunited with a distant loved one, take a small white
feather to a high place and, whispering their name to it three times, cast
it to the wind.

*"Put the knowledge
you learn to good use."*

THE RUNES

'Runes' is the term used for a number
of alphabets used by the ancient Anglo-Saxon,
Scandinavian and Germanic peoples.

In Norse mythology the Runes were won by the God Odin after he hung upside down on Yggdrassil, the Tree of Life, for 9 days and 9 nights. This image can be found in the first card of the Major Arcana of the Tarot; the Hanged Man or Fool. The Runes are also sometimes called the Futhark, after the first 6 letters of the runic alphabets. These alphabets are characterized by the fact that all of the symbols are created from straight lines alone. Most Runic alphabets consist of 24 characters, some of which would be represented in our alphabet by 2 letters, eg 'th' and 'ng'. Each character held a wealth of meaning, representing a vocal sound, a part of daily life, a tree, a herb, a colour, a type of magical being and its own magical intention. Runes were used for communication, divination and for magic. They were carved into monuments, stones and wooden staves. Today we usually make our Runes from flat pebbles or pieces of wood, although some will make them from gemstones.

Unlike other tools of divination it is important that you make your own Runes. Each should be created on a separate day, and time should be taken to understand all the meanings behind the character before moving on to the next. In this way your set of Runes will become your own. Develop your own interpretations rather than relying totally on those in booklets as some of these are a long way from their origins.

"Assess people by their actions,
not their words."

FOSSILS

Fossils are the remains or impressions of animals and plants which lived and died millions of years ago.

As well as the bones of dinosaurs, fossils are the specks of plants and insects found in Amber, as are the imprints of leaves and creatures seen in rock. They are found in a great variety of places; only recently I found a fossilized shell imprint on a stone in the gravel of my front drive. I've also found ammonites on beaches and in woods which are based in chalk soil. Should you be lucky enough to discover a fossil, check that you are not taking something of archaeological importance or interfering with an historic site.

Fossils were placed in Neolithic burial sites and were also traditionally used in magic for longevity. Today we use them in spells for psychic atunement, power enhancement, protection and past-life recall. Many Witches place a fossil on the Altar to represent the never-ending cycle of life, death and rebirth, and to maximize the energies of the Circle. To awaken a psychic state and revisit previous lives, sit cross-legged in the Moonlight with a fossil in your strong hand. Focus on the fossil and let go of your conscious mind. Let your mind travel back through time until you feel that you are in a familiar place. Explore this time and place as long as you wish; should you feel uncomfortable simply let go of the fossil. Past-life regression is best performed with someone to watch over you, who can take the fossil from your hand if you show any signs of distress.

"Past-life experiences are no
substitute for this life's ones."

ANCIENT MONUMENTS

It is not known how long people have considered
ancient monuments, standing stones and other
pre-historic 'building works' to be significant, but there
is no doubt it has been thousands of years.

Nor can we be sure why they were erected at such considerable effort. What we do believe is that they are a part of our history; a link to our ancestors. So, to us they become Sacred Sites which we visit and where we pay homage to our Gods. If you do visit a monument, try to do so when it will be quiet. Visiting Stonehenge at the height of the season, let alone at the Summer Solstice, may be interesting but it is unlikely to give you enough peace for contemplation or meditation.

However, it is well worth visiting at a quiet time. First, walk around the site, view it from many angles and imagine what it would have looked like to the people of the time. If it is allowed, find a quiet place within the site and sit down, visualize the building taking place and the co-operation of the people who must have been involved. Allow your mind to reach out and see if you can gain an understanding of what they may have been feeling, and why this structure was so important to them. Once you have finished give your thanks to the Old Gods for any knowledge they have allowed you. Do not place any physical offerings around the monument: workers spend many hours removing such 'litter'.

*"The support of friends carries
us through the hard times."*

LADYBIRDS

The ladybird family is very large; there are
several hundred species in Britain alone.
Their colouring varies from the familiar red
with a few black spots to ones which are black
with red spots, green with black spots and the
spots themselves vary from a couple to over 22.

The ladybird is the gardener's friend as both larvae and adults eat aphids, sometimes as many as 30 – 40 per day, each. If you find your plants infested with aphids then see if you can find a few ladybirds to deal with the problem for you, though never put them onto a plant which has been sprayed, or is about to be sprayed, with insecticide.

With their red and black colouring, ladybirds are associated with the Goddess as Crone and if you have one land on you, ask it one question and it will be answered before the following day. It is said to be lucky to have a ladybird land on you, although you should wait for it to leave of its own accord and not brush it off. Each spot will indicate a happy month to come. Ladybirds were also used in a charm to find a lover: one was taken from the grass and placed on the back of the hand, then invited to fly off in the direction of true love, and this would indicate which way you would find your love. Furthermore, if you count the seconds before a ladybird flies from your hand, this was said to indicate the number of months before you would marry.

"Don't waste time trying to impress fools."

USING THE RUNES

There are many ways of using Runes for divination,
from simply selecting one at random in answer to a
specific question, to layouts which involve them all.

One of the most effective is to place all the Runes in a bag, focus on your question and mix them with your fingers until they feel 'right'. Then draw out four Runes. As you draw the first say, *"This is the seed, from which the thing grew."* This is about the root cause of your issue. Draw the second and say, *"This is the tree which grew from the seed."* Here are the effects of that root. For the third say, *"This is my branch upon the tree."* This is your part in the issue, or the action you may need to take. For the last, say, *"This is the fruit, born of the branch."* This will tell you what the results may be. Interpret the Runes incorporating the aspect of the reading to which they refer and their action upon one another.

When using Runes in magic, they are read from right to left, or from bottom to top. A Runic spell usually consists of three characters and rarely more than five. You are using the symbolism of the Runes, rather than spelling out a word or words. The spell should always be created in a natural medium, like wood, stone or parchment. You can even write them in the sand and let the sea take them if that is appropriate.

Runes can also be used for meditation. Select three Runes at random and create a setting and story from their meanings.

*"Wrinkles are an outer
sign of increasing wisdom."*

MOON FOLKLORE

There is a wealth of folklore associated with the
Moon. Traditionally, each of the first 10 days from the
New Moon is considered to have its own attributes.

The first: A good day for new beginnings. To fall ill on this day meant it would last a long while. A child born at this time will be happy, prosperous and live long. Second: A good day for buying and selling, and for starting a sea voyage sea. A good time for hoeing and sowing. Third: Crimes committed on this day are certain to be found out. Fourth: A good day for building, construction and home renovations. Also a good day to be born on if you want to enter politics. Fifth: The weather on this day gives an indication of what to expect for the rest of the month. A good day for a woman to conceive. Sixth: The best day for hunting or fishing. Seventh: A good day for meeting and falling in love. Eighth: A sickness begun on this day was thought to be likely to cause death. Ninth: If the Moon shines on your face you may have twisted features or go mad. Tenth: People born on this day are likely to be travellers or have a restless spirit.

A New Moon on a Saturday or Sunday indicates rain, as does seeing the outline of the whole Moon at the same time as a New Moon. Furthermore, should the horns of a New Moon point upwards then the weather will be fair for the next lunar cycle, but if they point down then expect rain.

"To reduce stress,
start earlier."

VINE MONTH

Although associated with warm climes the Vine will
grow quite successfully in cooler places, although you may
have to shelter it in a greenhouse if you actually want
grapes you can eat. Properly cared for, Vines live a very
long time, some in France being said to be 400 years old.

To the ancient Celts the Vine was a tree of strength, growth and unity. It
was called the 'highest of beauty' and the 'strongest of effort' for its ability to grow higher than any plant which supported it, and to grow from
one tree to another. Whilst the fruit is used to make wine, the vine has
many other uses. The roots were plaited and twisted to make fine string
and strong rope. The leaves can be eaten in salads, and are strong in vitamins and minerals, ensuring a clear skin. They are also good for the blood
and calm the nerves. Boiled, they can be used as a lotion for sore mouths
or as a poultice on wounds and swellings. Grapes were recommended in
speeding the healing process. The tradition of giving grapes to someone
recovering from illness goes back a very long time indeed.

The fermented fruit of the Vine was considered to bring divine inspiration, although only in moderate quantities. In addition it was thought
to be a tree of teaching and knowledge. Interestingly, Vines are grown
around my son's school. Meditation under or by a Vine gives access to the
inner mind and is especially useful when seeking answers about the self.
Place grapes on the Altar in Rituals to Bacchus, Dionysus and Hathor.

*"Give thanks for sunlight,
sunshine is a bonus."*

THE FOX

The fox is the only wild member of the dog family left in Britain.

It is much maligned, partly because it will cause havoc if it gets into a hen coop, but probably equally because it provides an excuse for those who enjoy blood sports. However, despite its persecution in parts of the countryside, and because people do not seal their rubbish carefully, the fox is becoming increasingly common in urban areas. Contrary to urban myth, an adult cat is more likely to see off a fox than fall prey to it. Foxes are actually wonderful animals and excellent parents. We once had foxes in the garden and the sight of the cubs sitting in a circle around their mother in the Moonlight is one I will never forget. Later I had the task of hand rearing one and from the pet-owner point of view I can say that having a young one with the messiness of a puppy and the mischief of a kitten means that life has no dull moments!

In some parts of the world it is said that if a fox passes close to your home it means bad luck is on the way. However in Scotland to see a lone fox means good luck is on the way, whilst to see several indicates troubles are coming. To see a black fox was said to predict a death in the direction it was going.

Magically, the fox is an animal of skill, cunning, and knowledge. It has the power to travel from one world to another. Invoke its energy when you are seeking knowledge, especially of the otherworld.

*"Practical action works
better than wishful thinking."*

BLUE

Blue is the colour most usually associated with the Element of Water and it is ruled by Neptune. It is the colour of the West, the emotions and of Autumn. It is one of the colours of the Goddess in her role as the Mother. It is also a colour of peace, tranquillity, sleep and good health.

Blue is a good colour for the bedroom, despite its reputation for being 'cold', as it enhances sleep and pleasant dreams. If you have concerns which give you trouble getting to sleep, hold a blue stone in your hand whilst you wait for sleep to claim you. Wear blue when you need more peace in your life, or if you wish to calm those around you. Blue is also purifying, so place blue stones like Sodalite or Lapis Lazuli in the bath and burn a blue candle alongside whenever you feel the need. Blue is particularly kind to the eyes, and research has shown that if you alter your computer's settings so that you have dark blue text on a light blue background, you will be able to work for longer periods with less chance of eyestrain. I use this myself, although I would also advocate frequently switching your focus from the screen to something further away as an aid to your eyes.

Blue is an excellent colour to aid meditation. Paint a large sheet of paper in shades of blue from very pale at one edge to very dark at the other. Try to graduate the colours evenly. Place this in front of you and gaze at it to enter a meditative state.

"Never sign until you understand all the small print."

VAMPIRES

We are all used to the image of the black-clad,
bloodsucking vampire, who can be kept at bay
with a crucifix, some garlic and Sunlight.

These are the vampires of fiction. But there are real-life vampires. They include those people whose company, however pleasant, is physically, emotionally and spiritually draining, as well as those who are forever making demands on your time, energy and personal resources. The former are psychic vampires, and are often quite unconscious of the effect they have on those around them. The latter are users, and are generally typified by a 'poor little me' attitude to life and the world. Now obviously you could simply avoid both types, but if, like me, you have a good friend who is an unintentional psychic vampire, or if it's a family member or someone you work with, then you need to take other steps to protect yourself.

Try to ensure that you can limit the time you spend in close proximity to the person concerned, or at least that you know when you will be able to escape. This has the effect of giving your subconscious a promise of a break from the barrage. Before going into their vicinity, draw an invoking Pentagram over your head and visualize its protection folding around you. Carry or wear a piece of Smoky Quartz, which will both act as a defence against your energies being drained and draw off the energies surrounding the person. Lastly, practise learning to say no to people who prefer to have others run around after them all the time.

"No one human can be everything
to everyone, all the time."

ANU

There are two deities called Anu: the Babylonian Sky God and the Celtic Ancestor Goddess.

The Babylonian Sky God Anu, sometimes known as Anum, is one of the most ancient deities, his name being found on the earliest-known inscriptions. His worship dates back at least 5,000 years. It is thought that he was also the Sumerian God An. Together with his partner the Goddess Antu he presided over the universe. He was father of the Gods and ruler of destiny, and his name literally means Expanse of Heaven. He was also creator of the stars and arbiter of the Gods and Goddesses. Antu, also called Anatu and Antum, later became associated with Ishtar, originally as her mother and later in combined form. Antu was Ruler of the Earth in her own right and Queen of the Sky through Anu. He was the father of Enlil who was also known as Bel.

The Celtic Anu is also known as Ana and Cat Ana, and is thought by some to be a form of the Sun Goddess Aine. She is an ancestor Goddess of prosperity and abundance and there is a pair of mountains in western Ireland named 'the paps of Anu' after her. Aine was said to have been able to take the form of a red horse, that none could outrun, and gave birth to a son who became a wild goose.

Interestingly, worship of both the Babylonian God and Celtic Goddess named Anu takes place in the daylight and preferably in Sunshine.

"Look for beauty not for flaws."

HEDGEROW HARVEST

Throughout late Summer and Autumn the woods
and hedgerows bear their own harvest.
There are nuts, seeds and berries galore.

Many of these would have been a welcome addition to the diet of our forebears, being gathered and stored against the chill of winter. Today, although we are not dependent on finding our food in the wild, we can still look for and reap nature's harvest. Look for Blackberries, Beechnuts, Sweet Chestnuts, Hazel Nuts, Crab Apples and Sunflower heads in seed. If you are lucky you may also find occasional Apples, Pears, Plums and other fruits which have 'escaped' and can be found in the wild. If you are knowledgeable you might also collect Mushrooms, Red- and Blackcurrants too. You may well have other things to add to your harvest if you have planted and grown your own. Other fruits such as Quince, Elderberry and Sloes are also worth collecting for cooking and wine making, even though they may be too bitter to eat off the bush.

Where you have grown or come across a huge surplus of fallen produce, then it is often worth collecting extra to take home for freezing, bottling or drying as appropriate, or to feed the birds when the winter comes. However, do not pick a surplus from bush or tree, nor take everything you find on the ground, as this will be the source of food for the wildlife around. If you have grown herbs outside then this is the time to pick and dry the leaves as few will over-winter successfully.

*"Fresh air is a better
seasoning than any other."*

LAPIS LAZULI

**Lapis Lazuli is a beautiful deep blue stone with
golden flecks of pyrites running through it.**

It has long been a jewel of the Gods, royalty, worship and magic; its use
being known for over 5,000 years. In ancient Sumer it was carved with
representations of the Gods into seals. In China it was used as an offering to the Gods and it is one of the eight treasures of Buddhism. In
Ancient Egypt Lapis Lazuli was closely associated with the Gods and
sacred to Nuit and Isis. Ra was said to have hair of Lapis Lazuli, and talismans and amulets were often formed from it. Ground Lapis Lazuli provides the pigment ultramarine and was also used as eyeshadow, almost
certainly for Ritual as well as cosmetic purposes.

Magically Lapis Lazuli is associated with healing, joy, love, courage,
protection and psychic ability. It was thought to increase all powers of
sight; wearing it being thought to strengthen the eyes. Also wear Lapis
Lazuli to protect the eyes in bright or artificial light. This is not restrict-
ed to the physical plane; you can place a piece of the stone on your third
eye to awaken psychic powers. Warmed Lapis Lazuli has long been
placed over swellings to reduce pain and inflammation. A person with
any kind of sickness should hold a magically-empowered piece of the
stone to enhance the body's natural ability to heal itself. A necklace made
of Lapis Lazuli beads is worn as a protection, especially in the case of
young children, when it is thought to also enhance health and growth.

*"Take pride in your every
achievement, however small."*

THYME

**Common Thyme is one of the basic store
cupboard herbs, and is used to flavour meat,
fish, sauce, soup, casseroles and more.**

Thyme also has a long history as a medicinal herb. The oil is rubbed in to ease all manner of aches and pains including rheumatism. Added to hot water the vapour is inhaled to help soothe coughs, chest complaints and eases the onset of colds. Used as a gargle it will ease sore throats and inflammations of the mouth and gums. Thyme tea aids the whole digestive system, and is especially helpful in cases of trapped wind which afflicts those recovering from immobilizing illnesses. The leaves contain thymol which is a powerful antiseptic, so a solution of Thyme is useful in bathing, and even applied to dressings for all manner of wounds and skin complaints. It also acts as a deodorant. Thyme has long been associated with death, being planted on graves, and it is possible that this is linked to its early use in embalming. Bees are highly attracted to Thyme so plant it to encourage these garden workers.

Magically Thyme is used in spells for health, healing, sleep, love and purification. Burn Thyme in the sickroom to cleanse the air and to aid sleep and healing. Thyme and Lavender pillows have long been used to aid sleep, and will also help to develop psychic powers. The ancient Greeks used to burn it in the temple to purify the air, and today we use it prior to Ritual for the same purpose. It is said that if you wear Thyme you will be able to see fairies.

"Young people are old ones in training."

ELEMENT SYMBOLS

Balance of the Elements is
one of the keys to the Craft.

To remind us of this, and to welcome the energies of the Elements into the Circle, we place symbols of them on our Altar. Witches who regularly work magic will often have elemental symbols around the room they work in, or generally around the house.

Air is usually represented by incense on the Altar, as loose incense burnt on charcoal in a Censer or Thurible, or as cone or stick incense. Fire is represented by a lighted candle. Water is a small dish of water, perhaps with an Asperger to sprinkle it around the Circle. Earth is usually represented by salt, although an Altar Pentagram will also serve. Most Witches will leave the symbols on the Altar, but in some Coven work each symbol is taken from the Altar as the Element is invoked and carried around the Circle clockwise, before being placed in the appropriate Quarter; Air in the east, Fire in the South, Water in the West and Earth in the North, prior to working.

Many Witches also carry a small portable version of the Altar with its own elemental symbols: a feather for Air, a crystal for Fire, a shell for Water and a stone or small piece of wood for Earth. All these are wrapped in a small cloth which can then be used as the Altar surface. Of course you can always select other objects which represent the Elements to you. At least one Witch I know has a small bracelet with beads in the elemental colours which she wears when working magic.

"Only you can put heart into your life."

GODS OF THE SEA

For as long as people have lived beside, and ventured
out upon, the sea there have been Sea Gods deemed
responsible for creating the waves and who, if not
treated with respect, could rise up and take both
ships at sea and homes along the shore. They
were also responsible for the bounty of the sea.

Some of these remain known to us through classical mythology, like the
Greek Poseidon and Roman Neptune. Just a few of the others who are
less well known include: Tamm, a fierce sea God first of the Babylonians
and later of the Egyptians; Dagon the Phoenician Sea God, not to be
confused with Dagan, their God of agriculture; Proteus, an early Greek
form who, if caught, would prophesy. Interestingly, the Greek Oceanus
was not a God of the seas, but of the great river which girdles the universe
and gave birth to all waters, without becoming part of them. The
Scandinavian God Aegir would rise above the waves to capture ships.
Agwe is the Haitian sea God. The Celtic Manannan, or Manannan Mac
Lir, was the Irish and Manx God of the sea, the Isle of Man being named
after him. His Welsh equivalent is Manawyddan, who is not the same as
Dylan son of Arianrhod, who was known as Son of the Wave.

Whilst there would have been Gods of the Sea at almost every point
where mankind interacted with the waters, the names of most of these
have been, sadly, lost to us today. When you find yourself by the waters,
take a moment to meditate on the sea Gods and make a small offering in
their honour.

"Magical people do magical things."

ENSURING RETURN
TO A PLACE

Our lives today are far more
mobile than those of our ancestors.

We may move, not only from one dwelling to another, but from one town or even country to another. One of the effects of this is knowing that we may not be the only ones in the market for any particular property. Having myself moved a number of times I know how stressful it can be to find somewhere you want to live and be unsure of whether your application will be successful. When house hunting, take a small silver coin. When you have found the right place, circle the property clockwise once and then hide this coin in the earth as close as possible to the entrance of your chosen home. Ensure that no-one else knows of this; it must remain a secret. Then pick a small sprig of a plant growing close to the entrance and keep this with you until you have moved in.

We also travel for pleasure, to visit new places or catch up with friends. In our travels there are some places for which we develop a deep affection, almost amounting to a need to revisit. In some cases these are the homes of our spirit; this does not mean that we must live there, but that we will want to go back. If you identify such a place then make sure you can visit at the Full Moon. Go out in the Moonlight and bury in the ground a blue and purple glass bead and some honey. The next day, walk the boundary and drop 9 grains of rice as you go.

"Tell the people you
care for that you do.

HOPS

Hops have been a key constituent
in the production of beer since Viking times.

But Hops have many other uses. The stems are used in Sweden to create rough cloth, and also paper. The young shoots were eaten as a vegetable by the ancient Greeks. The leaves and flower heads produce brown dye. The fruit, or cones, of the female which are used in brewing are also steeped in hot water, which is used as a tonic to improve the appetite and as a digestive. At one time a cup of Hop tea taken daily was thought to produce good health and prolong life.

Strictly speaking Hops belong to the stinging nettle family and as such are in fact relatively easy to grow. Their historic susceptibility to aphids is easily solved if you 'import' some ladybirds as pest controls. Plant Hops in the ground or in deep tubs and give them wires or supports to grow along and they take off at a considerable pace. They can be trained up walls, into arches, or if you have enough you can make a semi-sheltered outdoor sitting area. The scent of Hops in flower is relaxing and quite soporific. Indeed Hop pillows are making a comeback as a really effective alternative solution to insomnia.

Hops are often used in healing incenses and are incorporated in sachets for household protection. Strings of dried Hops, often seen today as decoration in restaurants and bars, were thought to drive out evil spirits, dispel all bad humour and encourage liveliness of energy. Give chains of Hops as a blessing on a new home.

"Practise being kind on yourself."

METAL MAGIC

**Whether we work skyclad or robed we remove metal
from our bodies and clothes before our workings.**

This is because metals have their own properties and spheres of influence, and as we cannot always be sure of the content of many metallic items, we don't want, or need, unintended influences affecting our magic. One of the easiest ways of using metals is to wear or hold the appropriate kind and visualize the outcome you seek taking place.

Here are some of the most commonly used metals. **Gold** – ruled by the Sun and associated with the God; used in spells for power, money, success and wisdom. **Silver** – ruled by the Moon and the Goddess; used in spells for peace, protection, love, dreams and psychic powers. **Aluminium** – ruled by Mercury; used to enhance mental abilities, for travel protection and in image and mirror magic. **Brass** – ruled by the Sun; used in spells for healing, money and protection. **Copper** – ruled by Venus; used for harnessing and directing energy, for spells involving luck, love, healing and money. **Iron** – ruled by Mars; strongly protective and defensive, used for healing and grounding. **Lead** – ruled by Saturn; used in divination, defence and protection. **Pyrite** – ruled by Mars; used in spells for luck and money. **Tin** - ruled by Jupiter; used for divination, luck and money.

Traditionally, Mercury was used but it is highly poisonous, being absorbed through the skin and accumulating within the body, so is best left alone. Its closest counterpart Aluminium is safe to handle, although it is worth remembering it is recognized as being unsafe for contact with food.

"Surprise other road users by being polite."

LETTERS

Although the writing of letters by hand is a
dying art, it is worth preserving. A handwritten
letter is far more personal than one typed or emailed.

There are many traditions associated with letters. A love letter should always be written in ink; pencil means the writer's affections are likely to fade. Typed, it means the writer is trying to keep a distance. A typed envelope is worse, meaning the relationship will soon end. Should letters cross in the post it means a misunderstanding or quarrel is due. A love letter without a stamp, or unsealed, means the affair is cooling. To ensure your love will feel kindly about you, place 3 lavender seeds in the envelope, and never post one on a Sunday. If the affair is at an end tear the letters up, do not burn them, or your next relationship will fare badly.

I cannot leave the subject of letters without mentioning 'chain letters'. These come in two main forms: fun ones where the chain is intended to share information, jokes or suchlike, and those which demand money and threaten dire consequences if the chain is broken. If you choose to take part in the former, fine, I've taken part in a very enjoyable one myself. Should you receive one of the latter I strongly advise that you break the chain. If you are concerned about the consequences, the following will send any bad luck back to the originator. Take the letter and tear it up, pour salt and urine or vinegar over the pieces, and bury it on a piece of waste land.

"Never trust your secrets to a computer,
they have no morals!"

THE WITCHES' RUNES

The Witches' Runes are a traditional tool of divination for Witches.

They are usually made from 8 flattish pebbles with the symbols hand-painted on one side, but can be made from small circles of wood. These are probably the easiest of the tools of divination to make for yourself, as well as to learn and understand. They are used to answer particular questions rather than for a whole life reading. The Runes are gently dropped by the person seeking the reading, from cupped hands onto a cloth and any which are face down are discarded. The remainder are read with those nearest the subject, the leading runes, being the ones of most significance to the question being asked, and those near to one another influencing each other.

The 8 symbols which make up the Witches Runes are as follows: a golden-rayed Sun – the male principle, success, honour, fame and expansion. A silver crescent Moon – the female principle, conception, childbirth, change within the month. Two pink interlocking rings – romance, love, marriage, partnership. Two red crossed spears – strife, quarrels, healing after accident or illness. A blue reverse S, the curling wave – those close to you, relatives, travel and journeys. Three birds, one each in red, white and blue – unexpected news, documents, writing, major life changes. A yellow ear of corn – money, luck, prosperity, social advancement, plenty. A black rune with a white H or # marked on it – change, fate, reversals and sometimes misfortune.

"Counting chickens is for poultry farmers."

HAIR

*If there's one thing which is true about hair,
it is that almost everyone, sooner or later, will
become unhappy with theirs. It will be too long,
short, straight, curly, the wrong colour or not enough!*

Fortunately, today most of these conditions can be changed with cosmetics. For our ancestors, however, the hair you had was what you had mostly to live with, and was often considered significant. Red hair indicated a fiery temper, and was the sign of a Witch. Dark hair indicated strength whilst fair hair was thought to indicate timidity and weakness. Even today blond hair is often thought to suggest a lack of intellect. Curly and unruly hair indicated an outgoing but frivolous nature, while straight hair indicated seriousness, but if it hung lankly then it indicated cunning. If the hair grows to a point over the forehead, the widow's peak, it is said to indicate someone who will outlive their partner and was also said to indicate a Witch.

Hair on a man's chest was significant, being considered in most of the world as a sign of strength. Indeed, the Native Americans claim that a man with no chest hair is not to be trusted. However, one who is very hairy is unlikely to be faithful! Similarly a bushy beard was a sign of virility. Hair on the arms and the backs of the hands was a sign of wealth. For either sex losing your hair was considered a sign of a decline in fortunes, although in some parts of the world actual baldness was considered a sign of virility.

*"Happiness can be found in
enjoying what you have."*

THE BADGER

**Badgers live in woodland and on the boundaries of
farmland and, being nocturnal, are rarely seen.**

They are substantial creatures nearly 3 feet (1m) in length, covered with
coarse grey fur with distinctive black and white stripes on the head and
throat. I have been privileged to meet one, as it had become acclimatized
to humans after being hand-reared. As it literally galloped across the
ground and flung itself at me, I was surprised by its sheer physical power.
Badgers are communal animals, living together in extended families in
large sets dug into the earth. Badgers are omnivorous but mostly eat
worms, slugs and suchlike. Contrary to folklore it now seems that badgers do not pass bovine tuberculosis to cattle, it is the other way around.
It is illegal in this country to harm a badger, although badger watching is
an enjoyable pastime. Badgers' teeth used to be highly prized by gam-
blers as they were thought to make it impossible to lose a bet!

Because the badger is active at twilight and in the dark it is a good
guide for otherworld journeys and meditations. Visualize yourself setting
off across the fields at dusk, heading towards a small bank on the out-
skirts of a wood. When you reach your destination, sit down and wait for
the badger to come to you. When he does, follow him into the wood and
he will lead you to a clearing where you will be able to seek answers to
your questions. These may take the form of a person, marks on the trees
or ground, or a stone, which you later have to interpret.

*"Effective complaining
is a worthy art to learn."*

SEVEN STEPS TO
A HEALTHIER WITCH

First Learn to stand tall and straight and you will look and feel better. Once a day remove your shoes and stand with your back to a flat wall. Your heels, bottom, back, head, shoulders and arms should all touch the wall. Now, without rising on your toes stretch up as tall as you can.

Second Develop a natural rather than chemical scent. Switch from scented soaps, antiperspirants and deodorants to unscented ones, or use a deodorant stone. Use only a small amount of a very light scent, or an essential oil. Remember, if you can smell your scent, it's too strong.

Third Tired and sore feet affect the way you look and react towards others, so pamper them: remove dead skin, apply a lotion, keep the nails neat and wear shoes which really fit and are comfortable.

Fourth Practise smiling often, with your eyes as well as your mouth. It can help to imagine you have secret good news. Check this in the mirror, as you don't want to look like an idiot!

Fifth Ensure your hair is clean, shiny and well cut. A good cut saves a lot of daily fiddling and shiny hair looks a lot better than tortured and starched hair!

Sixth Drink lots of plain water, at least 8 glasses a day. Water cleanses the whole system and gives clear eyes and skin.

Seventh Go for a short, brisk walk every day, whatever the weather. It improves the cardio-vascular and respiratory systems, tones and strengthens the legs and gives you time to clear your head and focus your mind. Use this time to notice the natural world around you.

"Relieve stress by reading humour."

WATER MEDITATION

The Equinox marks the start of Autumn,
which is associated with the Element of Water,
that of our feelings and emotions, and is one
of the hardest to come to terms with.

I frequently find myself reminding people that there is no such thing as 'wrong emotions'. Your feelings, whatever they are, are yours, and are not easy to control. However, what we can control is how we express our feelings and whether we let them get in the way of our lives. To help us it is often a good idea to take a little time to explore our feelings, to 'wallow' in them as my mother would have said!

Reserve the bathroom for a quiet time when you will not be disturbed. Decorate it attractively, with blue candles, incense or burning oils, and perhaps even flowers. Run a warm bath and add a few sprigs of Lavender, Thyme, Chamomile and Jasmine; tie them into a clean flannel if you don't want bits. Also add about ½ teaspoonful of blue food colouring to the water. Take with you 2 palm-sized stones, one dark and one light in colour. Completely immerse yourself 3 times. Then take the stones one in each hand. Close your eyes and think through the things you feel strongly about in your life. As you hold the stones, place the negative parts in the dark stone and the positives in the lighter. After you have filed your emotions in this way immerse yourself 3 more times. Later, place the light stone in a prominent place, and bury the dark one deep in the ground to take away the negativity.

"Let the raindrops wash away your troubles."

AUTUMN EQUINOX

Autumn is well-named Fall, as it is the time
when greens give way to a glorious array of yellows,
golds, oranges and reds before the wind takes the
leaves to the ground. Autumn is the season of
winds, the harbingers of the storms of Winter.
It is the time of harvest and plenty, when the
crops ripen, before the hardship of Winter.

Even if we do not tend the land to produce our own food it is a time of
harvest. This is the time when we should look to what we have achieved:
the tasks and projects we have completed, the successes we have had.
Even where not all has turned out as hoped for, there is often much which
has been achieved. As the farmer is setting aside seed for next year, so we
too can sort out the seeds of ideas for new things to begin. Much like we
did in the Spring this is a time for sorting through our lives, discarding
that which is finished and preparing to start afresh.

Take time to consider and sort through your life. Celebrate your own
harvest, whether it is a sprig of herb grown on the windowsill or a friend
you have helped through a bad time, and mark every achievement great
and small. For each collect a seed or a nut and create a string of them.
Sunflower seeds are good for this. Paint each in a colour which reminds
you of the good things of your year and place it in a prominent place
where you can remind yourself of the positive aspects of life.

*"Your rights are no less or
more than those around you."*

DRUMS

Apart from the human voice, drums and percussion instruments are probably the earliest forms of music making.

Mankind has been using them since time immemorial in Ritual and magic. Drumming has also been used in many communities and belief systems for meditation and to raise spirits. Even the simplest rhythmic beat creates vibrations which resonate through the body and the earth, as well as creating sound. Drumming is not only the earliest form of music making of our species; it is also one of the earliest of the individual: give any small child a wooden spoon and an empty tub and you will soon hear drumming! Additionally, percussive sound is used by a great many other creatures: the rabbit drums with the hind legs to warn of danger, the song of the cricket is also percussive.

In the Craft drumming is one of the more popular musical ways of enhancing Ritual, and is often used as a technique for raising energy together with chanting and dancing. It is frequently employed at the Summer and Winter solstices to welcome the Sun. Whilst it is not necessary to be highly skilled to drum, it is helpful to have some ability to keep time and maintain a rhythm! There are very few people who cannot master this with a little practice and perseverance. Of course drums are not the only percussive instruments; there are many others which can be purchased, made or improvised, all of which can enhance your Craft work.

"Understanding how another feels helps you to know why they act."

SUN IN LIBRA

Libra is an Air sign, relating to the world of thought,
ideas, communication and humanity. It is also a
Cardinal sign bringing eagerness, initiative, action
and impatience.

Librans are generally self-expressive, communicative, mentally alert and extrovert. They tend to be charming, easy-going, diplomatic and compromising. They are happiest in harmonious company, preferring to conform and to avoid conflict and dissension. Librans are typified by the scales; they like to weigh things in the balance. They are intelligent and capable of seeing all sides of an issue, however this can lead to indecisiveness, and sometimes to misunderstandings through doing what they think others expect. Librans enjoy bringing people together and often have a strong artistic or creative streak. They are acutely perceptive about those they love and are often forgiving of faults, whether real or perceived. They tend to bottle up their feelings for fear of 'upsetting the balance'. On the negative side they can lack self-confidence, be fault-finding, indecisive, frivolous and shallow.

Whilst the Sun is in their sign Librans should be particularly wary of their tendency to compare both themselves and others to some kind of ideal, as this is bound to lead to disappointment. It is a good time for them to express themselves artistically. Those of other signs will also find this a good time for artistic endeavours, social activities and for considering decisions which involve many positive and negative components.

*"A balanced life is one with
time for yourself."*

HARVEST DRINKS

Wine- and beer-making have long been part of our
heritage and the Craft. Not only are they used in
celebrations but often form an offering to the Gods or
the land. These recipes both celebrate the harvest.

Harvest Mead: Take the flesh, rind and juice, but not the white pith, of 3
Oranges and 2 Lemons. Add 3 or 4 chopped up Apples, 3 Cinnamon
sticks, 3 Cardamoms, 12 Cloves, 3 Nutmegs and 8 pints (4.5l) water. Boil
and simmer for 30 minutes. Strain and add 4 pints (2.25l) cold water.
Leave until it is only just warm. Add a blend of 1oz (25g) fresh or wine
yeast in a small amount of tepid water and 4–6 lb (2–3kg) honey. Place in
a sterilized demijohn or wine bucket and leave, in a warm dark place,
until all fermentation has ceased. This can take up to 6 months. Pour into
sterilized bottles with cork stoppers (in case further fermentation takes
place). Leave another month before drinking.

Country Cider: Place about 12 lb (6kg) of washed and roughly chopped
Apples in a large wine bucket and mash them to a pulp. This a good job
for when you're feeling annoyed with someone! Add 8 pints (4.5l) warm
water, 2 lb (1kg) honey and a blend of 1oz (25g) fresh or wine yeast in a
small amount of tepid water. Stir well and cover. Stir daily for at least 2
weeks, then strain into a demijohn. Place in a warm dark place and allow
to ferment. Once the bubbles have stopped rising, bottle in strong jars
with corks and keep in a cool place for a couple of months.

*"Try new things, you
might find you like them."*

ELM

**In times past the Elm was thought
to be the tree where Elves made their
home, hence it was called Elven.**

It was said that if you visited an Elm at midnight on midsummer's eve then you might see the Elves, but be sure to take a gift lest they spirit you away, or bring you misfortune. The Elm was the traditional wood for the Maypole. It was thought that Elm would protect from lightning and it was incorporated into many churches to protect them. The wood of the Elm is very hard, close-grained, free from knots and not likely to split, and because of this it was used in ship building, for coffins, wheels, pumps, water-pipes and to make highly prized furniture. The bark was also used to make rope and twisted into mats. Medicinally, the Elm was used as a worm treatment, and water found in the galls of the tree was used as a beauty treatment for hair and skin. A short piece of Elm was carried to attract love.

The Elm holds an important lesson for us: Dutch Elm disease has ravaged the Elm in many parts of the world, all but wiping it out in some countries. It is the import and export of plants and plant materials which can play a significant role in the spread of disease and even the endangerment of species. We can each play our part in helping protect the world by not transferring plant products ourselves. Also, by not purchasing things made from them, unless we are sure they come from sustainable and well-managed sources.

"Learn to see the wood and the trees."

BUTTERFLIES AND MOTHS

Butterflies and moths were closely associated with death and dying.

In many parts of the world both white moths and butterflies were thought to be the souls of the dead, possibly those of your own departed watching over you. It was also thought that if the first butterfly you see is yellow then it presages illness in the family. Should the first butterfly be white it indicates a prosperous year to come. To see 3 butterflies on the same leaf was said to indicate death whilst many moths flying around the house indicate fever. Moths were thought to be Witches, and to see a great number indicated that the Witches had you in mind.

A somewhat macabre form of curse used to involve leaving a lighted candle near an open window at midnight on the dark of the Moon, on the side of the house facing your 'enemy's' home. Extinguish all other lights and depart to bed. If in the morning there is a dead moth trapped in the residue of the wax, this should then be made into a new candle, in such a way that the moth's corpse will burn before it is seen, and given to the person who you wished to harm. But you should be careful as, if your cause is not just, then the curse will rebound, possibly in a form of the Law of Threefold Return. Personally I do not recommend trying this, not only because of the Wiccan Rede, but also because leaving a lighted candle by an open window is virtually a guaranteed way of starting a fire!

*"Laugh with your friends
but at your enemies."*

THE FATES

Another form of the Triple Goddess can be seen in the three Fates of ancient Greece.

These are the spinners of destiny, who manipulate the threads of the cloth of life and death to ensure that each entity is guided in their passage through life. Originally the three were one, called Moira or Moirae. Sometimes they were seen as two: Life and Death. But later, they assumed their triple personality. Clotho was the spinner; she held the distaff and spun the thread of life. Lachesis was the measurer, who weaved the thread as it came off the spindle, into the overall pattern of life. Atropos, the inevitable, cut the thread with her shears, and was responsible for the summoning of Death at the appropriate time. The Fates had authority over even the Gods and could not be turned from their purpose.

In some legends the Fates were the daughters of Themis, the lawgiver, and were given the task of trying to ensure that people fulfilled their destiny to complete the planned pattern of life. In other legends they were the daughters of Nyx the Night Queen, herself the first daughter of Chaos. Nyx also gave birth to Erebus and mated with him to give birth to Day, called Hemera, as well as Age and Death.

Even today many small Rituals are carried out to appease the Fates: touching wood, crossing fingers, not speaking about things which have yet to happen. All of these are intended to avoid the Fates noticing, lest they should remember that they were not intended.

"You can't change the past,
but you can decide which bits to remember."

WOOD

Trees and their Wood have long had special meaning.

Trees unite and balance the Elements with their roots in the Earth, taking up Water, and their branches in the Air reaching to the Fire of the Sun. For early man trees provided the Wood which gave shelter, primitive tools and heat. Indeed it is probable that seeing a tree struck by lightning and catching fire was a magical thing to them. Trees gave foods, medicines, treatments, dyes, rope, mats and much more.

Early man also became aware of the energies of different types of trees, and the seasons in which they came into their power. It was felt that trees had spirits of their own, which should be treated with respect. This knowledge probably came from the Druids, who also believed that trees channelled the energy flow of the land itself. To the ancient Chinese Wood was one of their five Elements, together with Fire, Earth, Metal and Water. To all of this we can add our 'modern' knowledge that trees are in fact the lungs of the earth, producing the oxygen on which we depend and, helping to cleanse the atmosphere of some of the pollutants we emit.

In the Craft today we still treat Wood with respect. Whilst we use it for our Wands and Staffs, we take only that which is permitted or fallen; we do not waste or squander it. We tend the trees that are in our care and make offerings to the Goddess and the God for the gifts they give us.

> *"Listen for whispers of wisdom
> in the music of the trees."*

BLACKBERRY

**Whilst the Blackberry or bramble is not the most
popular plant in the garden it does have many uses.**

The ancient Greeks and Romans considered the berries a sure cure for
gout. It was long thought that to eat young shoots of the plant would
secure loose teeth. The leaves are used to speed the cure of burns and
scalds, and will relieve sore eyes. Dried leaves and fruit also provide a remedy for diarrhoea. An arch of Bramble was considered to have great healing powers for people, especially children, and cattle who passed through
it. This was said to be effective in cases of hernia, boils, rheumatism and
whooping cough. Many of these tales say you should pass through the
arch three times, going as near as possible in an East to West direction.

The Blackberry has long been considered a magical plant and used in
Ritual as well as spells. Place a Bramble on the Altar when working protective or defensive magic. Bury a silver coin under a Bramble arch when
the berries are ripening and at the New Moon to attract wealth. Having
it grow near the house is protective, which may be of some comfort if you
can't rid the garden of it!

Kittens born on 29 September are called Blackberry kittens and, if
tortoiseshell, were thought to be very lucky. However, all animals born
on this day were thought to be badly behaved and it is considered
unlucky to pick the fruit after this date.

*"Books are where things are explained to you,
life is where they aren't."*

J. Barnes

IVY MONTH

The Celts considered the Ivy a 'tree' of power,
able to overcome even the mighty Oak,
because it can bind, constrict and strangle.

It is also a tree of warning: dreams, visions of it, or even large amounts in
your area indicate that you may be taking a wrong path or contemplating
a wrong direction in life, and it is time to review your life and motivations, and perhaps seek a new direction. It is a plant of persistence, not
just for the ancient Celts. A quaint 19th-century story tells of an Ivy in
Oxford which penetrated the wall of a wine cellar, removed the cork from
a bottle of port and drank the contents. The bottle was later found con-
gested with the roots of the plant!

Ivy leaves made up the wreath of the Roman God Bacchus and were
often hung outside inns to advertise their trade. It was thought that wearing a circle of Ivy around the head would prevent intoxication. Drinking
from a bowl of Ivy wood was said to be a cure for drunkenness. A wreath
of Ivy was given to newly-weds as a symbol of fidelity. A young girl
would carry an Ivy leaf in order to meet her future husband. Should a
man gather 10 Ivy leaves at Halloween, discard one and sleep with the
other 9 under his pillow he will dream of his future love. To dream of
spirits, place an Ivy leaf on each corner of your pillow. Ivy is magically
linked with Holly and it used to be forbidden to bring Ivy into a church
because of its Pagan associations.

*"For really fast food,
eat fruit."*

THE OWL

Owls have long been associated with Witches and the
Craft, probably because of their great eyes, nocturnal
habits and eerie calls, especially that of the Screech
Owl, said by some to be the cry of a damned soul.

It is hardly surprising that the Barn or Ghost Owl should be considered
supernatural to anyone who has seen its silvery glide across the land. In
the Mojave tradition it was said that the souls of those who were not cre-
mated became night owls.

Owls are linked to the Goddess in many traditions, especially to the
aspect of Crone or Wise one: Blodewedd, Celtic Goddess and wife created from flowers for the king Llew Llaw Gyffes, was turned into an Owl
after arranging his death at the hands of her lover. Hecate is often depicted
accompanied by an Owl. Holzweibel, one of the Buschfrauen of central
Europe who live in the woods, who guard the trees and those who obey
their three rules: never to put caraway in bread, never to pull bark from
trees and never to tell dreams. Huitaca, Moon Goddess of the joy of life to
the Chibcha, residents of what has become Colombia, was also known as
Owl Woman. She followed her puritanical rival Bochia, undoing all he
preached. Marinette, night Goddess and Screech Owl sorceress of the
Haitian voudoun, searches the woodlands seeking offerings left by her followers. Pamphile, Greek sorceress who could summon the Moon and
became an Owl to fly the night skies.

Should you be lucky enough to find an Owl's feather, place it on
your Altar when working for knowledge and wisdom.

"Find and hold a happy thought to go to sleep with."

DAYS OF THE WEEK

Each day of the week has its own energies and influences.

In the Craft we work with these to enhance our magic: Monday is for dreams, fertility and divination; Tuesday for the resolution of conflict and for defence; Wednesday for travel, business, knowledge and exams; Thursday for wealth, ambition and career; Friday for friendship, romance and self-respect; Saturday for binding and banishing; Sunday for energy, honour and results.

There are many other traditional attributions. An old rhyme gives attributes for children born on each day of the week: "*Monday's child is fair of face, Tuesday's child is full of grace, Wednesday's child is full of woe, Thursday's child has far to go, Friday's child is loving and giving, Saturday's child works hard for its living. But the child that is born on the Sabbath day is blithe and bonny, happy and gay.*" In New England, America, each day is held to bring its own attributes: "*Monday for health, Tuesday for wealth, Wednesday the best of all, Thursday for losses, Friday for crosses, And Saturday no luck at all.*"

Sunday and Monday are named after the Sun and Moon, with Saturday being named after both the God and the planet Saturn. Wednesday, Thursday and Friday are named after the Norse deities Wodin, Thor and Freya. Tuesday also has a Norse derivation, from the God Tyr, whose name in Old English became Tiw.

"Every day is a good one to remind yourself how wonderful you are."

GARLIC

Garlic was given to horses and warriors to
confer strength and courage prior to battle,
and was thought to repel the blows of the enemy.

It was planted in the thatch over the door to protect the home and repel thieves. Today we plant it in hanging baskets or tubs by the door for the same purpose. Alternatively, garlic bulbs in the windows keep negative energies at bay. Sailors carried it against shipwreck. Brides would carry a piece for good fortune in their marriage and a clove was placed under children's pillows to protect them whilst asleep. To deter insects from entering the house, rub garlic around the edges of all doors and windows. If you are badly troubled by insects sprinkle garlic powder on the floors to drive them out, but beware: it will smell!

It is used medicinally in a number of ways. A garlic solution can be used as an antiseptic and to wash or dress wounds. Garlic syrup was used to treat many respiratory complaints, from sore throat through to consumption. Certainly taking garlic helps to prevent colds and defends against winter infections, and it is an excellent aid to digestion. If you want to minimize the smell, chop rather than crush it before adding to dishes.

Garlic is sacred to Hecate and the Greeks would leave it at the crossroads as a sacrifice in her name. Place garlic on the Altar when working magic for protection, healing, and when banishing unwanted influences. Rub a clove on the skin for protection prior to working on the psychic plane.

"Buy nice cards when you see them,
then you'll have them when you need them."

THE CAULDRON

**No picture of a Witch has been complete
without a large Cauldron bubbling and
steaming away since Shakespeare's Macbeth.**

It should be remembered that the Cauldron is simply the forerunner of the saucepan. What we now consider to be a 'cauldron' used to be an everyday kitchen pot for our forebears, and would have been kept filled with steaming broth.

Today's Witches use saucepans to cook in, whether food or lotions and potions. For us the Cauldron has other meanings and uses. As with the Chalice, the Cauldron is a symbol of the Goddess. However, whereas the Chalice usually only holds wine or other drinks, the Cauldron is used to contain fire, to prevent scorching carpets or the land. Leaping such a fire is a key part of many cleansing and fertility Rites. It can also hold water to act as a dark mirror for scrying, or in water rituals. A Cauldron can represent the Cauldron of Cerridwen which has the power of giving knowledge and life, or the Cauldron of the Dagda, one of the four treasures of the Tuatha de Danann.

When seeking a Cauldron, ensure that it is made of thick metal, usually iron, as thin metal may not take the heat of even a couple of nightlights. There are two basic styles of Cauldron: the kind designed to hang over an open fire which generally has a large handle and no legs; and the kind with 3 sturdy legs which can stand on its own, keeping the heat away from whatever is underneath. The latter is more useful unless you only intend to hang it over a hearth.

"Everyone makes mistakes, but try not to repeat them."

HEMATITE

Polished Hematite is a beautiful dark silvery grey with a high shine, used in ancient times as a mirror.

Unpolished the stone is the colour of dried blood; hence its name which comes from the Greek for blood and the fact that it is also called Bloodstone. When worked Hematite leaves stains which closely resemble blood. It is also known as volcano spit and is sometimes termed Black Diamond. Hematite used to be considered a stone of mourning.

Traditionally, Hematite was used to stem bleeding by pressing it over a wound, and for the relief of headaches, sore eyes and kidney complaints; in all cases being rubbed over the affected parts. Interestingly, recently it is being magnetized and incorporated into jewellery which is worn for the relief of rheumatic and arthritic pain.

Magically, Hematite is used for protection, healing, grounding, meditation and divination. Small chips in the doors and windows of the home deter unwanted energies. A piece of Hematite under the pillow will help to ward off illness, which is especially useful if someone in the house has a contagious illness. To rid yourself of unwanted emotions, take a piece of the stone in each hand and pour your feelings into them. Then bury the stones to the North-West of your home, sprinkling a little salt over them first. To meditate with Hematite, position a piece close to a candle so that you can focus on the flame reflected on the surface. Write a question on a piece of paper and wrap it around the stone for 24 hours before using the same stone in meditation as above.

"Never criticize until you're sure you could do better."

APPLES

The Apple appears in the lore
surrounding many beliefs.

The Norse Gods were said to eat Apples from a tree in the garden of Asgard to retain their youth and strength. The Christians believe that the fruit eaten in the Garden of Eden was an Apple. The Greek God Melanion (also known as Hippomenes) used Apples to win a race against Atlanta and thereby make her his wife. The Greeks also regarded Apples as one of the fruits of Diana and this was continued by the Romans in respect of Venus. The Celts held that a branch laden with Apples would enable a person to visit the underworld, and for this reason Apples often appear on the Altar at Samhain. If you cut an Apple open across the centre you will find that the core forms a five-pointed star similar to the Pentacle.

Apples are used in spells for love, healing and, as cider, to encourage growth in the garden. Sharing an Apple which you have jointly consecrated with your partner will ensure a happy relationship, and this should be repeated at every New Moon. To encourage growth in the garden sprinkle cider (preferably still and unsweetened) onto the soil after it has been turned over. To drive out illness cut an Apple into 3 parts, rub them all over and bury the pieces separately. "An apple a day keeps the doctor away" has some truth, as eating Apples helps the liver and digestive system. Drinking Apple juice or rough cider also prevents the formation of stones. And eating one last thing at night is said to cure sleeplessness.

"Be the first to apologize
and you open the door."

THE EIGHT-FOLD PATH

Gardnerian Witchcraft refers to
eight ways of raising energy for Magic,
sometimes called the Eight-fold Path.

Meditation or concentration require exceptional focus by the sheer force of will, and usually take a considerable amount of practice to master. **Trance and astral projection** also require skill, practice and training. **Using cords to control the flow of the blood** can actually be dangerous for the unskilled. If you wish to experiment with control of blood flow then there are techniques available in Yoga which do not involve cords and are therefore less risky. **The Scourge**: repetitive use of the scourge can be used to raise power. However, many in the Craft today do not find this acceptable. Certainly it requires skill on the part of the scourger and similar effects can be achieved by holding the same position whilst rhythmic chanting and clapping take place around the subject. **Incense, wine and other aids release the spirit**: nearly all Witches are against the use of any drugs, including alcohol in Circle. Personally I feel that it is far more effective to learn to create a state of altered consciousness without them. **Chants and invocations** work very well. There are no right or wrong chants and it is best to choose the ones which work for you. Chanting is also effective for the solitary worker, unlike most of the other techniques. **Dance** is also open to the solitary and if combined with chant is very effective. **The Great Rite** is a very effective way of raising energy but works best within a practising partnership.

*"Boasting is a symptom
of insecurity."*

THE BAT

Being nocturnal Bats have long been associated with evil.

In some parts they were thought to be Witches, and one flying close to you it was said to be a Witch over-looking or trying to bewitch you. Having said that I have heard it said that Bats flying close to the house indicate that the spirits of Witches past are looking out for you. Should one fly into the house it portends death or very bad luck for someone you know. In other places the Bat is considered lucky, and carrying a Bat's bone will ensure good fortune. It used to be thought that carrying the right eye of a Bat will render a person invisible. A Bat hitting the side of a building is said to foretell rain whilst seeing them fly near the house in the early dusk means good weather is coming.

Contrary to the many beliefs, Bats do not get entangled in long hair. Experiments have proven that not only do Bats try to avoid people, but that no amount of hair will prevent one from immediately freeing itself. Furthermore, although a couple of varieties will drink the blood of animals, most Bats are vegetarian and will not bite unless provoked. In many parts of the world it is considered very unlucky to kill or harm a Bat, and could even shorten your life. This is probably just as well as many Bats are endangered and need all the protection they can get. I recommend visiting a zoo with a walk-through Bat house as a way of getting closer to these timid creatures.

"Make the most of this life;
you only get one chance at it."

LILITH

**Lilith has long been considered
one of the first Witches, and has
become the archetypal wicked Witch.**

She was represented as being the terrifying power that the Sumerians called Lamasthu and the Greeks Lamia, and is known by many other names including Baba Yaga. It is probable that Lilith was a form of the Babylonian Goddess Ninlil. Lilith was described as a night demon, with a beautiful face, luxuriant hair and great wings; however, instead of feet she had talons. In common with other demonized Deities she was reputed to steal, kill or drink the blood of babies and small children, creeping to the cradle at night.

Lilith appears in early versions of the Old Testament as the first wife of Adam, before Eve. In these tales she was created equal to Adam but refused to take the subordinate position in the relationship, notably with regard to intercourse. As a result Adam cast her aside, whereupon she went to Jehovah and tricked him into revealing his secret name of power, much as Isis had done in the earlier Egyptian story. In return she demanded that he give her wings, but it is said that he also cursed her with sterility. Perhaps this is intended to give a reason why she should harm the young. She was considered especially dangerous to infants in the first week of life, on Sabbath evenings and to those born to unmarried women, conveniently reinforcing a number of strictures on the activities of women. Certainly Lilith did not fit in with the authorized image of womanhood: she had refused to show humility and obedience to either man or God.

*"Raindrops are kisses
from the skies."*

APPLES IN LOVE DIVINATION

The Apple has long been used as a divination tool, especially in matters of love.

Young women who wish to know who they will marry should peel an Apple in one strip with a knife and cast the peel over their left shoulder at midnight. The shape the peel forms will give the initial of their future husband. It was also said that to eat an Apple, again at midnight, whilst watching in a mirror will result in seeing your future partner's reflection behind you. In some places this was only thought to work on Samhain eve. To see how someone feels about you, warm an Apple in your hands then give it to them. If they eat it then they love you.

Apple pips are also used in love divination. Place two pips on a shovel in the fire, and if both fly off in the same direction you and the person you are thinking of are destined to be together. To see which of two loves is likely to bring you happiness, name a pip for each and place them on your forehead. The one which stays in place longest will be the one who will bring you happiness. To see which direction your future love will come from squeeze an apple pip between the forefinger and thumb of your left hand (or right if you are left-handed) until it flies off, and this will tell you where they will come from. To see if your loved one is true place a pip into a fire: if it bursts then they are held to be bursting with love for you.

"Tidy and fun are
rarely compatible."

WHISTLING

Whistling has long been considered to be unlucky in certain circumstances.

Sailors believed that whistling on board ship would attract the attention of mermaids who might send fierce winds to sink it. That said, sailors in some parts believe that the right whistle can summon the right wind. Miners too had, and in some places still have, a prohibition against whistling and also singing whilst underground. It was thought that this would invite the spirits inside the earth to keep the miners underground by causing a cave-in. In the theatre whistling is said to foretell doom to the production, and even today you might find yourself asked to leave, not being allowed to return until you had turned around three times and someone else had entered. The expression *"A Whistling woman and a crowing hen, are neither fit for God nor men"* can be found in many parts of Britain and America. There is some discussion as to whether this bodes ill for men in particular or mankind as a whole! Both my father and I were forbidden to whistle of a morning as my mother asserted, quite rightly, that it would bring rain.

Whistling, like other forms of vocal sound, can be used in the Craft as a way of invoking the Quarters, and of raising energy. To invoke the Quarters you will need to experiment and work out which note, for you, best conjures up the image of the Element in question. This is usually best done with your eyes closed until you find the note which gives you the colour and feeling of each Element.

"Be yourself, it's impossible to live as someone else."

BLACK

The primitive fear of darkness and the
unknown is largely responsible for Black's
association with all things negative.

In the Craft we understand the need for balance and hence the need for darkness to balance light, we do not fear it or consider the colour to be negative. In the spectrum black absorbs all light and energy, hence for Witches it is the colour which represents the absorption, balancing and control of energy and magical power. To the ancient Egyptians black was the colour of life, being the colour of fertile soil. It is a colour of concealment, and favoured by Witches working outdoors, making it easier to fade into the background. Black makes the wearer more receptive to psychic emanations and is worn for many forms of magical working, especially divination. Black stones are likewise receptive and symbolize self-control, endurance and the harnessing of power. Linked to the earth they are grounding and stabilizing. Despite the popular image, black candles are not a sign of working evil; they are mostly used for remembrance and sometimes in banishings. Black is a colour of the Goddess as both Mother and Crone.

In this day true darkness is very hard to come by, even without a Moon. At the dead of night there may still be residual light from nearby towns, if not from street lamps. In the home there is still the standby light of the video or computer. This is a shame for we need the absence of light on a very basic level, as it helps us to rest and renew our energies.

*"Practise being happy,
and you'll soon be good at it."*

THE ROSE

The Rose has long associations with love and
romance and it has also been used medicinally
and in cosmetics; red Rose petals being
favoured in almost every case.

Rose water is soothing, cooling and lightly antiseptic. It is useful for
reducing acne, soothing sore eyes and cleansing wounds, and it used to be
taken internally for chest and lung problems. Honey of Roses, which is
rose petal extract added to Honey, is helpful for mouth and throat problems, as is a gargle of Rosehip syrup with water. Rose extract mixed in
vinegar was recommended as a compress for headaches, especially
through too much Sun. Rose oil, on its own or added to a base cream or
lotion, treats dry, chapped and roughened skin, as well as allergies.
Inhaled it can help in cases of regret, bereavement and other problems
related to the past, as well as relieving fears and worries.

Magically the Rose is sacred to the Goddess in all her aspects. It is
used in Rituals and magic for love, self-respect, friendship, emotional healing, and psychic development. Drinking Rosebud tea at night, made with
carefully collected rainwater, is said to enhance psychic ability. Place a
handful of fresh Rose petals into your bath prior to undertaking any kind
of divination. To attract love into your life consecrate and wear a necklace
of Rosehips. Carry Rose petals for protection and luck. Scatter them
around the house for a calm atmosphere, or place a few in the pillowcase
for restful sleep. Grow Roses in the garden to attract friendly spirits.

*"Life's a question of mind over matter,
you mind because you matter."*

THE HUNTER'S MOON

The Full Moon closest to Samhain is the one where the Moon is nearest to the Earth and hence appears at its largest and brightest in the sky.

Indeed, on a clear night its light is bright enough to read by. This is called the Hunter's Moon in honour of the God in his aspect of Hunter and Guardian of the Gates of Death, and as leader of the Wild Hunt.

The Wild Hunt commences at Samhain and continues throughout the winter months, in which the God as Hunter leads the host of the souls of dead warriors. The Hunt peaks at Yule when the unwary can be caught up and swept away. Some Witches perform a Ritual which echoes this. They set a course through woodland. Individuals set off one at a time with the intent of completing the course accurately, without stopping, pausing, or looking behind. An experienced Witch will summon the Spirit of the Hunt to pursue them and to try to lead them astray. Those who complete the test are said to be blessed by the Lord of the Hunt. The Wild Hunt used to be run on the night of the Hunter's Moon, rather than at Samhain, as is more common these days. This allows the run to take place separately from the festivities of the Sabbat.

Even if you don't choose to run a 'Wild Hunt', try to get outside on the night of the Hunter's Moon, raise your arms to the Moon and gaze deep into her face to feel closer to the Goddess and the God and to recharge your physical and psychic batteries.

"Use the mirror to see your good points."

HEATHER

Heather describes a family of plants,
Ericae, which bring strength and tenacity.

The scent of fresh Heather is said to be beneficial for headaches, heart complaints and nervous disorders. Honey made from the pollen helps menstrual problems. Many ancient peoples used to make Heather ale and it was also added to mead. It was, and in some places still is, also used to make thatch, ropes and brooms. It has even been polished and made into jewellery.

To the Celts Heather was associated with the passage through death into a new life, or destruction which brings something new. They also linked it to the otherworld. In Gaelic the word for Heather is *fraoch*, which means fierce and war-like. In Irish legend Fraoch was the son of the great warrior Cuchulain, born of Aoife the Warrior Queen. The tale goes on to say that Fraoch's gessa was never to tell his name, and he was killed when he challenged his father to battle.

White Heather has long been considered lucky, a tradition which some use to their advantage by gathering and selling it. It was also attributed with preventing a drunkard from drinking, and with protecting against rape and other crimes of violence. Heather is burnt on its own to conjure spirits, and with ferns to bring about rain. Lying on a bed of Heather is said to induce psychic powers and otherworld experiences. Burn Heather after cleansing to prepare the way for the new to begin; this is especially useful when moving into a new home, or starting a major undertaking.

"It's simpler to remain silent,
than to try to get the words back."

SMUDGE STICKS

Smudge sticks are usually short, fat bundles of herbs, tightly tied, which can be lit to produce a form of incense.

They may be a single herb, a combination, or include other ingredients such as resin. Smudge sticks are primarily used in personal workings to cleanse, purify or bring about an altered state of consciousness. It is thought they originated in the Native American tradition, where they were used to invoke spirits and enable journeys to the spirit world.

The most common ingredients in smudge sticks are Sage, Thyme, Rosemary, Lavender; indeed any woody herbs which will burn slowly and steadily. There may be resins such as Copal or Frankincense, or a few drops of essential oils such as Jasmine or Sandalwood. To make your own, gather the herb with stems about 6 to 8 inches (15 to 20 cm) long. Spread them out in a warm, dry place until they are thoroughly dried, as moist herbs will give off far too much smoke. Bind the stems tightly together in a bundle with threads, around their lower third to half. Your bundle needs to be dense, otherwise it will burn too quickly. You may like to experiment with different herbs and tying techniques before you find the one(s) which work(s) for you. When you are ready to use your smudge stick, light the top then blow out the flames, so that it smoulders and smokes. Waft the smoke around your body from head to toes to cleanse and then from toes to head to work your spell. Some people like to enhance the movement of the smoke with a feather.

"Regret is a waste of time,
but repair is worthwhile."

YARROW

Yarrow is a highly prolific plant,
considered a weed by most gardeners.

However, if you have the space it is worth cultivating a small patch. You can prevent it taking over by removing the flowers before they seed, although you will have to be diligent! Some of its folk names give an idea of how highly it used to be prized: Soldier's Woundwort, Knight's Milfoil, Herbe Militaris, Bloodwort, Staunchweed, Sanguinary. Others give an indication of its association with the Craft: Devil's Nettle, Devil's Plaything. Yarrow was used to stop bleeding and to dress wounds to speed healing: the leaves were rolled up and inserted to stop nose bleeds. Conversely, it was made into a poultice and placed over the nose and sinuses to induce a nosebleed to relieve severe headaches. Such poultices can also be used to ease bleeding piles. Yarrow tea is excellent for heavy colds and cleanses the urinary system. Yarrow was used to make beer which was thought to be more intoxicating than that made from hops.

Magically Yarrow is associated with Venus and is used in workings for love, courage and protection, and to develop psychic powers. Carry Yarrow for protection and to attract friendship and love, and to regain contact with lost relatives. Place it under an external doormat to deter unwanted callers. A tea made from Yarrow flowers is said to improve psychic powers. Burn dried Yarrow leaves to cleanse the house or make the stems into a smudge stick to exorcize negativity from a person. If a couple eat Yarrow at their wedding it is said to ensure 7 years of happiness.

*"No one ever died from
too much sleep."*

OPALS

Opals with their beautiful iridescence have long been
considered magical, and their flashing colours were
thought to reflect the wearer's mood. The Opal
contains all the colours of other stones and can be
employed in their place if correctly charged.

Around the middle of the 19th century, Opals became thought of as
unlucky, especially in engagement rings. This may be due to their fragili-
ty, as if an Opal is soaked in water, perhaps immersed in the bath or washing up, it may fracture or crack. It is also thought that Sir Walter Scott's
early 19th-century novel Anne of Geierstein may have led to the stone's
poor reputation. In this, a half-mortal, half-fairy woman disappears after
holy water is sprinkled on her Opal. However, as Opals have been used
for around 5,000 years I think we can disregard this recent superstition,
although do take care not to get them too wet. Also, do not expose them
to too much heat as this will also make them brittle.

Opals are energizing stones, so wear them when your personal
resources, physical or otherwise, are flagging. They also confer protection on the Astral plane. To enhance psychic powers wear Opal earrings
or a circlet with an Opal set in the centre. Opals were traditionally given
to ensure the safe return of travellers and as a token of love. Opals were
also thought to lose their colour, or 'fire' if the wearer was poisoned.
Black Opals have long been considered to confer magical powers on their
wearer, but be aware that Opals, like some other stones, are often artificially 'enhanced' or even created these days.

"The finest gem is the laughter of a child."

BLACKTHORN

The Blackthorn grows mostly in old hedgerows.

Its dense thickets of thorns provide birds and wildlife with a safe sanctuary to live and breed, and the fruits give them food. The wood is used to make walking sticks and occasionally in the manufacture of decorative woodwork. Boil the leaves in water to make an excellent mouthwash and gargle, for the relief of mouth and throat complaints. The bark was traditionally used to make tea to relieve fever. The fruit, or Sloes, are dark purple berries which are bitter to the taste, but which make an excellent jam. They are best-known as an addition to gin, which produces a tonic to help cure diarrhoea. To make Sloe gin, take a couple of handfuls of berries, wash them and prick them all over. Add to a bottle of gin, seal and wait at least 6 months before using. A sweeter form can be made by adding 2 tablespoons of sugar. The juice of the berries makes both a good ink and a dye.

The Blackthorn is also called 'Mother of the Wood' and 'Wishing Thorn' and is one of the traditional trees which had strips of cloth, or hair, tied to their branches when seeking the aid of the Goddess. Its wood is prized for making divining rods and wands. It is also a tree of protection, so if you have boundary hedges consider adding Blackthorn to provide a psychic and physical defence. Place pieces of the wood around the home to protect all who live there and a piece in the car will add to its protection and security.

> *"When in two minds,*
> *look for the third option."*

OLD SAMHAIN

*Samhain is the most important festival
in the Witches' year. It marks the end of
one year and the beginning of the next.*

It is also a time outside of the 'normal' year, an intercalary day, when the veil between the worlds is at its thinnest and the spirits of those who have gone before may return. Candles are lit to guide the spirits of our loved ones home. It is sometimes called the Festival of the Dead. Samhain is a time of reflection and remembrance and marks the approach of Winter. In the agricultural cycle it is the end of the harvest and the time when stocks would have been assessed to see whether they would last until the new growth of Spring. If there was not enough fodder, then some cattle may well have been slaughtered rather than using up supplies. At this time the Goddess takes on her robes of Crone or Wise One and the festival is sometimes called the Feast of the Crone. It is a time for divination and scrying as the Crone is keeper of all riddles and secrets. The God also takes on his dark aspect and becomes leader of the Wild Hunt.

Many other cultures and beliefs have similar festivals at around this time. There is the Hindu Divali, the Christian All Souls, and in South America there are carnivals and families will visit the graves of their families, picnicking and partying by the graveside. Additionally, the commemoration day in the UK for the dead of the First and Second World Wars falls shortly after Samhain.

*"Curses are better than
boomerangs at coming back."*

ANUBIS

The jackal-headed God of the ancient Egyptians is one
of the best-known ancient deities since the discovery of
artefacts in Tutankamun's tomb, including a large image
of Anubis, also referred to as Anpu, Anup and Wip.

Anubis was born of the contrived union between Osiris and Nepthys. In
order to conceal his birth from her husband Set, Nepthys wove a basket
of papyrus and cast the baby adrift on the Nile. He was found washed up
in the rushes by Isis and her dogs, and was raised by her to become her
attendant and guardian. He was also watcher and guardian of her dogs,
from whence he got his name. In some versions he is credited with assist-
ing Isis and Nepthys to repair and resurrect the body of Osiris. He is
Guardian of the Gates of Death, whose task is to ensure that none cross
over, in either direction, who should not do so. He presided over the
embalming and funeral processes of the dead. With Upuaut, 'Opener of
the Ways', he oversaw the halls of the dead, leading them to judgement
and supervising the weighing of the heart. It is considered that his worship predated that of Isis and Osiris.

Anubis was also considered a particular guardian of children and his
statue was often placed by the bed to protect them. If you have a picture
of Anubis place it facing, or over, the front door for household protection. Intriguingly, Anubis is also considered to help in locating lost
objects. If you misplace something then touch Anubis' ears whilst visualizing the object and you will soon be able to find it.

"To cure frustration,
go and strangle your pillow!"

ASTROLOGY

Mankind has always sought answers in the stars, and the first recorded study of their influence dates back to around 5000 BC.

Modern Astrology derives from the observations and workings of ancient Sumeria and Babylon. From there Astrology spread through all civilizations and religions, only falling out of favour under Christianity. In early times the study of the movements of the stars was limited to those planets visible to the naked eye: Sun, Moon, Mercury, Mars Venus, Jupiter and Saturn, plus stars of the celestial constellations, and was far more complex than most Astrology practised today. Having said that, using just the known planets of our solar system, today's Astrology can be startlingly accurate.

In order to calculate a birth (or Natal) chart the Astrologer needs the subject's date, time and place of birth. From this they work out the exact position of every planet in the Astrological houses at the time of birth. From this they determine much about the subject. Progressive Astrology can then take this information and, working with current and future planetary positions, make certain deductions as to the likely courses of aspects of a person's life. However, these, like any divinations of the future, are only guidelines, for we each still have the ability to take charge and control our future. If planning to consult an Astrologer, I always counsel going to one who has been recommended by someone you know and trust.

"Anything that seems too good to be true almost certainly is."

SUN IN SCORPIO

Scorpio is one of the Water signs, reflecting the
emotions, the world of the intangible, sensitivity,
psychism, perception and mysticism. It is also
one of the Fixed signs, bringing stability,
stubbornness, resilience and persistence.

Those born under Scorpio are generally self-repressive, emotional, intuitive, steadfast and intense. The typical Scorpio can be quite secretive,
keeping personal affairs and feelings hidden from those around them.
Outwardly they may appear fearless with a strong desire to succeed. They
can be purposeful and dynamic. They are perceptive about others and
their personal magnetism makes them good at persistent probing to get to
the basis of things. Their perceptiveness allows them to understand and
comfort others in times of difficulty, and they are unlikely to violate a confidence. On the negative side their intense feelings can make them highly
caustic and scornful when angered or crossed in any way. They can be
highly jealous, destructive, stubborn, suspicious and even vindictive.

Those born under this Sun sign should utilize their ability to reason
whilst being aware of their negative qualities. They should be aware that
relationships only flourish if both parties can share their thoughts and
feelings. Those of other signs will also find this a good time to work on
psychic abilities as the energies of the period, including the influences of
the Hunter's Moon and Samhain, will enhance these.

*"Put on an extra jumper before you
turn the heating up."*

CHANGING LUCK

Whilst genuine negative attacks are extremely
rare, an accumulation of generalized negativity
can lead to periods when much seems to go
wrong in life. This can be a series of small
misfortunes or even a few major happenings
which lead us to feel that 'nothing ever goes right'.

Sometimes it could be negative energies directed at us from others, possibly unwittingly: they may be jealous or resentful, even of imagined slights. It may arise from our own negative feelings, or the struggles and stresses of life can just build up a negative residue around us. There are several steps which can remove negativity, and bring positive influences into our lives.

First, address any debts, letters that should have been replied to, favours returned, calls made, and anything financial. Then thoroughly tidy and clean. Negativity accumulates in dust, dirt and clutter. Generally put your living environment in order. If you come across gifts from people with whom your relationship has soured, consider whether these provide negative links with them, and if so get rid of or thoroughly cleanse them. When all is in order cleanse and bless the home with salt water and then burn a purifying incense throughout. Reinforce or replace any protections around the home. Lastly, gather together family and friends for a celebratory meal or party to fill the home with positive influences, but invite only those who you feel will contribute positively.

"Magic will not work unless you put
effort and energy into it."

YEW

The slow-growing Yew is one of our oldest trees. It is an
evergreen with a flaking reddish bark. The female tree,
for there are male and female, bears a bright red fruit.
It reaches a maximum height of around 50 feet (350m),
after which it tends to increase in girth, often having
more than one trunk growing from one set of roots.

The Yew was sacred to the Druids and ancient peoples, and was thought
to be a guardian of the dead. It is often found growing in churchyards and
there are many reasons for this. Churches were often the only places with
solid walls around them preventing the ingress of livestock. The Yew,
being a favoured tree for making bows and arrows since the Stone Age,
therefore had to be protected from cattle and the like. Conversely, as it is
highly poisonous, valuable livestock had to be protected from eating the
Yew. However, as some churchyard Yews are thought to be around 4,000
years old, it is more probable that the Churches were built near Yew as a
sacred place.

All parts of the Yew are poisonous, especially the fruit and seeds, and
protective gloves should be worn if it is necessary to handle it. There are
no recorded historic medicinal uses for the tree, although it is being
experimented on with reference to treatments for cancer today. Magically
the Yew is linked to the salmon, the word Eo being an ancient word for
both, and hence is a tree of knowledge. Because of its links with death it
is particularly useful as a focus for meditation on the afterlife.

"You are unique, so value yourself."

PAST-LIFE RECALL

A belief in reincarnation implies that we
have had previous lives and many people
seek to know more about who they may have
been, and what they may have done before.

Some even believe that the wrongs they committed follow them and are responsible for the problems they experience in this life. Whilst some belief systems think that Karma is ongoing, this is not a belief of most Witches. It may be convenient to think our troubles are caused by previous, separate, selves, but the Craft belief of personal responsibility means that we should accept that our problems are our own. However, past-life recall can be interesting and sometimes useful as it may reveal traits, or reasons for them, that we are unaware of.

There are many ways of attempting such recall: meditation, pathworking and hypnosis. One of the most effective is known as the Christos method. This requires at least 2 people in addition to the subject. The subject lies on the floor with their head on the lap of the narrator and their feet in the lap of another. The narrator leads the subject through a series of visualizations whilst continuously drawing a circle on the subject's forehead over the third eye. At the same time the person supporting the feet massages them gently. When the subject is fully relaxed the narrator guides them in exploring the time before their current life. The narrator can break off if any distress is sensed.

"Look after your friends;
you never know when you'll need them."

GRAVEYARD WORKINGS

The idea of Witches gathering in graveyards,
and their use of parts of dead bodies and 'graveyard
dust or dirt', was instigated by the Witch Hunters and
became embedded in imagery of the Witch by
early engravings inspired by the same accounts.

It is, to say the least, unlikely that early Witches would have gathered so close to churches, and besides, they would not have desecrated the resting place of their friends and family. Having said that, many old beliefs include the sharing of festivals and times of great change with those who have gone before, so some gatherings may have included a visit to deceased family members.

Equally, many of the old texts include ingredients that sound as though they are linked to the dead. In some cases ingredients are deliberately concealed by the use of false terminology, sometimes as a sort of copyright protection where only the author knew the true meaning. In other cases this would be done as a way of implying a greater degree of difficulty or risk to the worker of the spell. But in many cases the names are actually country terms for plants. For example, Dead Tongue, or Dead Man's Fingers are names for Dropwort, which was used as a rat poison. The problem with using old spells and recipes is that the same country names can sometimes refer to different plants; both Patchouli and Valerian are called graveyard dust and graveyard dirt in different places. For this reason it is often better to look to the properties of the plants you can recognize rather than using guesswork.

"Never waste your magic on the trivial things."

REED MONTH COMMENCES

The Reed of the Celts has counterparts
in other cultures; for the Romans it was flax,
and for the Egyptians, Papyrus.

In all cases it is very much a plant with many uses making anything from thatch to weaving, from paper to musical instruments. It was also used in making arrows and to heal wounds caused by them. It is a plant strongly linked to water, being sometimes called the Water-Elder. It is also associated with the pathway between the worlds. Indeed it is thought that growing the plant in, or very close to the house was to open the door to death. The Greeks considered the Reed sacred to Pan; Pan Pipes being made from a series of Reed tubes tied together, which could be played to invoke him. However, this is not something which should be done lightly as Pan is a deity who can bring mischief and the uncertain. They also considered it to be strongly linked to Hecate, and placed Reeds at her shrines.

The Reed is associated with willpower, creativity, imagination, insight and love. Weave a circle from Reeds and keep it by you when you need help with new projects or new ideas. Wearing a ring or bracelet of Reed will help to strengthen your willpower. Whenever you gather Reeds you should ensure that you make an offering lest you offend the spirits which dwell within the Reed beds. It is also a good idea to ensure that you do not gather Reeds at times when waterfowl and other species are using the beds to raise their young.

"Dictionaries are consciousness expanding."

HALLOWEEN

Whilst Halloween is another name for Samhain there are many seemingly non-Wiccan practices to celebrate alongside those attendant on our beliefs.

Many Witches take advantage of the commercial aspects of the Halloween season to bring out of storage and decorate their homes with all the Witchy things which normally might cause raised eyebrows among non-Wiccan friends and neighbours. Many of us, especially those with children, will be holding parties, possibly fancy dress, and may also be organizing Trick or Treating.

Many of the customs of this season come from the traditions of Samhain. Carved pumpkin lanterns with lights inside guide the spirits of our loved ones home, should they wish to visit, and protect against unwanted spirits. Dressing up was done to scare off malevolent spirits and energies. The wearing of masks was thought to mislead troublesome demons and spirits and was a form of protection. Trick or Treating has its origins in a time when it was considered acceptable to enact a revenge causing nuisance to those with whom you had a conflict. This meant that the time approaching Halloween was one when debts would be paid and things borrowed would be returned. As an aside, this tradition can be safely and sensibly practised by the simple addition of a sensible adult accompanying the 'Treaters' on their rounds. It was also a time when divination or fortune telling was practised, especially with regard to love and marriage.

"Do what you can, let the impossible look after itself."

CREATING RITUALS

Whether you are alone or in a group some parts of a magical working or Ritual remain the same.

The first and most important is purpose; not only should there be one, but it should be carefully thought through to ensure that the desired results are achieved without unwanted side effects. The next is timing; magically in terms of the phase of the Moon, day of the week, and in terms of ensuring sufficient undisturbed peace and quiet. Then there are considerations of space, tools and magical items. There is little point in creating a Ritual which is prohibitively expensive or requires items which are out of season.

The basic structure of any magical working is always the same. Everything should be in place. In a group working, everyone should gather and be briefed on what is to happen, and why. The Elements should be invoked, the Goddess and God invited, the Circle cast. This need not involve using tools, speaking out loud, or physically drawing Pentagrams in the air, but can be achieved mentally, given sufficient focus, control and practice. Once the Sacred Space has been created and all is in balance, then energy is raised and the purpose of the working can be carried out. Then the Rite of Wine and Cakes can take place. At the end, the Elements should be dismissed, the Goddess and the God thanked and the Circle taken down. All should be cleared away and something eaten and drunk to aid grounding. Groups may wish to feast at this point. Lastly, all should be written up in each Witch's journal.

> *"Teach your children massage,*
> *and one day you'll be grateful."*

SAMHAIN EVE

**As the biggest festival of the Witches' year it
really is one to share with others if at all possible.**

In many Covens everyone attends this Sabbat, including those from
Daughter Covens. Around this time there are sometimes conferences and
other open functions. However, not everyone is able to find a gathering
to attend, yet they still wish to celebrate Samhain. There are many focuses to choose from for this festival, like the Wild Hunt, the formation of
light and dark Circles, seeking the wisdom of the Crone, and remembrance of loved ones who have departed. These can be undertaken individually or combined in a larger celebration.

Take a Cauldron or largish dark coloured bowl and fill it with water.
Add several drops of black ink to create a Dark Mirror. Place it in such a
way that the Moon is reflected in its surface, or light a candle which will
do likewise. Also, beside the Cauldron burn an incense containing
Mugwort and Sandalwood. Extinguish all lights in the house, or room,
except the candle. Kneel before the Cauldron and visualize the Goddess
as Crone and the God as Leader of the Wild Hunt. When you are ready
place 9 drops of silver ink in the centre of the water saying, *"I call upon
the Wise One and the Leader of the Wild Hunt to give aid to my sight. As
I drop this silver into the blackness may she give to me the gift of sight.
Blessed Be."* With the forefinger of your right hand swirl the waters gently 3 times and then gaze into the depths to ask your questions.

"Most of life's evil spirits come in bottles."

SAMHAIN

As the last of the Autumn leaves were falling
and the harvest gathered in the people would
prepare for the storms of Winter.

At this time the land starts to become bare of the colours of life. In your garden you need to be clearing away dead leaves, and cutting back plants for Winter. Protect or bring in delicate plants before the real chill sets in, and remove any remaining fruit before the first storms. Houseplants should not be too close to windows as at this time of year they can easily chill. Consider feeding birds and wildlife, so long as you are sure you will continue to do so throughout the coming winter.

 Wrap up warmly and take yourself out into the woods to notice the changes around you. Take some dried fruit and a little cider or wine as an offering. Seek out the oldest tree you can find (almost certainly the one with the widest trunk) and make your offering to the land. Then sit beneath it with your back to the trunk for a while. Close your eyes and visualize all the seasonal changes of Spring, Summer and Autumn which have led to this point. Then recall all the things in your life which have likewise started, grown and come to fruition this year. In your mind see the Goddess as Wise One and the God as Hunter walking through the woods, and thank them for all that has come to you. When you are ready open your eyes and seek out a token of the season to take home with you.

"The Goddess will walk with you,
if you invite her."

MOONSTONE

**Together with Amber and Jet, the Moonstone
is a stone strongly linked with the Craft.**

It comes in a variety of hues but is generally white, blue or pink. It is sacred to the Goddess, especially the Lunar Goddesses Diana, Artemis, Arianrhod, Hecate, Selene and Isis. In ancient Egypt it was also sacred to Anubis under his name of Anup. It has been a magical stone in many belief systems, including Christianity, for over 4,000 years.

Traditionally the Moonstone is used for healing on the waxing Moon and for divination on the waning Moon. It was worn by lovers; if they were apart at the Full Moon, the Moonstone would provide a psychic link between them. It was believed that the Moonstone changed colour during the cycles of the Moon, but I have not noticed this effect. However, I have found that it changes, not colour but iridescence, depending upon the psychic energies of those I am with.

The Moonstone has many magical attributions. If two lovers each hold a Moonstone at the Full Moon their relationship will be strengthened and they will be able to more easily understand one another's feelings. If you have a disagreement with a loved one, at the Full Moon hold a Moonstone in both hands whilst focusing only on the love you feel for them. When it is fairly crammed with your love wrap it in silver tissue and give it as a gift to your loved one. Placing one under the pillow will bring peaceful and restful sleep, especially if regularly charged in the light of the Full Moon.

*"Read the introduction,
it's usually written for a reason."*

WORMWOOD

Wormwood is one of the members of the Artemisia family.

It is best-known as the key ingredient in Absinth, a drink which used to cause blindness because it was frequently made with impure alcohol and often coloured with copper. Modern Absinths do not suffer from these problems. A highly bitter herb, it was favoured for strewing on the floor to prevent fleas and other insects from infesting the home. Indeed, a collar soaked in an infusion of Wormwood will deter fleas from dogs and cats. Wormwood tea was used to dispel melancholy and to remove the yellow tinge of jaundice. It used to be thought that the herb encouraged the digestive system and cleared the mind. Traditionally, it was thought to counteract the effects of poison, although that may be due to its emetic properties. A sprig of Wormwood used to be worn to protect against Witchcraft.

Magically Wormwood is used in spells for love, protection and to enhance psychic powers and call spirits. To enhance your psychic skills place a sprig under your pillow and burn the herb when performing acts of divination. A teaspoonful of Absinth placed under the tongue will also enhance divination. Burn it with Sandalwood to induce others to communicate with you. Give the whole plant to your loved one to consolidate the bond between you. Place a sprig of Wormwood in the car to help to prevent accidents. Place it on the Altar when working spells for love and relationships.

*"Consideration oils the
wheels of life."*

THE DARK MIRROR

The true Dark Mirror is made by coating the back of a curved glass, such as is found on the front of old-fashioned mantle clocks, with soot.

The resulting black shiny surface is then used for scrying. However, this is extremely messy and requires an open fire. A similar version can be made by applying black paint to the back of a glass, and many of the Dark Mirrors sold today are made in this way. The more natural way is to fill a bowl with water and add black ink to create a pool of blackness, similar to that created by a deep pond at night. This latter is most probably the form used by our ancestors. One of the most famous Dark Mirrors was owned by Dr John Dee, court magician to Queen Elizabeth I. This is made from highly polished Obsidian, and can be seen in the British Museum. Dee used this not only for scrying, but also to summon spirits which, he claimed, appeared in its surface and spoke to him. Certainly Obsidian is an excellent medium for meditation and divination but I cannot say that any spirits have appeared in my Obsidian ball.

Dark Mirrors are used in much the same way as the Crystal Ball. Sitting before it, you have to unfocus your conscious mind and allow the subconscious to take over. Some Witches see images in the surface or, more often, just under it. Others find that images and/or words simply appear in their mind. Often it helps to work by candlelight, or to have candlelight reflected in the surface.

"In some, the difference between the subconscious and unconscious is indeterminate."

SILVER

Silver is the metal of the Moon and sacred to the Goddess, and has been so for thousands of years.

As it can be found in its pure form, silver was one of the earliest metals used in decoration and jewellery. It was also used for Ritual implements and offerings. Highly-polished silver was used as early mirrors and up until quite recently the backing of mirrors was very thin silver. It is the metal of choice for most Witches' jewellery, especially for Pentacles, Pentagrams and the symbols of Degrees of Initiation. Many High Priestesses wear a silver crescent Moon on the forehead during Ritual. Silver is associated with the Element of Water and with the emotions, and is made into friendship rings and exchanged between those with strong ties.

Silver is used in magic for protection, travel, money, love, and to develop psychic abilities. It is also used to invoke the Goddess; silver bells being to invite her presence. It enhances psychic powers as it opens the door to the subconscious. Some may find that wearing silver leaves them too open to psychic emanations but this can be counteracted by also wearing some gold. Silver is also soothing and calming: if feeling over-wrought lie down with a silver disc over your third eye. If this is not possible, for example at work, visualize a silver disc spinning over the same spot. To ensure that money comes into the home, keep a silver coin above the door. Silver is protective, especially of travellers, so wear or carry a disc with the symbol of the Goddess upon it.

> *"Magpies collect shiny things,*
> *Witches collect practical ones."*

HECATE

**To the ancient Greeks, Hecate was one
of the pre-Olympian deities ousted by Zeus,
with whom she alone shared the ability of
granting or withholding anything she wished.**

It is thought that her worship was pre-Greek, originally Thracian. Hecate
is also known as Queen of the Night and is the third aspect, or Crone, of
the Persephone-Demeter triple Goddess. She is both a Lunar Goddess
and an Earth Goddess, ruling the spirits of the dead. As Queen of Death
she held magical powers of regeneration, and could release or hold back
the spirits of the dead.

Hecate is Goddess of the Crossroads, guarding all ways, and offerings were made to her there. It was said she could see 3 ways at once and
she was sometimes depicted as having 3 heads: those of a serpent, a horse
and a dog. In other depictions she is a beautiful, if severe, woman riding
a horse accompanied by an owl and a large black dog. She was also said
to walk the roads of ancient Greece, accompanied by her Sacred Dogs
and carrying a torch. She is a Goddess of household protection, with her
image being placed at the side of the door, and offerings of food were left
to her on her feast nights. Hecate suppers were held in her honour, and
magical knowledge was exchanged at these gatherings, for Hecate is a
Goddess of Witchcraft, sorcery and all things magical and she was
thought to confer these talents upon her followers. Public feasts were also
held in her name at which sacrifices of black lambs and honey were made.

*"You can't run away from
the things you carry with you."*

RAVEN

The Raven is the largest member of the
Crow family, being some 25 inches (70 cm) in
length. It is all black, including the beak. It has
long been considered a bird of magic and omens.

Probably the most notable story concerns the Ravens at the Tower of London, about which it is said that should they be lost or fly away then Britain and the Royal family will fall. These days their wings are clipped to prevent them leaving! The Native Americans call the Raven 'the messenger of death', and they believe that it can scent death and will arrive whenever it is imminent. It used to be thought that to hear a Raven calling over the house indicated one of the inhabitants would soon fall ill. Indeed its call is said to be, "corpse, corpse". Ravens seen facing towards a clouded Sun indicate that hot weather is on the way, but if seen preening then the weather will be wet. Seen flying towards one another they are said to presage battle.

The Raven is sacred to the Celtic Battle Goddess the Morrighan. It was said that she would watch over the field of war in the guise of a Raven, waiting to feed on the bodies of the fallen. The Raven was also thought to be a messenger for the Morrighan, and as such was under her protection. Should anyone kill a Raven it was thought that She would visit destruction on their household. The Celtic Goddess Natosuelta was a Raven Goddess of Gaul, and was both Creator and Destroyer of the world.

"Never drop anything on the street
that you wouldn't drop on your carpet."

BRIDGES

**It used to be said that Witches
could not cross running water, and bridges
were built with a cross in the construction,
sometimes literally, as ornamentation,
to prevent them using the bridge to pass.**

It was thought that should Witches attempt to use such a bridge then they would be forced to turn back when they reached the centre. It is probably for this reason that it used to be a superstition that to turn back halfway across a bridge was to court disaster.

In some places it is thought to be unlucky to say goodbye to a friend on a bridge as it meant you would never see one another again. It is also considered unlucky to be under a railway bridge when a train passes overhead. However, when I was young we would rush to be underneath to hear the thunderous noise. (Which could explain a lot!) In Wales it was considered to court misfortune to talk whilst passing under a bridge. This latter may be related to the belief that it was bad luck to disturb the spirits which lived underground. If you cross a bridge over running water you should throw a coin into the waters to appease the spirits which dwell underneath. It used to be said that you should not cross a bridge if a part of it was obscured by fog or mist, in such a way that you could not see all the way across. To do so could result in you ending up, not on the other side, but in the otherworld.

*"Take comfort in the knowledge that unpleasant people
inevitably get their just desserts."*

BAY

The Bay tree is most often seen these days pruned into a sort of pom-pom on a stick, and is often seen standing outside restaurants to advertise their trade.

However, if allowed to grow naturally it develops a bushy habit and can grow as high as 60 feet in a warm climate. It is used as a flavouring in a number of dishes, although it is almost always removed before eating.

The Bay is sacred to Daphne. It is said that Daphne led secret Rituals to celebrate womanhood. Apollo, the Sun God, suggested that the women should celebrate naked to ensure there were no male intruders. When the women shed their clothing a man, Leucippus, was unmasked. However, Apollo then accosted Daphne and demanded that she sleep with him. As she fled his violent advances she called out to Mother Earth to help her and was transformed into the Bay laurel.

The priestesses of Apollo used to chew Bay to induce prophetic visions. Today it is still used in brews to enhance psychic abilities. It should, however, be used sparingly as too much can be toxic. Bay used to be the laurel of the victor's crown. It can be worn for protection and a Bay tree in the garden provides protection for the whole household. Incense made with Bay will drive out negativity and break curses. If a couple wish their relationship to endure they should jointly break off a sprig of Bay and break it in two, keeping half each. Hang Bay around the house, not only to protect psychically, but also to deter flying insects from entering.

"An hour with a good book
improves even the worst day."

NUTMEG

Nutmeg is the seed of the fruit of the
Nutmeg tree: the outer covering of this
fruit is Mace which is also used as a spice.

Nutmeg and Mace actually have the same properties although it is the seed which is more often used. Nutmeg is used to soothe the digestive system, reducing nausea, vomiting and flatulence, although too much can act as an emetic. It is often grated and sprinkled onto warm drinks for those recovering from illness. Grated Nutmeg added to ointment is very effective for piles. Nutmeg oil is used externally to warm and stimulate, and is of some benefit in relieving deep-seated aches and pains.

Magically Nutmeg is taken, usually in a warm drink, to enhance psychic powers, as an aid to divination, and when taking otherworld journeys. It has the effect of loosening the hold of the conscious mind and of allowing the subconscious to come to the fore. A little is sometimes added to incense which is burned during readings. A necklace made of Nutmegs, interlaced with other herbs, such as Juniper berries, Star Anise and Cardamoms, is sometimes worn when undertaking psychic readings. Whole Nutmegs are carried as good luck charms and often placed under the cot of an infant to protect it. It is said that carrying a Nutmeg protects against rheumatism and boils. They are also pierced and threaded to make a charm against cold sores, sties and dental pain. To bring money roll a green candle in freshly grated Nutmeg, so that it sticks to the surface, and burn it on a Friday.

"Willpower gets stronger the
more it's exercised."

THE DAGDA

To the Celts the Dagda is the Father of the Gods.

His name translates as 'the Good God'. The Celtic tradition has a number of 'father' Gods, such as the Dagda and Nuada. They shared certain traditions and attributes which were undoubtedly pre-Celtic, and this combined with the complex religious lore of the Celts themselves. Thus the concept of a shadowy and all-powerful primal ancestor God is likely to be both Celtic and pre-Celtic. The Dagda is sometimes referred to as Eochaidh Ollathair, 'All Father', and as Ruad Rofessa, 'Lord of Great Knowledge'.

The Dagda is depicted as a man in rustic garb, carrying a gigantic magic club. With one end of the club he could slay his enemies, whilst with the other he could heal. The Dagda also had a magical harp which was stolen by the enemies of the Tuatha De Danaan; the Fomorri. He also possessed a Cauldron, brought from the city of Murias; this was one of the treasures of the Tuatha. At the second battle of Magh Tuireadh the Dagda appeared in the form of Ruad Rofessa. He carried a Cauldron which held eighty gallons of milk, plus whole goats, sheep and swine, all of which went to make his meal. His ladle was large enough to hold a man and a woman. It was said that no man ever went hungry from it. This symbolism is suggestive of a leader or God who nourished his people. As the Tuatha De Danaan departed to the underground Sidhe, they changed from Gods into fairies and the Dagda resided as their leader.

> *"Never use words in magic if you*
> *don't understand their meaning."*

APPLE RING

Apples are a key part of the Samhain season, which is occasionally called the Apple Sabbat.

The five-pointed star found in the cross section is also a symbol of the Craft. They have a long tradition of being used in love divination and celebratory games at this time. Apples are frequently placed on the Altar at this time, whether whole or in part. They are sometimes used as a substitute for the biscuits, and rough Cider in place of wine, in the Rite of Wine and Cakes and Cider.

One of the ways of producing a long-term reminder of the season is to create a dried Apple Ring. You will need to slice several Apples, across the core, to create sufficient equal-sized apple rings. Place the slices on kitchen paper and put into a very low barely warm oven, until they have completely dried out. If the oven is too warm they may curl, but this can be rectified if you then place them under a heavy weight for a day or so. As they dry the Apple slices will darken, becoming quite brown, but if you prefer a paler ring then paint both sides of each slice with lemon juice as soon as they have been cut. Once your slices are completely dry and flat, arrange and glue them into a ring. This should then be placed in a warm dark place, again under weights, for a further few days to ensure it has fully dried. At this point it can, if you wish, be varnished. Your Apple Ring can then be decorated and hung up by a ribbon if you wish.

*"Disagreeing is best done
without shouting."*

ASPEN

The Aspen, or Poplar, can grow to a height
of 100 feet (30m) in some parts, although
it is more normally around 60 feet (20m).

It is also known as the Quaking or Shivering Aspen, from the way in which its branches and leaves will move in even the slightest breeze. In the autumn the leaves turn a bright yellow. Separate trees bear the light-brown male, and the green female, catkins. Its bark contains salicin and populin, and is useful in the treatment of fever, as a tonic and to ease urinary problems.

The Aspen is a tree of knowledge, particularly self-knowledge. It is also a symbol of achievement in combining physical and mental understanding, and of achieving personal humility. In the Celtic tradition the Aspen is linked to Scathach, the female warrior who trained Cuchulain and bore his son. The Celts used the wood of the Aspen for shield-making. It is said that to burn Aspen is to invite ill luck and sickness into the home. It was also thought that the tree could never be struck by lightning. An Aspen growing in the garden will protect the house against thieves. Use Aspen wood in anti-theft spells; keep a small piece of the wood in your car to protect it. The Aspen also has the power to increase eloquence, so place a leaf under the tongue to clarify the mind and facilitate communication. Add the buds or catkins to incense to attract money. Aspen used to be added to flying ointment, and such a mixture can facilitate astral projection and otherworld experiences.

"Stand up straight,
you've earned the right."

POTATOES

The humble Potato may seem an unlikely
magical tool but our forebears would have
worked most frequently with the things which
are to hand, for these would have been those
whose properties they were most familiar with.

As the Mandrake is in fact a member of the Potato family it is perhaps not so surprising that the Potato can be used in its own right. Potatoes make excellent poppets or fith-faths for working image magic. When working healing inscribe the name of the subject on a Potato and bury it in the ground at the Full Moon: as the Moon wanes, so will the disease. Potato juice mixed with red ink is excellent for writing magical talismans.

A Potato which has naturally gone hard and black has long been carried in the pocket as a cure for rheumatism. Somewhat more scientific is the practice of drinking raw Potato juice which has a high concentration of potash salts. Hot Potato water compresses also relieve the pain of rheumatism and arthritis. Pounded raw Potatoes also make a soothing dressing for burns and scalds. A slice of raw Potato will reduce the inflammation of a bruised or blackened eye. The floury centre of baked Potato, when mixed with oil, is helpful in healing over-chilled and frostbitten skin. Be sure to make a wish when eating the first new Potatoes of the season.

Two things which any eater of Potatoes, whether Witch or no, should be aware of are that green Potatoes can be toxic, and a Potato boiled without its skin loses one third to one half of its goodness in the water.

*"Silence is often mistaken
for wisdom."*

RITES OF PUBERTY

**Rites of Passage held at puberty were
very much a part of the lives of people in the past,
but fell out of use during the last millennium.**

But there was a time when the onset of puberty, marked in girls by menstruation and in boys by other physical changes, was something which was marked by separation, tests of courage and same-sex or even whole-village celebrations. In many cultures tattoos and other body art would have marked these changes, as would perhaps the taking on of a new name. Sometimes use of this new name would be confined to the gender group of the adolescent, which is similar to the way a Witch name is kept within the Coven or group.

However, in recent years Rites of Puberty are returning: currently these are mainly low-key events and are generally more popular amongst girls than boys. The purpose of such Rites today is to mark the onset of adulthood, unlike earlier Rites which marked the end of childhood, as we have less urgency in moving our young into full responsibility. It is important that today's Rites should be followed by a genuine appreciation that the young person is maturing, and they should have increased responsibilities, and respect for their views and privacy. To do otherwise negates the purpose of the Ritual. In keeping with this it is a good idea that the young person is included in the planning of the content of the Ritual or celebration. In Wiccan families this event is sometimes marked by inclusion in the Rites and Rituals of the Craft within that family.

"Other people's opinions are just that."

LABRADORITE

Labradorite is usually a darkish-blue or greenish-grey,
but occasionally white, stone with lustrous metallic
tints of all the colours of the rainbow, but
mostly blue and/or green, and from which
the mineral term Labradorescence comes.

Needless to say, Labradorite is named after Labrador, Canada, where it was discovered in the 18th century, although there are reasons to believe that it was known in ancient times and 'forgotten' for some time. However, it can also be found in many parts of the world. Labradorite comes from the same feldspar group as Moonstone and the two are occasionally confused. The stone, like Moonstone, is sensitive to pressure and to psychic change. Although there are distinct differences between the two stones, there are some which cross the boundary and are called Labradorite-Moonstone. These are highly prized in magical work.

Wear Labradorite to enhance wisdom; it cannot replace learning but allows the wearer to access and make the best use of the information they have, whether consciously or unconsciously held. Labradorite opens doorways; it enhances spiritual growth and allows access to the subconscious mind. Gaze into it to enhance meditation or use it for scrying. Wear, or carry, it in interview situations and whenever communication is important. Wear it also to enhance self-confidence and 'presence'. Place it under the pillow to encourage psychic and revelatory dreams. Labradorite also protects against others accessing your thoughts and so can be worn when you have a secret to protect.

"Secrets are only secret until they are shared."

LIFE BALANCE

The term 'work-life balance' is currently fashionable,
reflecting the dawning realization that there
may be more to life than the acquisition of
wealth and possessions.

The concept of balance is one of the keys to the Craft. Furthermore the Craft is about living as a part of life rather than apart from it. These two concepts should be applied to the balance we seek in our daily lives, as an emphasis on any one part of life can be detrimental to the other parts.

It is useful, occasionally, to step back and assess our lives; to examine whether we are doing the things which benefit us, or expending our energies on the things which are no longer relevant or important. There are many ways of doing this but the one I use involves writing down lists of the ways I spend my time, and then reviewing them against another list of the things I feel are important in my life. Of course we cannot only do that which we enjoy, as there are some things which have to be done. But, unless you are very organized you will find that there are some things on which you spend time and effort which are neither necessary nor desirable. These are the things on which we expend useful time and energy, but from which we need to consider extricating ourselves. This does not mean you should completely stop being helpful to others, but that perhaps you should bring this into balance with the rest of your life.

"Learn to say 'no' to those requests and
demands which do not enhance you."

THE STAG

Stag is a term for the male deer.

Horned deer have been connected with magic and the Gods since the earliest of times. Antlered human forms are to be found in cave paintings and as religious icons around the world. Gods have been depicted or associated with the Stag from the Inuit to the Inca.

Probably the best-known forms today are Cernunnos and Herne. Cernunnos literally means 'horned one', and he is often referred to as the Horned God or Stag Lord. He is usually depicted as a seated human form with antlers, holding a snake in one hand and a torc in the other, and often accompanied by wild animals. He is a God of animals and fertility. The best-known depiction of Cernunnos is on the Gundestrup Cauldron. Herne is the more anglicized form of the same God. It is thought that his name comes from the call of the hind in the rutting season. Herne the Hunter is said to appear in Windsor Great Park at times of national crisis. In Wales a similar God form who also leads the Wild Hunt is called Gwyn. Little written information is available to us on either Herne or Cernunnos, probably because it was the Horned Gods which gave rise to the concept of the devil bearing horns and even having cloven feet. However, he is mentioned in the Song of the Irish bard Amergin as the Stag of 7 tines, ie branches on the antlers. Probably the best way of coming to an understanding of this God form is to spend time meditating on him in the woodlands which are his home.

"If you smother love it will die."

MISTLETOE

Mistletoe which grows between the earth and the air was especially sacred to the Druids.

It was gathered with a golden or silver sickle, or curved knife. It had to be cut with a single stroke and must not be allowed to fall to the ground. Should it do so it was thought to portend a great disaster to the land. They believed that it had great powers of protection, especially when it grew upon the Oak. Such Oaks were considered especially sacred. It was gathered and distributed to welcome in the New Year, and this custom is still enacted when we add it to our Yule or Christmas decorations. Mistletoe also features in Norse mythology, being the plant which was used to kill Balder.

One of the folk names for Mistletoe is All Heal. Mistletoe leaves were used to treat internal haemorrhage, epilepsy, convulsions, delirium, urinary problems, nervous disorders and many other ills. A tincture of Mistletoe was also used to treat heart irregularities. Today it is usually only used homoeopathically, as too much of the plant or the berries can cause convulsions.

Magically Mistletoe is used in spells for protection, hunting, fertility, healing and exorcism. It is also called the Golden Bough and Witches Broom. It is carried to ensure fertility, possibly the origin of kissing under a sprig. Placed over the bed it induces peaceful sleep. Wearing a ring made from the wood is said to protect against illness, and hanging it around the house will protect against spirits. Burn Mistletoe to drive out negativity and to break negative spells.

"Punctuality shows you care."

ONIONS

Onions have long been credited with healing and protective properties.

Eating Onions, especially with garlic, is very helpful in preventing and combating the common cold. It is said that placing a sliced one in the sick room will speed recovery, and modern research has shown that slices will attract germs. Cut Onion was also rubbed into the skin to prevent pain being felt, particularly by schoolboys expecting the cane! They are also helpful in easing the pain of wasp stings. Hot Onion was often used as a poultice to draw bruises and boils, and to ease earache.

Magically Onions are also used for healing as well as for protection, love and prosperity spells. A sliced Onion can be used to clean and cleanse magical tools, especially those made of metal. For magical healing rub half an Onion over the affected part and then burn it. It was said that placing half an Onion under the pillow will bring dreams of a lover to be. To decide between two or more partners carve their names into separate Onions and put them in a warm place. Whichever sprouts first will have the strongest love for you. Onion skins should never be dropped on the ground as this will remove your prosperity; to draw money to you, burn them. My mother used to say that if you have Onions in your house then you will never lack food on the table. To protect the home hang a string of Onions in the kitchen, or take a small one, cover it with black-headed pins and place it in the window facing the road.

"Pursue perfection,
but don't expect it to be easy."

NUT, PIP AND SEED DIVINATION

Nuts, pips and seeds have long been used in love divination.

To choose between a number of possible partners, name pips and place them on a hot shovel to see which jumps off first. To see whether a love was true a pip would be placed into the fire; if it burned brightly then so would the love. Few people today have open fires; however, a heated frying pan or a hot charcoal briquette can be used instead. The rhyme, "*Tinker, tailor, soldier, sailor, rich man, poor man, beggar man, thief,*" is another form of love divination, the stones of fruit being thus counted to determine which occupation a future husband would have. To determine how long it would be before a girl would marry she was supposed to place 10 Apple pips into the fire; those which flew out of the flames would then give the number of years before her wedding, unless it was all 10 which would indicate she would die an old maid!

Nuts are also used to determine the answers to questions. Take three Hazel nuts, paint a cross on one, a circle on another and leave the last plain. Place them in a bag and when you seek to know whether to take a particular course of action take one out at random. The circle will indicate that what you do will bring you benefit, the cross that it will bring strife, and the plain one that you do not have all the information you need to make a decision.

"Clouds are just sunshine in hiding."

JASPER

Jasper comes in a wide range of colours, most frequently red, green and brown.

It is usually striped or spotted, and completely plain Jasper is very rare. Green Jasper is sometimes called Prase, grey Jasper is called Hornstone, and black Jasper is Touchstone. It has been used magically for around 5,000 years, particularly for Amulets, and is specifically mentioned in the Book of the Dead.

Jasper was thought to guard against snake bites and to draw poison from wounds. It was also thought to ease the pain of childbirth, and to protect both mother and child. Jasper Amulets are made in different shapes or have the shapes inscribed in them for different purposes: red Jasper with a lion's head to guard against poison and cure fever; mottled Jasper with an equal-armed cross, representing the Elements, to protect against drowning; a stag or dog to cure possession and prevent insanity; a bird with a leaf in its beak for prosperity; a hare for protection from evil spirits. To the Native Americans Jasper is the Rain Bringer and pieces of the stone were worn and scattered on the ground during rain-making Rituals.

Jasper is a stone which enables control of the mind; it stimulates thought whilst helping to restrict impulses. It was thought that it would prevent hallucinations. Wear Jasper in magical work to enhance your focus and to increase control over your own energies. Jasper is also a grounding stone, so rub it over the wrists and forehead after magical working to bring you back to yourself.

"You have the power to change your life,
if you only grasp it."

SUN IN SAGITTARIUS

*Sagittarius is a Fire sign bringing energy and
inspiration. It represents enthusiasm, spontaneity,
intuition and idealism. It is a Mutable sign bringing
flexibility, resolution and problem-solving.*

Sagittarians are generally self-expressive, energetic, spontaneous,
assertive and extrovert. The typical Sagittarian seeks freedom and space,
physically and mentally. They are ambitious and optimistic and will frequently take on large and complex tasks with enthusiasm and energy.
Sagittarians make good mediators, having a good insight into the feelings
of others. Intellectually strong, they enjoy challenges and learning.
Whilst not innovators, they are good at examining and interpreting the
thoughts of others. They can be idealistic and are inclined to hold strong
beliefs. They are also disposed towards outdoor activities and sports.
They are ardent lovers but do not like feeling tied down. On the negative
side they can be know-it-all, outspoken, tactless, boastful and inconsid-
erate. They can also alienate others by moralizing when they hold the
same traits themselves. It can be easy for Sagittarians to be unfocused or
to flit from one thing to another.

During this period Sagittarians should focus on undertaking problem-
solving, intellectual and physical pursuits. But they should be wary of
allowing their love of freedom to cut off those close to them. Non-
Sagittarians will find this a good time for honest examination of personality
traits and addressing outstanding problems in that area.

*"It's not the chocolate that's fattening,
it's the quantity."*

MAKING INCENSES

Whilst incenses can be bought, it can be more meaningful to make your own.

Not only can you be completely sure that all the ingredients are the ones you need for your magic, but the actual work of making it becomes a part of your spell. Loose incense is the easiest to create at home. Of course many plants and herbs can be burned on their own, but blended incenses are often far more effective. The main components of incense are resins, such as Copal or Frankincense; woods, such as Sandalwood and Pine; and plant materials, such as flowers and leaves. Try to ensure that no more than one third of your mix is resin, otherwise you could find that it generates far too much smoke for comfort. Also ensure the other ingredients are completely dry, for the same reason. When making incense your equipment should be scrupulously clean and dry, to avoid incorporating traces of things which may not be helpful for your magic. Plant ingredients should be relatively fresh, or freshly dried, as they lose their properties over time. A quick guide to this is the smell: if it smells musty it is unlikely to be useful. All the ingredients should be finely ground or chopped, but not reduced to powder, before blending. Incenses should always be kept in a cool, dry and dark place, and for no longer than a few months.

To burn your incense you will need a fire-proof container and some self-igniting charcoal. This should always be kept completely dry, ideally in a container together with a small sachet of silica.

"Only give the benefit of the doubt the first time."

ELDER MONTH

The Elder is a very useful tree.

Its flowers can be eaten and made into wine. A tea or syrup made from the flowers is good for coughs and sore throats. The berries, which are high in vitamin C, can be eaten in a variety of ways and also make a fine wine. The berries and leaves, also high in vitamin C, can be made into jam. The leaves can be boiled and cooled and used as a dressing to relieve earache. Elderflower water is excellent for the skin, cleansing, soothing and, for those with pale skins, whitening it. It also helps to reduce acne and prevent it from scarring. The bark was boiled to make a laxative tea. Its wood can easily be hollowed out to make whistles and, for children, pop-guns.

The Elder is a tree of wisdom and knowledge associated with the Crone. It used to be thought of as a tree of death and of sorrow. It is said that to cut the tree, or to burn its wood, is to invite ill luck. In Northern Europe it is said that the Elder-tree Mother inhabits the tree and if any wood is cut she would follow the wood and haunt the owner. Even fallen wood should only be taken with permission. Elder leaves were thought to keep off Witches and were hung on doors to protect all within. The pith of the branches was supposed to make a wick which, when lit, would reveal all the Witches in the neighbourhood. Meditate under a fruiting Elder if you seek answers from those who have gone before.

> *"A life without some disappointment*
> *is a life with nothing in it."*

DIVINATION

**The term Divination covers a number of ways of
finding out things which are otherwise hidden from us.**

There are many different forms of Divination. Some are fairly limited,
answering only questions with yes/no responses, for example the
Pendulum. Others only deal with certain specifics, like Divining Rods.
Some will only answer specific questions, others are better for general
readings, like the Tarot. Some forms are more useful than others for in-
depth examination of a person's character and potentialities, like
Astrology or Palmistry. Probably the earliest forms of Divination used
water, as in the Dark Mirror, and fire, as in scrying in the flames. No one
method is any better, or more accurate, than any other, it is simply a question of finding the method which you feel most in tune with. In all cases
the cards, ball, runes or whatever, are only the means by which the reader can access their inner mind. It is this which actually produces the
insights which make the reading meaningful.

One common misconception about Divination is that pictures are
actually seen, or voices heard. This is rare, as for almost every reader it is
more a question of just finding that the knowledge is already there in the
mind. For most people, the 'secret' to learning to read is simply a question of learning to trust these feelings. A second misconception is that our
fates are fixed and the reader can tell us exactly what will happen. But any
form of Divination can only give the potentials that are available. Your
future is still subject to your own free will.

*"Hang on to your sense of humour;
you're bound to need it."*

SWALLOWS

In Britain the Swallow is particularly welcome as its arrival heralds the start of Summer.

Swallows like to build their nests just under the eaves, or other over-hangs, on houses, and it is said that this confers great luck on the home, bringing health, prosperity, success and happiness to the inhabitants. However, should they abandon it before the end of season then it bodes ill. Swallows flying low are said to herald the onset of rain, whilst when they are high in the sky then a long spell of good weather can be expect-ed. Some farmers still believe that to kill a Swallow will ruin the milk of their cows. Should a woman tread on a Swallow's egg it is said she will never bear children. To see Swallows fighting indicates troubles are on their way.

Swallow feathers are used in magic related to the Element of Air, and are said to bring clarity of mind. A duster made of Swallows' feathers, which would probably be too small for proper housework, can be used to sweep negativity from the room or home. A trio of feathers tied together can be used to waft incense smoke around the Circle to invite the Goddess. The direction of flight of Swallows in the morning gives an indication of the sort of day ahead: if they head South you can expect to be busy; East, you should approach the day cautiously and with much thought; West, emotions will run high, and you should beware of upset-ting those close to you; North, expect news or information.

"Life is not out to get you,
even if it sometimes feels like it."

WORKING OUTSIDE

**The Craft is often referred to as a nature-based
belief system, and for most Witches it is important
to perform at least some Rituals and magic
outside amidst nature.**

However, very few Witches are lucky enough to have a garden in which
they can work without the risk of being overlooked or overheard. For
this reason we look to the wild places around: woods and wooded park-
land for preference. For these places are more secluded, and Witchcraft is
not a spectator sport!

Try using an ordnance survey map to try to find your special place.
Look for footpaths which do not lead to places of interest, and investigate
several locations. Once you have located a potential site, or sites, you should
visit in several seasons to check suitability. It can take up to a year to find a
suitable location, as one which is private in Winter may be overrun by
tourists in the Summer, or one which is fine in the Summer can be inaccessible when the ground is wet. When you have selected one, make a point of
visiting it and tending it. Take some offerings and spend a little time in meditation before your first working. The first real working should be a consecration and blessing of the space. Invoke the Elements, invite the Goddess
and the God and seek the blessing of each. Then place a protective Circle
around the area you intend to use. Whatever your workings, always ensure
that you do not harm the environment, for example with fire. Also ensure
that you do not leave any traces, such as candle wax, behind you.

> *"There's a wonderful future if
> you only grasp it."*

THISTLES

There are a wide variety of thistles, almost all of which are disliked by the gardener.

Not only that, but once allowed to seed they spread rapidly and are extraordinarily hard to eradicate. Having said that, they have many uses. Blessed Thistle leaves were eaten to purify the blood, aid the digestion and cure headaches. This was also said to strengthen the brain and improve memory. The leaves were made into an infusion to be taken last thing at night to produce sweating for the cure of fever. Both the leaves and stems of the Marian, or Milk Thistle were eaten, especially when young and tender. It was thought to be helpful to nursing mothers, to cure jaundice and to dispel melancholy. The Saxons believed that if worn it would 'set snakes to fight'. It was also used to prevent and treat plague. From ancient Greek times Scotch Thistle juice was used to treat rickets, nervous complaints, cancerous growths and ulcers.

Thistles are used magically for defence, curse-breaking, purification and healing. Any species of Thistle grown around the home protects it against theft and negativity. They also bring strength and energy to those within. A bowl of Thistle heads in the room will enhance mental and physical energy. Carry a Thistle for protection and to attract positive change into your life.

If you want to grow Thistles, but do not want to be overrun by them, then plant them behind a barrier in the soil. Also cut them back before they flower, or at the latest before they seed, then dry the leaves and keep them for use.

"It's nice to be popular, but it's better to be respected."

HANDKERCHIEFS

The traditions associated with the handkerchief
come from the time when they were made of
cotton or linen, rather than disposable. However,
many of these traditions are valid whether you
use a tissue or a handkerchief.

Almost everyone knows that you tie a knot in a handkerchief to remind
you of something you don't want to forget. But this is far more effective
if you whisper "*rabbits*" three times into the knot as you tie it. This is
actually a remnant of an older belief that you could protect yourself from
demons and ill-wishing by carrying a handkerchief with a knot in one
corner. The knot should never be untied, so you will need another handkerchief for your nose! The larger form of handkerchief or neckerchief
was also worn to defend against ill luck. It was believed that to put a fold-
ed handkerchief into your pocket was to invite bad luck, so it should
always be unfolded first.

Cotton, silk and linen handkerchiefs are used in the Craft for a number
of purposes. They can protect Tarot cards and hold other divination tools.
They make excellent totem bags, and can be stitched, or tied, to make
pouches to contain all manner of spells. Never allow a used handkerchief to
fall into the hands of anyone who might wish you ill, as it is said to give
them a direct link to you. To ensure that your lover remains faithful, carefully extract three, and only three, threads from a handkerchief with their
initial sewn into it. Burn the threads and then give them the handkerchief.

"Better a handkerchief in the pocket
than a drip on the nose."

GREETINGS CARDS

The sending of cards is a fairly modern tradition, and
used to be only for people that you would not be
actually seeing. It was considered polite to give your
greetings in person, whenever you could. However,
today clever marketing from the manufacturers
means that we tend to send cards to everyone,
even when they live in the same house.

Whether you celebrate Yule, Christmas or another festival in December
you will probably be sending greetings cards. If you do this now then not
only do you save a panic later, but also you will have the time to do a bit
more than just scrawl your name. For those people with whom you are not
in regular contact, try writing a few lines telling them what's happening in
your world at present. You could also enclose a small token, perhaps a
pressed flower, to bring them cheer. Of course if you have the time it can
be nice to make your own cards, and there are kits which can be bought to
help with this. For special people make your card into a spell for them.
Decorate it with flowers or other plants which will bring them good fortune, like Fern, Oak, Holly, Poppy, Rose petals, Violet. Alternatively, select
plants for harmony, like Lavender, Passion Flower and Gardenia.

So get out your address book, dust off your memory and write your
cards, now, before the festive season gets fully under way. You'll thank
yourself for it later! And don't forget to have a few cards over, just in case
there's someone you forget.

> *"Thinking time is*
> *never wasted."*

EARTH MEDITATION

As we move into the Winter we also move into the
season of Earth, the realm of the physical. For the
land this is a resting time and for us it is a time of
reflection and remembering our achievements. The
earth is also a medium for repair and rejuvenation.

If the weather is warm enough this is best done barefoot outside. If it is
too cold or wet then bring some earth indoors in bowls or on trays.
Try to ensure that it is relatively dry. Sit in such a way that you are comfortable, with the soles of your feet and your hands touching the earth.
Close your eyes and breathe deeply to relax. Feel the earth with
your hands and feet. Take some time to experience its texture against
your skin. Take the forefinger of your strong hand and draw a circle over
your third eye, then replace your hand on the soil. Continue breathing
deeply and evenly until you can smell the earth. Now visualize the energy of Earth, the pulse of the land. Allow your breathing to slow to this
rhythm. Visualize the energy of the land as a deep green pulsing light,
rising up through your hands and feet, regenerating and revitalizing you.
See it pushing out all weariness and stress. When you truly feel in tune
with the land, allow your breathing to resume its normal pace, open
your eyes and rub your arms and legs to ground yourself. Tidy up after
yourself but keep a little of the soil in a small pot on your windowsill
throughout the Winter months.

"Productive is good,
effective is better."

NUMEROLOGY

*Numerology is a form of divination using
numbers, and is believed to have been first
utilized by the ancient Greeks.*

Its most common application lies in determining basic personality types and compatibility between individuals. In such basic numerology the name of a person is given a numerical value. This should be the name by which they are known, which is not necessarily the same as their given name. Each letter is given a value using the system A=1, B=2 and so forth up to I=9; after that the letters start again at J=1, etc. These numbers are then added together, and where the result equals a number over 9, the digits are added together until a number with the value 9 or less is achieved.

The basic attributions of the primary numbers vary from one system to another but one of the most common systems is: 1 – creation, intellect, the Sun; 2 – duality, the female, the Horned God; 3 – The Triple Goddess, fertility; 4 – the Elements, the seasons, employment, the physical realm; 5 – the points of the Pentacle, male and female combined; 6 – wholeness, domesticity; 7 – the Moon, wisdom, knowledge; 8 – Justice, the law, business; 9 – magic and spirituality. Added to this, even numbers are generally considered female and odd numbers male. The number 10 is thought by some to be unreadable, or to indicate that the information should remain hidden. It can also be taken to indicate that this is effectively a blank sheet, or a person who is flexible.

*"Sometimes money comes in handy,
so use it wisely."*

PIGS

**Whilst most modern Witches may
have little, if anything, to do with pigs,
they were important in times past.**

Many poor people owned or shared a pig, and these were often allowed to run loose in the village. Wild pigs, or boar, were also a feature of country life. The pig features in the legends of several of the Gods and Goddesses. There are a number of deities associated with the boar or pig. For example, Frey, brother to Freya, who accompanied her as a wild boar; Henwen, British magical Sow Goddess who gave birth to all manner of living things: Mala Liath, Scottish form of the Cailleach who protected wild boar; Moccus, Celtic Pig God; and Varaha, a form of the God Vishnu who takes the shape of a boar. It is thought by some that the pig, or boar, sometimes represents the personification of the male aspect of the Goddess in legends.

Pigs do not deserve the reputation ascribed to them. They are not dirty animals, although they do roll in mud to protect their skins from hot sunshine. They are devoted parents, and the young are only at risk of crushing in overcrowded conditions. They used to be considered reliable forecasters of the weather, carrying straw and sorting their bedding when chill winds or storms were on the way. It was said that if you met a pig on your outgoing journey then you should abandon the trip and return home. This especially applied to fisherman who would never mention the word pig at sea.

*"Don't run yourself down, there's bound
to be someone else who'll do it for you."*

THE CAILLEACH

The Cailleach is one of the Greater Goddesses of the Celtic world.

She was known by many different names: Cailleach Bheur or Carlin in Scotland, Sally Berry and the Hag of Beare or Digne in Ireland, Cailleach ny Groamch, and Black Annis. She has survived from before the Celtic period. The Cailleach could endlessly renew her youth, although she was also the hag, or Crone. She was reputed to have red teeth and one exceptional eye in the centre of a blue-black face. Her hair was long and matted and covered by a kerchief. She wore grey clothing and a plaid shawl. She was Goddess of Earth and Sky, Moon and Sun, and controlled the weather and the seasons. She was said to be cunning and to lure workers with the promise of great wages if they could out-work her for 6 months. But none could outwork a supernatural being and many died trying. This would appear to be an addition to her tale which was invented by the advocates of the incoming Celtic deities. In one of her personas, Cailleach Boi, she was the wife of Lugh.

As Black Annis she lived in a cave which she had dug out with her fingernails. Children who strayed were lured there to be scratched to death. It was a custom at one time to drag a dead cat before hounds, as a ceremonial cat hunt which ritually marked the end of winter and Black Annis' time of power. As Gentle Annie she was said to bring good weather to those who followed her path.

> *"Sometimes you have to make a few fresh starts before you can get going."*

JET

Jet, which is also called Witches' Amber and Black Amber, is actually a form of bituminous coal, millions of years old.

It is frequently copied in black glass, but it is easy to detect the difference for true Jet becomes charged with static when rubbed, so that tissue will stick to it. It is much sought after for Wiccan Ritual jewellery, and a necklace made of Amber and Jet is often worn by the High Priestess. Jet is associated with the fifth Element, Spirit. It is sacred to the Goddess Cybele and the God Pan, and is associated with the Goddess as Crone. Wear it to enhance intelligence, and knowledge of the spirit world.

Jet has a long association with magic, Ritual and with death. It has been found in pre-historic burial mounds and the Victorians made much use of it for mourning jewellery. It has long been used to protect and defend, particularly against spells and spirits. When Jet is worn or carried continuously it takes on something of the owner, so for this reason it is not a good idea to lend this stone. Should you buy it second-hand it should be thoroughly cleansed before use. Jet has long been thought to have properties of curing toothache, and was boiled in wine to create a healing elixir. Like Amber, Jet can be ground and added to incense, when it will break even the strongest of curses. Jet incense is also burnt to increase psychic abilities. Jet absorbs all negative influences and should be thoroughly cleansed if you have been wearing it in negative company.

"Why dwell on the past, when the future's got so much more promise."

FEVERFEW

Feverfew is a member of the Chrysanthemum family, and is also known as Pyrethrum and Batchelor's Buttons.

It is eaten to stimulate the appetite and ease the symptoms of colds and to reduce fever. It is also helps in nervous complaints, depression and as a general tonic. Added to boiling water with some sugar or, preferably, honey it eases coughs and breathing difficulties. A single young leaf chewed will help to heal headaches and migraines. The leaves rubbed into the skin, or a tincture made from them, relieves the sting and itch of insect bites. It can also be added to pouches of herbs worn to deter insects, or made into a weak solution and applied directly to the skin to prevent bites. This latter can also be sprayed onto dogs to deter fleas. It can be used to bring on and regulate menstruation. Planted around the home Feverfew purifies the atmosphere and guards against illness. Feverfew used to be added to all manner of drinks to guard against illness.

Magically Feverfew is used mainly in defence and protection. A few fresh leaves in the car guard against accidents. Carry the dry leaves to protect against colds, fevers and other contagious diseases. When working outdoors, bury groups of 3 leaves along the access routes to your working space to deter passers-by from finding you. These protected routes should go back further than the site is visible. If you can actually plant Feverfew in these sites without disturbing the local ecology it will provide a long-term protection.

"Deal with the little things
before they grow larger."

RINGS

The most common example of traditions associated with rings and hands is that of wearing wedding and engagement rings on the third finger of the left hand.

It was thought that this finger connected directly with the heart and wearing a ring here would prevent a person, originally a woman, from being distracted by the charms of anyone other than her partner. But the ring, being a circle, has far older associations than this. It has long been used to represent protection and defence. Of course in the Craft the circle represents the Circle of protection and power in which we work. It also means the circle of our fellowship, which includes all Witches, past, present or future.

To Witches the forefinger of the strong hand is important for its ability to direct energy. The Athame, when used, is simply an extension of this. The forefinger of the opposite hand is therefore used to attract energy. For this reason many Witches will wear a Pentagram ring or one with a special gemstone on this finger. The third finger of the strong hand is usually the place where a High Priestess will wear the ring symbol of her office, if she has one, although in some traditions this is the little finger. Another form of ring sometimes worn by Witches is shaped like a snake or serpent. This is worn to enhance the ability to work with the male aspect of the life force, sometimes called Kundalini. In the Craft silver is usually the preferred metal for all Ritual jewellery, including rings because of its links with the Goddess.

"Take greatest care of the things you value most."

BROWN

**Brown, and all shades of it, has long
been a colour associated with those who
are poor and who work on the land.**

These people would not have had the resources or inclination to spend money on fancy colours for workday clothing. It was also worn by those who eschewed wealth and worldly success. It indicates a desire for links with nature and the land. Brown is the colour of the Earth, and in some systems brown candles are burnt, instead of green, to invoke this Element. Brown candles are also used in healing spells for animals and other living things.

Brown stones such as Agate, Jasper and Tiger's Eye used to be worn for protection and victory in battle. They were also worn or carried as a wealth talisman, often engraved with symbols of success. Brown stones are also very good for grounding and centring and to re-balance the energies after magical workings. Brown robes are often favoured by Witches who work a lot of earth-healing magic and by those who practise Hedge-Witchcraft. It is also a very useful colour for outdoor workings, showing little dirt as well as blending easily into the background. Brown is a colour which should be worn by anyone who customarily has their 'head in the clouds'. It is particularly useful for those who are habitually clumsy or badly co-ordinated. Although considered by some to be a bland or dull colour, some of the richer shades are particularly useful if you are feeling stressed or overanxious. Create a circular swirling pattern of shades of brown with finger paints when you need to recharge your batteries.

"No one is perfect, but we can try."

FERNS

There is a large variety of Ferns, which have adapted to all kinds of living conditions which deter other plants.

In common with many plants used for healing, Ferns have a folk name which associates them with evil: Devil's Brushes. Some were thought to protect against Witchcraft, like Bracken, while others were thought to grow best in the presence of Witches, like Moonwort. Almost all Ferns were used medicinally. Male Fern was used for worming, especially in the case of tapeworm, in both people and animals. Black Spleenwort for coughs and chest complaints. Wall Rue cleanses the head from scurf, and was used to treat rickets. Common Maidenhair encourages hair to grow thick and strong. True Maidenhair was added to syrup for chest problems, jaundice and liver troubles. Hart's Tongue was used for digestive troubles, especially diarrhoea. Bracken was used for worming and as a purgative. Its seeds were thought to confer invisibility and perpetual youth. Be warned, though, that Bracken is nowadays thought to be carcinogenic at certain times of the year.

In the Craft Ferns are used in spells for rain-making, luck, protection and driving out negatives. It is said that burning Ferns will bring rain. Ferns of any kind growing in cracks near or on the doorstep protect the household. It used to be thought that treading on Ferns would make you confused and lose your way, but if carried they will lead to the discovery of treasures. As Fern is linked to the Element of Air, these are most probably riches of the mind, like knowledge, rather than a pot of Gold!

"Don't waste your eyes, use them all the time."

BERYL

Beryl is a semi- precious clear stone which usually comes in greens, yellows, golds and occasionally pinks, and various shades thereof.

The Beryl is closely related to the Aquamarine, and indeed green Beryl is sometimes heat-treated to create Aquamarines. In its clearer forms Beryl has been used to make eyeglasses, although these were very brittle. Dr John Dee's famous crystal sphere, now housed in the British Museum, is made of Beryl.

Beryl opens the subconscious mind, facilitating psychic development, and is especially good for scrying. However, it is a stone best used by the solitary worker or those in a partnership, as it also opens the mind to love, which can be distracting. Having said that, it can also be worn to protect against fascination, or a person seeking to take advantage psychically. Being a psychic stone it has also been used to make psychic mirrors as well as spheres. The former were placed against a white cloth, rather than being backed by soot as in the dark mirror. Beryl is also associated with the Element of Water and is considered protective for travellers, especially at sea. Indeed it is thought to halt sea-sickness. Beryl is good for bringing clarity of mind and should be worn to facilitate discussion and communication. It also aids study and the retention of information. Beryl is also physically energizing, but should not be employed continuously for this, as the weariness it banishes will be stored up and will sooner or later catch up. Beryl should be carried, not worn, to banish gossip. Exchanged between long-term partners Beryl will renew and refresh the relationship.

"You may as well accept ageing; it's going to happen anyway."

MAKING A SABBAT WHEEL

One addition to the Altar is the Sabbat Wheel.

This is a stone or wooden disc inscribed, or otherwise decorated, with images to represent the Sabbats. If made of a soft stone, such as slate, then the images can be sketched on with pencil and then carved into the surface. A circular wheel is easy to make, and a simple plain breadboard can form your basis. First, divide it into eight equal segments, like the spokes of a wheel. Symbols can then be burnt or carved into each of the segments, drawn or painted, or even created from gemstone chips, seeds, etc. Alternatively, you could press plants which represent each Sabbat and glue them into place, sealing it with a coat of clear varnish. Some ideas for the decorations are: Imbolg, candle, Snowdrops; Oestara, eggs, the Hare, Primroses; Beltane, Maypole, Besom, Chalice and Athame, Hawthorn blossom, Bluebells; Litha, the Sun, Green Man, Oak leaves, Sunflowers; Lughnasadh, a single stem or a sheaf of wheat, harvest loaf; Madron, scales; Samhain, Apples, Winter Jasmine; Yule, the Sun, Holly. For flowers and plants it is more meaningful to actually collect them in season in your garden or locality.

Another version of this is to embroider illustrations of the Sabbats, placing each in an eighth segment of a circular tablecloth. If you have doubts about your ability to sew directly onto cloth, then embroider pieces of cloth which are then sewn in place. This also allows several members of the group to contribute and means that each illustration can be placed on a cloth of an appropriate colour if desired.

> *"List-making only works if you get*
> *on with the contents."*

MAGICAL PARTNERS

Magical Partners are people who work within the Craft together, whether in the same place or on the Astral plane.

Where they belong to a Coven they will also work with the group, and sometimes with others of the Coven. A true magical partnership is made up of two people who are in tune with one another, and who have absolute trust in each other. Ideally, there should be one male and one female to balance the energies. However, it is possible for a man to learn to draw on his feminine energies and vice versa, although this generally only comes with experience. Because of the level of trust and honesty necessary, magical partnerships generally work best for people who have known each other for quite some time, and have shared life, as well as Craft, experience. When selecting a magical partner you have to ask yourself if you would trust this person with your deepest secrets, as well as with access to your energies; emotional and mental as well as physical. In turn you should be prepared to drop anything to help them, with the knowledge that they would not call upon you without cause.

To find out if a potential magical partner will be right for you, the first thing to do is to seek the guidance of the Goddess. At the Full Moon take one silver and one gold candle. Place a pin into each, at the same height, and light the candles at the same time. If the pins drop at the same time it means you should be compatible, otherwise you should rethink carefully.

"Nothing is impossible, but some people are!"

Traditional

BEARS

**When bear-baiting and bear-dancing were acceptable
forms of entertainment, bears were commonly seen
on the streets of Europe and the States.**

It was said that any child who rode upon a bear would never contract whooping cough. Thankfully vaccination has replaced cruelty to animals! In America it was thought that wild bears only bred every 7 years and that this caused such a disturbance in the world that local livestock would not be able to reproduce at this time. Having said that, to see one was considered a sign of good luck. To the Native Americans, however, the bear was a symbol of great strength combined with gentleness, although the latter only to its own, not to humanity. Today, bears have a key place in the raising of our children. It is almost inevitable that the first gift for a newborn will be a teddy bear. Bears also feature strongly in children's literature, AA Milne giving us examples of both the cute and the fierce: from Winnie the Pooh, the faithful childhood companion, to the Bears on the Squares who watch for, and may attack, the unwary.

Magically speaking, Bears have long been a symbol which encourages us to explore the unknown, and possibly dangerous, from a safe perspective. To meet one when making an otherworld journey indicates that you are about to tread where you have not been before, but that so long as your intent is true, you will be protected. Should the bear come forward to be your Totem animal then not only is it a great honour, but you can be assured that your magical study is progressing.

*"Tortured feet put lines
on the face."*

ALTERNATIVE THERAPIES

In the last couple of decades we have seen the rise of
a number of alternative therapies, sometimes referred
to derogatorily as 'new age remedies'.

But this title is not only somewhat offensive, it is highly inaccurate. Most of these remedies have been around far longer than the modern medicine we compare them to. Some have come to us from parts of the world where they have been practised for thousands of years. In many cases they do not have the same immediate effectiveness as modern drugs, but on the other hand they frequently do not have the same unwanted side effects. However, it is important to ensure that the therapist is bona fide, where possible qualified or recognized by some kind of authority. Regrettably this is an area where many charlatans set up shop. The best recommendation is one which comes from a trusted friend.

It is also important to ensure that the proposed therapy is compatible with any other treatments you are receiving. St John's Wort, for example, can interfere with the effectiveness of the contraceptive pill. Ask both your therapist and your doctor, and if buying over-the-counter remedies check with the pharmacist, if there is one. Do not forget to check the ingredients of any potential remedy. Some, especially eastern products, still rely on the use of animal products, sometimes from endangered species, and some-times cruelly obtained. Having said that, learning the healing skills of our forebears is very much part of understanding the Craft, whether those skills be herblore, aromatherapy, reflexology or Reiki.

"Capture happy moments,
let sad ones pass by."

GODDESS AND GOD SYMBOLS

**Most Witches like to have a statue of the Goddess
and/or the God on their Altar; indeed some have
many statues around the home which can be
placed there for particular Rituals.**

Today we are lucky as there are many relatively inexpensive statues available. The last 10 years have seen something of a revival of interest in Greek, Roman and Egyptian deities as decorative objects for the house and garden. Indeed many china or gift shop sells attractive images of Anubis and Bast, not to mention figurines representing the signs of the zodiac, many of which are taken from Greek images of the Gods. Images of the Green Man and Woman can be found in garden centres.

Of course there are many other ways of representing the deities. The Goddess can be represented by a holed stone, by the herbs and plants which are sacred to Her, or by a silver candle. The God can be represented by any phallic-shaped piece of wood or stone, by natural things or by a gold candle. But by far the best thing to do is to create your own images. There are a great many things you could use for your image: clay, papier maché, or even wood, but probably the best to start with is children's clay which dries without the need for firing. Such images will not only be imbued with your own energies, but their creation becomes an act of worship and a means of opening the way to greater understanding of the form you work on.

*"Never light a fire unless you
are certain you can put it out."*

CAT'S EYE

**True Cat's Eye is a form of Chrysoberyl, a
name which comes from the Greek for gold,
and has been known since earliest times.**

This is not the same as the Quartz cat's eye, the Tiger's Eye. Cat's Eye is usually found in green, orange or yellow, and is characterized by a fine silver-white line which appears to move as the stone is moved. This line is far clearer in Chrysoberyl Cat's Eyes than in the Quartz varieties.

The Cat's Eye is used in spells for wealth, beauty and protection. To enhance your looks place a Cat's Eye in rainwater and stand this in the light of the Full Moon for 3 nights. Use this water to wash your face and also to rinse your hair. Carry the stones to draw respect towards you. The Cat's Eye used to be considered a charm against evil spirits and to protect against Witchcraft. A Cat's Eye set in silver is worn to enhance psychic power and to protect against the spells of others. It was also thought to protect mental health and cure depression. Certainly, rubbing one in a circular motion on the forehead reduces stress and anxiety. Wear it when seeking to enhance your mental powers, whether psychic or otherwise. The Cat's Eye is also used in money magic, so to protect your finances keep a Cat's Eye in your purse or wallet. It helps to protect your money and to make good any recent losses. It used to be thought that wearing a Cat's Eye would render the wearer invisible.

*"Remember to look up from the
path to check the destination."*

MAKING A YULE CAKE

Here is a recipe for a Yule Log to share with friends and family, whether Wiccan or not.

Preheat the oven to 425 degrees F, 220 C or gas mark 7. Grease and line with greaseproof paper a 13 x 9 inch (30 x 20cm) cake tin.

Put 3 eggs and 4oz (100g) caster sugar into a bowl placed in a pan of hot water. Whisk until light in colour and stiff enough to retain the mark of the whisk. Remove from the pan of hot water and continue to beat until cool. Sift 3oz (75g) plain flour and fold 2oz (50g) into the egg and sugar mix. Add 1oz (25g) cocoa powder to the remaining 1oz of flour and fold this in too. Blend in 1 tablespoon of hot water. Pour the mixture into the tin, ensuring it is evenly spread without knocking out the air. Bake for 7 to 9 minutes until well risen. Heavily dust another sheet of greaseproof paper with caster sugar. As the sponge comes out of the oven turn it out onto the sugared paper. Cut off the crispy edges and roll the hot sponge and paper into a fairly tight roll. Whip ½ pint double cream until really stiff. Once the sponge is cold, slide the paper out and uncurl the sponge enough to fill with cream. Cut the roll diagonally and place one piece against the other to make a branched log shape. Melt 2oz (25g) chocolate in a bowl over hot water, add ½ teaspoon glycerine and about 2 ½oz (85g) sifted icing sugar. Pour this over the log and use a fork to make bark-like markings. Dust with icing sugar and decorate with holly leaves.

"Stick to your guns,
don't fire them off."

DRAWING DOWN THE MOON

Drawing Down the Moon is a Rite in which a
Priest invokes the Goddess into a Priestess.

In some groups it is performed at every Esbat, or Full Moon ritual. Others only perform it occasionally, or when they need additional energy for a specific working. Performed correctly, the spirit of the Goddess actually enters the Priestess and speaks through her. Sometimes the words she speaks will come to her at the time, but she will usually commence by reciting the Charge of the Goddess. Drawing Down the Moon also provides energy for magical workings, which is channelled through the Priestess. As the Rite is exacting it is usually performed by the most experienced Witches in the Coven or group. It is also far more effective if the Priest and Priestess have an existing working relationship as they will be in tune with one another.

Drawing Down the Moon can be performed by a Priestess on her own, although she will find this far easier if she has had experience of performing the Rite with a partner beforehand. This is best done actually standing facing the light of the Full Moon. In this case the Priestess will not need to declaim the words of the Charge out aloud. Whether a solitary or group Rite it is important that the Priestess earths herself thoroughly afterwards, preferably with a hot drink and something to eat. Whilst it is possible for the Goddess to be invoked into a Priest, it is more usual to perform Drawing Down the Sun for a male.

"Life is always wonderful,
but not necessarily always pleasant."

PREPARING A YULE LOG

The Yule Log is key to the celebration of this festival.

If you are lucky you will be able to find a good log in your local woodland. If you are not fortunate in this respect you may find you have to buy a small bag of logs and select one from these. Your log should be of a size to take enough candles so that everyone attending your Yule Ritual will be able have one. It should also have one surface flat enough so that it will not rock when the candles have been lit. Once you have your log, carefully remove dirt and surface insects. If you have planned ahead then leaving your log in a warmish environment will help to evict any insects which may have burrowed under the bark. Ideally the candles should be gold, for the Sun, but if gold are not available then orange or another 'Sun colour' can be substituted. You want one for everyone taking part in the Ritual and one extra.

There are two ways of fixing your candles to the log. The first is to use a power drill to make a suitable-sized hole for each candle. Otherwise, you will need a hammer and a quantity of smallish nails. For each candle, hammer in 3 or 4 nails in a pattern sufficiently tight to wedge the candle between them. Do not drive them all the way into the wood. This takes some practice and you may find you need several trial runs. Your log is now ready for Yule.

"Help comes most readily
to those who ask for it."

YULE

**Yule, the Winter Solstice, is the start of Winter and the
time of year when we celebrate the rebirth of the Sun.**

Since the Summer Solstice the days have been getting shorter and the
nights longer, but now the tide is about to turn and we celebrate the return
of the Sun King. As Yule is a Solstice it can fall on any date from 20 to 23
of December, although many will celebrate it on the 21st anyway.

After dusk gather your group together and place your Yule Log on a
safe table in the centre of your gathering. Check that all the candles are
secure and that the log is stable and cannot be upset by children or pets.
Each person in turn should state something positive they are thankful for
in the previous season. Then, again in turns, they should state something
they wish for the coming season and light their candle. It is worth
remembering to light the candles furthest away first, so that no-one has
to stretch over an already lit candle. Whilst the candles are burning, you
could also slice and eat a chocolate Yule log, or simply discuss the things
you hope to see in the coming season. The candles should be extinguished
before they reach the wood as they may set it alight!

If you have an open fire there is an older way of performing this Rite
in which you first burn last year's Log on the fire and from its flames you
light the candles on the new Yule Log.

*"The cold and dark of winter are as necessary
to life as the heat and light of summer."*

A SUN SYMBOL

One of the ways to welcome the reborn Sun is to
create a Solar image. The following is a version which
can be enjoyed by even the very young, but you can
adapt it and make it as complex as you wish.

Take a cardboard circle; a paper plate is fine. Cut it into a Sun symbol and
decorate it in yellows, oranges and golds. You can use shiny paper, glitter, paint, even used sweet wrappers. If you have a little time and some
patience it can be fun to create your image from gluing a combination of
pastas, beans and pulses and then painting them in the above colours.
Once your Sun is completed it can take part in a very simple Yule Rite.

Just before dawn (around 8am) on the Winter Solstice take your Sun
symbol and a dark cloth. Cover the Sun with the cloth and then chant the
following, "*Return, return, the Earth, the Air, the Fire and the Water*,"
three times. You can accompany this with clapping or drumming if you
are sure it will not upset others who may still be asleep! Once the Sun has
risen, remove the dark cloth from the symbol and bow 3 times to the Sun,
saying, "*Welcome to the returning Sun King. May he lighten our days and
bring warmth to the land. Blessed Be.*" Your Sun symbol can now be
hung in a prominent place in the house.

> "*Everyone is not always
> as truthful as they could be!*"

SUN IN CAPRICORN

Capricorn is one of the Earth signs
bringing physicality, resourcefulness, practicality
and a down-to-earth attitude. It is also a Cardinal
sign indicating a desire to take action, impatience,
eagerness and a need to be in control.

Having said that, Capricorns are generally restrained, patient, cautious and methodical. They tend to be rational, prudent, and admire disciplined behaviour. They will persevere with a problem or task, taking it one step at a time until they reach their desired result. They do not give up ideas or dreams easily. They can appear cool and calculating, but this is because they tend to hold back their feelings, and can appear unaffected by even the strongest of stimuli. On the negative side they can be harsh and exacting on those around them. They can be narrow-minded, critical, selfish and pessimistic, particularly in respect of human nature. Their desire for control can also lead to them being quite manipulative, especially of emotions.

This period is one where Capricorns should restrain their expression about others; it is very much a time when they should think carefully about the effects of what they say and do, before they say or do it. Those of other signs can use the energies of this time to great effect in honest examination of their relationships with those around them. They will also find that this is a good time for tackling outstanding tasks and chores, especially those which previously seemed over-complex.

*"Never mind the others,
do what you know is right."*

BIRCH MONTH

**The common Birch, sometimes called the Silver Birch,
has a white trunk with orange-red-brown branches,
and is often referred to as Lady of the Woods.**

The subspecies is darker and has downy instead of knobbly twigs. The Birch was well-known to the ancients, its bark being used for writing, the wood for building boats and houses. These days it is used for a number of purposes from broom handles to bobbins, the lighter branches being employed in thatching. The twigs also go into brooms and have been used in the manufacture of cloth. Charcoal has been used in making gunpowder. A few Birch leaves added to hot water and inhaled under a towel help to relieve headaches, head colds and the symptoms of flu.

The Celts saw the Birch as a tree of new beginnings and opportunities. This may seem strange for a tree which is not placed at the start of either the traditional or modern year. However, if taken in the magical context this ties in nicely with the resting period of Winter as it is an excellent time to start new magical workings and studies. Place a piece of the wood on your Altar when working for inspiration, confidence and insight before commencing new areas of magical study. Birch is one of the woods from which the traditional besom was made. The wood is used in spells for protection and purification. Make an Asperger from Birch for use in house and personal cleansing Rituals. Seek the guidance of the Goddess under the branches of the Birch whatever the time of year.

*"The thing to remember about martyrs is that
they're only recognized when they're dead."*

CHRISTMAS

Christmas is not a Wiccan festival; however, it is such an intrinsic part of life today that almost all Witches will celebrate it.

It's hard to avoid such a dominant celebration. Certainly, anyone with children would have to be either very lucky or extremely firm in order to persuade their young not to celebrate it. In our house we celebrate Yule and then go on to celebrate Christmas too.

There are a number of interesting customs and beliefs associated with Christmas. It is said that you should eat a mince pie on each of the 12 days of Christmas, preferably given to you by someone else, to ensure 12 months of good luck. Moreover, it is bad luck to refuse a mince pie if it is offered to you. The pies should never be cut as this would bring conflict into the home. The Christmas pudding, when made at home, should be stirred 3 times Deosil, or clockwise, by everyone in the house to ensure their wishes come true. Should a fly be seen in the house between Christmas and the New Year it is said to forecast a good year. To see a person's shadow without a head on Christmas day was believed to indicate a death in the coming year. The turkey wishbone should be pulled by two people using only their little fingers. The one who wins the nub will then have their wish come true. At midnight on this day you should open all the doors in the house to let evil spirits depart.

"Learn to recognize when to go with the flow, rather than fighting the tide."

THE WREN

One of the smallest birds, the Wren has long been associated with Witchcraft and Paganism, both to its detriment and benefit.

On St Stephen's day, 26 December, a ritual known as 'Hunting the Wren' was enacted. The poor Wren was hunted, killed, decorated and paraded through the streets to bring good fortune to the people of the town. In some areas it was simply kept caged for the remaining 12 days of Christmas and in others it was decorated with ribbons and allowed to fly free.

It is thought by some that this treatment of the Wren was to offset the Pagan associations of the bird. On the positive side, folklore has long held the Wren to be a lucky bird: a Wren's feather falling on you indicated a long and prosperous life, to have one in your garden indicates a happy home and just to hear its song was considered lucky.

Perhaps surprisingly some families still re-enact Hunting the Wren as part of the season's festivities, only in this case the Wren in question is a paper one! A small bird shape is cut out of paper and painted. It is then secreted somewhere in the house. At dusk the children are sent to hunt the Wren. The first to find her is given the Wren to place in their room. When I was young, our extended family would gather on Boxing Day. The youngest child was selected as the Wren and then a fairly straightforward game of hide and seek would commence, ending after every child had been the Wren.

> *"Despair uses up the energy to make change."*

COCKERELS

The Cockerel has long been considered a bird of sacrifice in a number of belief systems.

It was also revered, as it was believed that its early morning crowing drove away all the spirits of the night. White Cocks were considered very lucky, and to hear one crow on your way to work meant a fortunate day. Black Cocks, however, were said to be the consorts of the devil. A Cock crowing in the evening indicates bad weather. If it crows facing the house then a stranger will be visiting. The Cock was felt to be a bird of healing and would be rubbed over the body of a sufferer. The unfortunate bird was then cast into the sea, or driven out of the district.

The Cockerel was also considered to be a bird of light and was associated with the Sun. In the Craft it is considered to embody the spirit of the Corn. The last sheaf of harvested corn was even called the cock-sheaf or harvest-cock. A Cockerel was often sacrificed at the end of harvest as an offering to the spirit of the corn. During the Witch Hunts, Witches were accused of sacrificing Cockerels to feed their familiars, it being thought that the Cockerel was a symbol of the Christian God. Effectively, this meant that you should be very careful not to be seen feeding chicken meat to your cat! It was also claimed that Witches would sacrifice a Cock to raise a storm. Witches' Sabbats were also thought to go on all night, only breaking up when the Cock crowed.

*"There's a difference between needing support
and being propped up."*

THREES

**Three has long been considered a significant
number. It is considered both lucky and
unlucky on different occasions.**

Certainly my parents' generation believed that bad things would always
happen in threes, whether breakages or deaths. A further example is the
belief that it is unlucky to light 3 cigarettes from a single match, although
it is thought by many that this is because in warfare the enemy would
sight on the first light, take aim on the second and then shoot on the
third. Interestingly, it was also thought to be unlucky to have 3 lighted
candles or lamps in the same room. Three, however, is considered positive in terms of trying to achieve things, as in third time lucky. A very old
form of divination involved 3 dishes; one filled with clean water, one with
dirty and the third left empty, placed in front of the fire. A blindfolded
person dips their left hand into one at random. If they select the clean
water then they will be married, the dirty they will be widowed and if it
is empty then they will never marry.

Of course, in the Craft 3 is significant because many Goddesses have
three aspects: Maiden, Mother and Crone. Hence, many spells will
require that something is done 3 times, or over 3 nights, and chants are
usually repeated thrice. Furthermore, there are 3 degrees of Initiation. In
some traditions of the Craft it is said that magic should always be worked
in 3 parts: one for yourself, one for someone else and one for the land.

*"Look after the planet;
you may need it one day."*

CERRIDWEN

The Welsh Goddess Cerridwen had two children: Creidwy who was beautiful and Afagdu who was ugly.

To compensate him for his looks Cerridwen created a potion of intelligence and inspiration. For a year and a day she simmered this in her Cauldron and charged a boy, Gwion, to stir it. One day when she was out gathering more herbs for the brew, some of the hot potion spattered onto Gwion's hand, which he put into his mouth to ease the pain. Gwion was suddenly gifted with the qualities Cerridwen had planned for her son. Knowing she would be angry he ran off, but Cerridwen chased him. To elude her, he changed himself into a hare but she became a greyhound. He became a fish, she an otter, and when he became a bird, she became a hawk. Finally he became a grain of wheat and she a hen, at which point she devoured him. Nine months later she gave birth to a baby boy, which Cerridwen cast adrift in the water. This child was found by a prince who raised him, and he grew up to be the great poet Taliesin, meaning 'shining one'. He was the earliest recorded bard, and there is still a place in Wales called Taliesin.

This tale of life, death and rebirth all leading to inspiration reminds us that we must be prepared to embrace all the aspects of life in order to progress. The Cauldron of Cerridwen is often invoked in the Craft as the source of inspiration.

"If in doubt about a spell,
don't do it."

CINNAMON

The Cinnamon we use is actually the bark of the tree, which is usually purchased in sticks or powdered form.

It has a strong scent and flavour. Sugar can be flavoured with it by simply placing a stick of Cinnamon into a jar of sugar and leaving it there for a month. In the past it was used medicinally to relieve vomiting, diarrhoea, flatulence, indigestion and heavy menstruation. It has antiseptic properties, and powdered cinnamon in water can be used to bathe wounds. A few drops of Cinnamon oil added to the bath are very warming and will alleviate the symptoms, particularly shivering, of colds and flu. To warm the atmosphere, burn oils of Cinnamon, Clove, Ginger and Orange. This is also very good for preventing the transfer of cold germs from one person to another.

Magically Cinnamon is used in spells for love, lust, healing and to develop psychic powers. Burn crushed Cinnamon sticks to raise your spiritual awareness and before acts of divination. Cinnamon is linked to both the Sun and the element of Fire, so add the powder to sachets and other powders to increase their energy. To improve your romantic life anoint a red candle with a little Cinnamon oil and burn it when meeting your loved one. Place flakes of Cinnamon in your purse or wallet to draw money. To protect the house tie a red cord around a bundle of three Cinnamon sticks and hang it by the side of the front door, on the opening side. This can also be placed in the car to protect the occupants.

"The purpose of an advert is to make you want what you don't need."

JANUS

The Roman God Janus gave his name to the month of January. Janus was the God of doorways and the turn of the year.

He was portrayed as having two faces, one on each side of his head, so that he could look both forward and backward at the same time. His wife was Jana, a woodland and Moon Goddess who was also called Dione. In some tales she was also his mother. Janus evolved from Dianus and was the God of the Oak, and in his morning aspect he was called Matutinus. In early Roman times he was a Sun God who opened the gates of heaven. Until the arrival of Jupiter, Janus was the primary God of Rome. His festival was celebrated from dusk on New Year's Eve to sunset on New Year's Day, although the dates would have been different from ours as the calendar had not been adjusted at that time. His shrine in central Rome was closed at times of peace, although this was said to be only 3 times during 7 centuries. It was also said that it was closed at the time of the birth of Jesus.

The ancient Egyptians also had an Earth God called Aker. He was represented as having the foreparts of two lions, joined together, each with a human head. He opened the gates to the underworld and presided over the place where the East and West horizons of the underworld met. He was invoked to neutralize poison from snakes and flying insects. Like Janus he also looked both ways.

"There is no ending and no beginning,
for all life is a circle."

THE PHASES OF THE MOON

To Witches the phases of the Moon
are very significant.

Each has its own energies which can be drawn on to work different kinds
of magic and to help in daily life. Each is also linked to a different aspect
of the Goddess. Whilst it is not essential to work in tune with the Moon,
if you do so, then things will flow more easily. The phases of the Moon
have not been included in the body of the book as they do not fall on regular dates in the year. Thus you can apply the energies of the phases as
they really are to any of the other topics covered here.

The New Moon, which commences when it is seen as a reverse C in
the sky, lasts through its waxing (increasing) period. This is associated
with the Goddess as Maiden, with her youthful energy and enthusiasm.
It is the time for starting new things, for beginnings of all kinds. It is
the time for planting seeds, whether literally or metaphorically. Tackle
complex, difficult or tedious chores at this time and they will be easier,
especially if you dedicate them to the Maiden. Honour her with a single
yellow flower or candle on your Altar. Use these energies for planning,
learning, and taking on new ideas. Work spells for these things and for
energy, enthusiasm, inspiration and to draw things to you. If working
healing at this time, emphasize the aspects of healing energy and drawing
health towards the person.

The Full Moon is associated with the Goddess as Mother. The period of the Full Moon is considered to include the night either side of its
peak. This is when the lunar tide of energy is at its height. Some Witches
consider that the energies rise to the moment of fullness, when there is a
pause before they begin to flow in the other direction. This is a time for

production, growth and development. Build on the things which were started at the New Moon. This is a time for consolidation. Honour the Mother with red, and with the fruits of the season. Work magic for development, protection and the curing of ills. Physical, mental and emotional healing can all be undertaken at this time.

The waning, or decreasing Moon lasts from Full to the 3 days just prior to the next New Moon. This is the time when the Goddess moves from Mother to Crone; the time for banishing, for sending things away and for looking within. This is the season for clearing out, cleaning and cleansing. It is also a time for analysis, understanding, attaining knowledge, divination and enhancing psychic development. Honour the Crone with purple. Work magic to rid yourself of old habits or ways of thinking. Also work to drive out doubts, uncertainties, and all negativity. Healing at this time focuses on driving out illness.

For 3 nights before the New Moon, there is no Moon visible in the sky. This is termed the Dark of the Moon. This is not a good time for working magic as the energies can be uncertain. It is a time for reflection rather than action.

Also by Kate West

Real Witchcraft: an Introduction, co-written with David Williams, 1996. A basic introduction to the Craft. Reprinted 2003 by I-H-O Books, Mandrake Press.

Pagan Paths, Pagan Media Ltd, 1997. Six Pathworking cassettes covering the Elements, the Goddess and the God. These are available from the Children of Artemis, www.witchcraft.org

Pagan Rites of Passage, Mandrake Press, 1997. A series of booklets giving information and Rituals for the Rites of Passage of Handfasting, Naming and the Rites of Withdrawal.

The Real Witches' Handbook, Thorsons, HarperCollins, 2000. Real Witchcraft for real people with real lives; this book shows how to practise the Craft in a way sensitive to those around you.

The Real Witches' Kitchen, Thorsons, HarperCollins, 2002. Oils, lotions and ointments for Magic and to relieve and heal. Soaps and bathing distillations for Circle and Magical work. Magical incenses, candles and sachets to give or to keep. Food and drink to celebrate the Sabbats, for personal well-being and to share with friends.

A Spell in your Pocket, Element Books, HarperCollins, 2002. A handy pocket-sized gift book for the Witch on the move.

The Real Witches' Coven, Element Books, HarperCollins, 2003. A complete guide to running a Coven. Problems and solutions, and real-life examples of what can, and does, happen in a Coven. For the new, or would-be, High Priestess and/or High Priest this covers all the aspects you need to know. For the experienced High Priestess/High Priest, there are new insights and stories you will relate too. For the would-be Coven member, this tells you what to expect!

The Real Witches' Book of Spells and Rituals, Element Books, Harper Collins 2003. Spells for all occasions, Rituals for seasonal festivals, Rites of Passage and Initiations, and much more.

The Real Witches' Garden, Element Books, Harper Collins 2004. Ways of using your garden to enhance your Craft, and your Craft to enhance the garden. Whether your contact with nature is a window sill or an acre, here are ways of getting closer to nature and unlocking the magical power of the land.

INDEX